Called to Be Church

Called to Be Church

THE BOOK OF ACTS FOR A NEW DAY

Anthony B. Robinson & Robert W. Wall

WILLIAM B. EERDMANS PUBLISHING COMPANY
GRAND RAPIDS, MICHIGAN

Wm. B. Eerdmans Publishing Co.
2140 Oak Industrial Drive NE, Grand Rapids, Michigan 49505
www.eerdmans.com

23 22 21 20 19 18 17   9 10 11 12 13 14 15

Library of Congress Cataloging-in-Publication Data

Robinson, Anthony B.
    Called to be church : the book of Acts for a new day /
    Anthony B. Robinson & Robert W. Wall.
        p.   cm.
    ISBN 978-0-8028-6065-1 (pbk.: alk. paper)
    1. Bible. N.T. Acts — Criticism, interpretation, etc.
    2. Church — Biblical teaching.   I. Wall, Robert W.   II. Title.

BS2625.6.C5.R63 2006
226.6'06 — dc22

                                          2005033665

For Carla Wall and Linda Robinson

Loving companions, exemplary teachers

Contents

Contents

Preface

Called to Be Church is the fruit of a friendship almost three decades long. Ours is an enduring friendship of two people who come from different sides of the theological track, from different denominational backgrounds, and who serve the church in different professional roles.

Robert W. Wall is a biblical scholar and a professor at Seattle Pacific University. As a teaching elder of the Free Methodist Church, he is labeled "evangelical" in some circles; and yet his politics and theology are most significantly shaped by the teachings of John and Charles Wesley and their ideals of a sanctified discipleship. His published scholarship ranges widely, including several studies on the Acts of the Apostles. His commentary on Acts in volume 10 of the *New Interpreter's Bible* (L. E. Keck, ed., Nashville: Abingdon, 2002) is the interpretive foundation on which much of the present book rests.

Anthony B. Robinson is a pastor and teacher. He has been a minister and senior pastor in four congregations of the Congregational/United Church of Christ. In conventional terms he would be described as "mainline" or "liberal." Theologically, he has been shaped by the Reformed tradition of Calvin and Edwards. Today he writes and teaches on congregational renewal and leadership, often culling from the book of Acts lessons that encourage a change in thinking and direction.

This book is a testimony to God's capacity to transcend the labels and categories of which we often make so much — entirely too much in our experience. We hope its publication serves the church as one modest public sign of what many have come to see as an urgent matter within the American church: to overcome ecclesiastical barriers and religious stereotypes in order to serve Christ's church and its mission in today's world more faithfully. In this new day, the old liberal-conservative dualism is not at all helpful and is even counterproductive to a mutually enriching conversation between earnest believers of different faith traditions. Our partnership in this non-dogmatic venture testifies to what Wesley called a "catholic spirit."

Not only does this book bring together two friends in Christ from different religious backgrounds; we are teachers whose common calling is embodied in different ways and settings. Rob is a scholar of the Christian Scriptures and teacher at a liberal arts university, while Tony is a pastor and teacher of Christian congregations and their leaders. Their complementary perspectives on Acts, shaped by a common vocation worked out within different locations, are set out in the opening two chapters: Tony asks the pastor's question, "Why Acts? Why Now?" to which Rob responds as a biblical scholar by "Introducing Acts to a Congregation of Faithful Readers." In the chapters that follow these two perspectives fashion a conversation over selected stories from Acts: Rob "interprets" each story as sacred Scripture, and Tony "engages" the story by adapting it in response to a wide variety of hard issues with which today's believers struggle. The book thereby combines scholarly and pastoral perspectives on Acts with the aim of providing today's congregations and classrooms with intellectual and spiritual beginning points, not simple conclusions. For this reason, we have added discussion questions at the end of each chapter to facilitate conversations among our readers that will move what they have read in directions that enable them to carry what they have learned from Acts into the marketplace where they work, the congregations where they worship, the dorm rooms where they live. Only in this sort of dialogue with Scripture can a people belonging to God hear a new word that helps to redeem this hard moment for God's sake.

For this reason, we pray that our exploration into the contemporary meaning of this precious story will provoke and evoke, challenge and encourage, and in the end lead us to a closer walk with Jesus Christ as pastors and scholars, students and parishioners. Thank you for joining us and enlarging our partnership!

We wish to acknowledge the encouragement and work of our editor at Eerdmans, Reinder Van Til. Reinder, more than anyone else, has championed this project from the beginning, participating in its conception, birth, and growth to maturity. We are in his debt as authors, and more so because our work together is deeply rooted in friendship. We also wish to acknowledge with thanksgiving those students at Seattle Pacific University who studied Acts with us — at various levels of enthusiasm! — during winter quarter, 2005, with an ever-critical eye toward the production of this book: Seth Addington, Serena Bye, Jordan Lee, Megan Millar, Laura Murrell, Kystel Porter, Ryan Provonsha, Carolyn Robbins, Jamie Spiro, Nick Waltz, Harmony Zieman, and Rhoda Zopfi. Their puzzlements, probing questions, and insightful comments helped to motivate and guide this project. Finally, we wish to dedicate this book to our wives, teachers and educators themselves, Linda Robinson and Carla Wall. We are routinely inspired by their ministries of teaching to still different kinds of congregations, and most especially by their loving partnership with us in life and faith.

PENTECOST, 2005

1 *Why Acts?*
Why Now?

The Contemporary Context

Over the past two decades there has been an explosion of interest in Jesus, a burst of fascination that has taken both scholarly and popular forms. There have been countless books and magazine articles on who Jesus was, what he really said, and what he actually did. There have been public seminars and on-line conferences about the Jesus of history and the Jesus of faith. Hollywood films and educational videos have brought Jesus to the big screen and small screens, while he has been celebrated in popular song and consulted via W.W.J.D. bracelets. Jesus has been big!

Such interest, study, and debate has been strong — even astonishing — when we consider that not too many years ago our era was confidently foreseen by experts and scholars as one that would be decidedly and thoroughly secular. According to the twentieth-century theorists of secularization, religious faith should by now be relegated to museums. But, on the contrary, spirituality is everywhere and Jesus is big. Inevitably, of course, this embrace of Jesus has been uneven; still, Christians cannot but rejoice in the focus of so much thought and interest, curiosity and debate, concerning Jesus of Nazareth.

This explosion of Jesus interest comes as part of the larger — also unanticipated — fascination with spirituality. Who would have imagined that, rather than being driven out of the public arena by business or psychology, spirituality would be emerging in the workplace and in the worlds of counseling and personal growth? Again, this flowering of spirituality in recent decades has also been uneven. Spirituality can be as shallow as comedian Dennis Miller's quip suggests: "Spirituality is whatever it is you're feeling when you're feeling good about yourself." Or it can mean something quite deep and powerful.

It is especially striking, then, that neither the scholarly and popular fascination with Jesus nor the widespread exploration of spirituality has spawned or been accompanied by a similar interest in the church, in congregations, or in the community of faith in general. In fact, the now common distinction that many people make, "I am spiritual, but not religious," probably has as its subtext and meaning, "I am spiritually interested and engaged, but I am not a part of a church or congregation or any organized religious community." If books about Jesus and spirituality flood the shelves, the section on "church" remains puny by comparison.

To be sure, a corollary of the new interest in Jesus has been a certain amount of interest in the formative era of the church, particularly the process by which some texts became canonical while others did not. The new or renewed attention to Jesus has also led both scholars and general readers to a new interest in noncanonical writings, such as the Gospel of Thomas and the so-called Gnostic Gospels, as well as other documents that did not get included in the canon of Scripture. Because documentaries and TV specials seem fascinated with Jesus' world, this particular and limited aspect of the church's story has received new attention.

There also has been in recent decades a rather abundant literature on church growth and decline; but even that is nothing approaching the combination of scholarly and popular interest in Jesus specifically or spirituality broadly conceived. In addition, many new expressions and forms of church have emerged today, including but not limited to "the new orthodox," "ancient-future," and "mega- and emerging" churches. Finally, there has been some investment — though limited — in "congregational studies" among scholars and researchers. Yet, while there have been these forms of interest in particular aspects of the church — the canonical process and noncanonical texts, church growth and decline, new forms of church, and congregational studies — the theology and life of the community of faith has been largely neglected. We should probably not be surprised that Jesus has proved rather more fascinating and compelling than the church; but the contrast does seem telling. One is reminded of the tart remark of the English romantic poet Percy Shelley: "I could be-

lieve in Christ if he did not drag along with him that leprous bride of his
— the church."

Moreover, the contemporary focus on Jesus and the fascination with
spirituality may be particularly congenial to a culture that often emphasizes the individual at the expense of the community. It seems to fit a society that encourages personal, even private, spirituality while spurning the
difficult work of forming and sustaining communities and institutions.
While Jesus' life and teachings do, in many ways, challenge such individualism, it remains true that the study of Jesus, whether as savior or sage,
teacher or magician, storyteller or prophet, has often seemed to lend itself
more to an individual, "spiritual" appropriation of him than to a consideration of the nature of the Christian community or the church. But this
risks a distortion of the Christian faith and the biblical story — a distortion that accommodates it to a culture of individualism.

Such a privatized faith was memorably portrayed in one of the films in
Woody Allen's corpus, *Hannah and Her Sisters,* where Allen himself portrays a man wracked by guilt and self-doubt, as he often does in his movies.
The man decides to give Jesus a try, and we see him making a solo visit to a
priest or pastor — and then staggering away with an armload of books. He
will approach Jesus individually, through books. At no point in this character's attempt to become Christian or at least a religious person do we see
anything that looks like a community, anything that looks like church.
Both spirituality and Christianity are portrayed as individual, even solitary, interests. The contemporary fascination with spirituality and the interest in Jesus seem too often to fall short at just this point, because they remain individual and personal pursuits, private and solitary.

The consistent witness of Scripture, however, is that God's intention is
to form a people, a community, a visible body. Beginning with Abraham
and Sarah in Genesis and continuing through to Paul's letters and to the
book of Revelation, the nature and life of the community of faith is the focus. God means to have a people who will be a blessing to all the peoples of
the earth (Gen. 12:1-4). Contrary to what many contemporary Westerners
or Americans may imagine, the concern of Scripture is not the spiritual
state of individuals, their holiness, or even their salvation. The focus is
God's *ekklesia,* God's community taking form in the world, which even
provides a new world and a new vision for those who share in it. From
Genesis through Revelation, God is hard at the task of forming a people of
God, Israel and a new Israel, and finally the body of Christ. John the Bap-

tist begins his ministry by announcing, "God can raise up a people from these stones" (Luke 3). Jesus sends his disciples out to make more disciples, to baptize and teach in every nation (Matt. 28).

This move to community, to a people, and even to enduring institutions that carry and express our shared memories and hopes, is a central but neglected theme of the Christian faith. We often tend to focus on ourselves, to measure ourselves against one another, to plot our progress on some sort of spiritual growth chart. But a good case can be made that God is less concerned with how "I" am doing than with how "we" are doing. Indeed, a good part of the raison d'etre of any congregation is the challenge to call us out of ourselves into some larger community, to some greater venture, to learning about Jesus by learning to be part of his people in the world. And yet the church may be the most neglected aspect of contemporary Christian thought.

Jim Wallis, founder and editor of the *Sojourners* magazine and community, once put it this way: "The greatest need in our time is not simply for *kerygma*, the preaching of the gospel; nor for *diakonia*, service on behalf of justice; nor for *charisma*, the experience of the Spirit's gifts; nor even for *propheteia*, the challenging of the king. The greatest need for our time is *koinonia*, the call simply to be the church, to love one another, and to offer our lives for the sake of the world. The creation of living, breathing, loving communities of faith at the local church level is the foundation of all other answers."

Moreover, the relative neglect of church, of the Christian community, and of religious institutions has come at a time of particular challenge for the church and for congregations. Huge shifts have been underway in the lifetimes of those of us who have lived during the second half of the twentieth and first decade of the twenty-first century. We have lived through the end of an American Christendom to see the emergence of a society that is officially secular but at the same time religiously pluralistic. In this same period we have witnessed the waning of the modern era and of its most compelling values. We shall return to these themes and shifts, but for now we simply observe that these shifts constitute a sea change in our culture and for the church. It is a time of significant challenge and change for congregations, for denominations, and for lay and pastoral leaders.

In the face of this relative neglect of the church as a subject for theological study and spiritual reflection, the book of Acts is uniquely positioned to be helpful, provocative, evocative, and compelling. It shows us the Christian faith as a life lived in community, a community that is engaged in the world. It shows us the church that is both grounded in Scripture and alive to the Spirit. In Acts we see a church that transcends so many of the false polarities and dichotomies of our own time and experience. In Acts, for example, there is no dichotomy between spirituality and social-cultural engagement and witness; the two are one, inextricably woven together. Similarly, there is no choice to be made here between the "by grace through faith alone" direction of some aspects of the church and the "without works faith is dead" conviction of other parts of the historic church. In Acts we see a church that is not only the creation of God and the gift of the Spirit but also a community engaged in a full-orbed and demanding practice of holiness and a new way of life. Here we see the church advancing the ministry of Jesus, doing what he did, saying what he said, disturbing and delighting a world that is both sorely in need of the gospel and yet resistant to it. It is our conviction that this book of Scripture, the Acts of the Apostles, is uniquely relevant to a time when the church and congregations both need to be rediscovered and transformed. Acts is a book for the church and for congregations today.

Acts as Gift and Challenge to the Church

If part of the gift of the book of Acts is that it transcends false dichotomies to offer a fuller vision of the church, it also offers particular gifts and challenges to distinct expressions of the contemporary church in North America. Acts will problematize, or challenge, the specific ways that the various forms of the contemporary church — such as mainline Christians, evangelicals, Pentecostals, and Roman Catholics — have understood faith and church. All of these embodiments of the contemporary church in North America will find their faith and life deepened and guided in well-defined ways by the richness of Acts.

For example, we see Acts as a powerfully theocentric antidote and therapy for some mainline churches that have become anthropocentric and too often moralistic in their preaching and teaching of the faith. The great strength of mainline congregations has been their emphasis on public faith and public morality — on active engagement in the world. But too often this has resulted in a kind of neo-Pelagianism that has turned a religion of grace into a religion of good works and achievement. In contrast to this overemphasis on what *we* are to do, to think, to feel, or to believe, Acts places a clear and significant emphasis on the *divine* initiative, on revelation, on God's grace, and God's unexpected intrusions. The God of Acts is an active God, a God who will direct the church. This is not a God who, having set the world and church in motion, has retired to Florida and left us in charge.

Thus, as the Gospel of Luke ends and as Acts begins, we do not find the church busy at its tasks. Rather, the apostles are told to return to Jerusalem and wait — wait for the Spirit from on high. This is a way of saying to the church, "You're not in charge here." It is God's Spirit who will make the first and decisive moves. What a strange, and yet strangely welcome, word this may prove to be for many mainline Protestants who have been depleted by years of relentless activism. Wait on the Spirit! The first question is not, suggests Acts, what should we do? Instead, it is: what is God doing? Where is the Spirit moving? This may prove to be not merely a helpful corrective but a transformative one for some congregations. Acts provokes a shift of focus in such churches — a focus toward God's will and the Spirit's way.

If Acts problematizes the activist faith of mainliners, it also challenges the historic strength — which sometimes becomes a weakness — of the more evangelical churches and Christians. The core theme of American evangelicalism is the change in the personal lives of people through the transforming power and presence of Jesus Christ, the living Lord. We rejoice in this gospel of transformation; and yet we regret that too often it can remain merely personal and does not also find expression in relationship, in community, and in the public practice of faith. We understand and affirm the power of God's saving grace, but we believe that Acts moves the church to complement grace with response, with new life in Christ that is embodied in the particular way of life and the practices of the community of faith.

In Acts we find those whose lives have been transformed participating in a visible, public community of faith, one that is characterized by "resurrection practices." The faith is not internal or personal alone; it is public, visible, and shared. Acts portrays the life of those who have experienced God's grace as one of the sharing of goods, of bold witness, of turning away from idols, and of sharing in the life of the community of resurrection — which is itself a visible witness to the world. Another way to put this, one that is relevant to both mainline and evangelical forms of Christianity in North America, is that in Acts the "gentilizing" of the gospel is just as much an issue as Paul makes of the "Judaizing" of the gospel in some of his letters. In this context, "Judaizing" means adding Hebrew legal requirements to the conversion process that might jeopardize the power and centrality of God's grace. This remains a constant concern. But we have been so focused on that danger of reinstituting "the law" ("Judaizing") that we have not seen another, equal danger: that the church would not embody its faith in a visible and public life of discipleship. The book of Acts recognizes the threat to Christian faith and life of "gentilizing," that is, of forgetting our Jewish inheritance and of its call to be a distinct and visible body that is a salt to the earth and a light to the world.

The biblical scholar James Sanders has observed that, as Christianity developed, Christians embraced the *mythos,* the story, while Jews took the *ethos,* the way of life. Christianity, at least in some quarters, was principally about beliefs, often at the expense of practices, of a way of life. Today, as American Christendom wanes, and as we wonder what it really does mean to live and lead a Christian life — and to do so in community — Acts provides guidance and direction.

Acts not only offers challenges and guidance to historic mainline and evangelical Christians; it can also broaden and deepen the faith of the one branch of the Christian church that has paid significant attention to this book of the Bible, namely, Pentecostals. Too often Pentecostals have turned to Acts in order to support and establish charismatic expressions of Christianity, but without allowing Acts to be heard in its own voice, breadth, and depth. Acts is much more than a kind of blueprint for receiving the Holy Spirit, or for organizing the church and establishing such offices as deacons. It represents a thoroughgoing vision of the church that will challenge Pentecostals to a more whole version of the faith. In Acts the Holy Spirit is not limited to particular gifts and expressions, such as glossolalia (the gift of speaking in tongues). Rather, the Holy Spirit directs the mission of the church, and the Holy Spirit is the power through whom Christians move from being spectators to participants, from objects to agency.

All of these themes in Acts — its theocentrism, its emphasis on public discipleship and holiness, and its full-orbed presentation of the Spirit — speak powerfully to the contemporary Roman Catholic experience as well. If Acts' theocentrism is a gift to the mainline churches, and its emphasis on practices and a way of life is a gift to evangelicals, the Roman Catholic

Church may find here the invitation to church that is both firmly rooted in God's promises in Scripture and yet open to the movement and surprises of the Spirit.

Contemporary Questions and Acts

Not only does the book of Acts provide an antidote to the recent neglect of the church by portraying vital communities of faith; and not only does Acts speak a word of challenge to particular historic expressions of the church in North America; Acts also addresses a number of issues and themes that are of particular interest in our time. These include, but are not limited to, the role of women in the church and as ministers of the gospel; the place of possessions in the lives of believers and in the community of faith; matters of sexuality and their bearing on Christian discipleship; conflict and decision-making in the church; and leadership for the church. All of these themes, questions, and issues are alive in the church of Acts and are very much alive and vital for the church today. In Acts we find a church that is engaging these questions, and we find a church that knows and experiences conflict, but is able to face and resolve conflict.

Perhaps no single issue, however, is more relevant to the church today than how Acts shows the church negotiating life and faith in a multicultural world. Much ink has been spilt, many conferences held, and many sermons preached on "Christianity in a multicultural world" in our own time. We have been informed by sociological studies and historical analysis; we have listened to contemporary testimony regarding racial and ethnic prejudice; we have learned from ethnographic and anthropological studies. But few have paid sufficient attention to the church's primary text and experience in this matter, which is to be found in the Acts of the Apostles. Here we see the gospel surge across its first cultural boundaries into Samaria, a population that Jews regarded as particularly suspect and untrustworthy. But the movement of the church and the gospel across cultural boundaries and borders does not stop with this near, if distasteful, neighbor. Before long, Paul — of all people — is commissioned to be the apostle to the gentiles, and hence the gospel moves into the gentile world. It is in Acts that the apostle Peter is led to the home of the first gentile to be converted to Christianity. But it is not only this first gentile, Cornelius, who is converted: if we look closely, we can witness the ongoing conversion of Peter himself, as God leads him over thresholds he never imagined he would cross. Both then and now, the church has found and will find itself grappling with crucial questions in its life and development: what is precious and what is expendable? What is earthen vessel and what is transcendent power (2 Cor. 4)? How much is the gospel bound up with any particular culture? In the emerging multiculturalism of our world and continent, Acts can help.

Our New Time and Acts

For all of these reasons, we believe that the book of Acts can go far to correct the current neglect of the church, to overcome false dichotomies and distorted emphases that limit the church and congregations today, and to point toward the shape of a new and transforming church for our time. Finally, we believe that the very shifts in our culture that make it such a challenging time for the church have created unique opportunities for us to read Acts freshly and faithfully.

The first of these huge shifts has been the gradual end of the era of American Christendom. By "American Christendom" we mean both an era and a manner in which American society and Christianity have been woven together in mutually supportive and reinforcing ways during most of the twentieth century. "Christendom," of course, had its genesis long before its particular American form, but Christianity in North America has been woven into the culture in ways that make it less visible but perhaps more enduring than the more formal state churches of Europe. While Christendom continues to be with us in many ways, it is dead and gone in other ways. No longer are stores closed on Sunday in tacit support of the church and Christianity. No longer do public schools give privileged status to Christianity or its leaders. No longer does the church benefit from a pervasive expectation that part of being a good American is being a participant and member of a church or synagogue. On the contrary, in these early decades of the twenty-first century we live in an officially secular, religiously pluralistic society.

While many have argued — and we tend to agree — that the loss of privilege and place on the part of Christianity, and particularly mainline Protestant versions of it, represents a wonderful opportunity, it still is an enormous shift and a significant challenge. Many of our churches, denominations, and church leaders learned how to be the church during the era of American Christendom. Particular values and strategies served us well in that era. Today those same values and strategies for being and doing church are no longer as useful as they once were; in fact, some of them may even be counterproductive. In Acts we may find gestures toward new strategies and ways for our time.

During the era of American Christendom, the book of Acts was often held at arm's length or simply ignored in many of our churches in North America. There were notable exceptions, particularly among the various Pentecostal churches; but by and large, Acts played a distinct second or third fiddle to the Gospels and to the letters of Paul. Why was this true? The answer is not particularly mysterious or elusive. Acts portrays the church during a time of great dynamism, a time when the church was often at odds with the dominant culture and its prevailing values, ways, and gods. In Acts we see the church as the first counter-culture. The church in Acts is the church of which Jesus himself spoke: it is the salt of the earth, the leaven of the loaf, and the light to the world. It is not the church of Christendom, of the Constantine-initiated Holy Roman Empire, when religious and civil authority was one and the same. Nor is it the particularly American version of Christendom, where Christianity has been woven into the warp and woof of the culture and institutions of the society.

During Christendom's heyday, the book of Acts often seemed not only strange but not especially relevant or even helpful. We Christians were busy running America, joining the United Way and the city council, and putting our stamp on universities and hospitals. In many ways, we *were* the establishment. What use did we have for Acts — with its wild stories of apostles on trial, preachers being run out of town, shipwrecks on missionary journeys, and the rush of a Pentecostal wind? The answer is, not much. Mostly, Acts seemed a little too wild — too triumphalistic in some stories and too magical in others. As one preacher lamented in the late sixties, "It's difficult to get from the book of Acts to the church today." To the extent that the church was in — or was — the social mainstream, it just didn't seem as though we had a lot in common with the church in Acts.

The good news is that things have changed. For better or worse, and surely it is some of both, we find ourselves in a new world that looks more like the church before Constantine inaugurated such a huge shift in our social place and role. Today the church has been "disestablished," and Acts has new relevance, meaning, and power. Indeed, Acts just may be the most relevant book of the Bible for the church as it tries to negotiate its way faithfully in a new time.

Not only is the church today living in the era after the heyday of American Christendom; it is also the era of postmodernity. Like Christendom, modernity is still with us in countless ways, but in other ways it is over. Just as many of our churches learned to be and do church in the period of American Christendom, the great cultural ethos in relation to which we positioned ourselves was modernity and its core values born of confidence in science and technology: reason, progress, optimism, tolerance, and individualism. One could say that the mainline and liberal churches opened their minds and hearts to modernity and took it as their task to make Christian faith and theology sensible to the modern person and world. At the other end of the spectrum — but in some ways no less influenced by modernity — was the fundamentalist movement. If the Protestant mainline opened its arms to modernity and its hallmark values, fundamentalism tended to circle the wagons against modernity. Modernity seemed to threaten much that fundamentalists held dear. Still, fundamentalists were greatly influenced by modernity, because as they looked for evidence and proofs for their faith from biblical texts and concepts, they adopted — often seemingly unawares — Enlightenment notions of truth as correspondence.

Between the liberal and fundamentalist responses to modernity, the Roman Catholic Church and the more evangelical Christians took a more cautious and perhaps balanced approach to modernity and its values. But, though the responses have played out in different ways, no form of Christianity has been exempt from the challenge and influence of modernity, with its tendency to pit reason against revelation, science against faith.

Like American Christendom, however, modernity — or what some call the "Enlightenment project" — no longer has the taken-for-granted status that it so long enjoyed. The shift from modernity to postmodernity means that reason and rationality are no longer the only legitimate ways of knowing. Today people are open to, indeed fascinated by, other forms of knowing, including the mystical, the emotional, and the sensory. We hear much today about "different forms of intelligence," expanding beyond modernity's singular devotion to reason and rational ways of knowing. Modernity's optimism about solving most human social problems and gaining control over nature through science and technology has also given way — often to a skepticism about modernity's great promises of conquering nature and solving humanity's perennial problems. Indeed, sometimes modernity's optimism has been replaced by postmodern pessimism: the grand narrative of Western and modern culture, with its story of explaining mystery and mastering the unknown, no longer seems as compelling as it once did. If moderns looked at mystery as something to solve or control, postmoderns tend to look at mystery as something to be experienced.

One could go on, but the point is that in the twentieth century we learned in many ways how to be the church in the modern era. With the modern age on the wane, we are compelled now to learn new ways to be and do church. Acts may prove especially relevant and helpful in our new time. If the Spirit-driven mission, the mysterious appearances and offstage exits of various *dramatis personae,* the dreams and visions, and the overall magical quality of the Acts of the Apostles was a stumbling block in the modern era, perhaps all of that makes the book particularly intriguing and appealing in a less certain and possibly less arrogant time. For a culture that has perhaps drunk too deeply at the wells of reason and rationality, Acts offers intrigue, adventure, and the church as a place and people of mystery and magic. That is, Acts — like much of the Bible — is a postmodern book!

In our new post-Christendom and postmodern time, congregations and pastoral leaders will find in the book of Acts a resource and companion for being the church in new and adventurous times. Here, for example, we will find a church that is formed and empowered by the winds and fire of the Spirit. Here we will find a church that, rather than having a "mission program" or a "mission budget," is itself a mission, a community of transformation. Here we will find a community that embodies its faith in public practices, resurrection practices that constitute a visible and discernible way of life. Here, too, we will see a church engaged in the work of making disciples. Overall, our experience with the church in Acts will be an encounter with a fluid, dynamic, on-the-move body, one that struggles with internal and external challenges but always does so with a sense and experience of a faithful God, a living Lord, and a powerful and active Spirit.

What a refreshing contrast this can be for many contemporary church leaders and congregations, who find themselves drained of energy and enthusiasm, wondering what the source of their power and life may be, and whether there is something at stake in their ongoing existence. We do not mean to suggest that Acts will simply make us feel poor or inadequate by comparison; that is neither our intention nor the intention of the book of Acts itself. Rather, in this book we may get clues to a new vitality, a new dynamism, a new way of being church for our time, one characterized by a sense of adventure in place of our frequent preoccupation with survival, one characterized by a sense of hope and purpose in place of our despair or lack of direction. Moreover, we may find in Acts hints and guesses for deepening our experience as a community of shared goods, where particular practices and pathways of life together are lived out in ways that are both formative and transformative. There is, to put it succinctly, a sense of joy and excitement and adventure about being the church — and Acts can help!

We do not mean to imply that Acts provides some kind of straightforward or technical manual for doing church, a how-to guide with ten steps for better churches. It is nothing so technical — or ultimately so useless — as that. Acts is a narrative through and through. It is not a how-to guide so much as it is a witness and a story. It is a story that is uniquely designed to provide encouragement for us.

Will we find in the book of Acts ready "answers" to all our questions about being the church? Probably not. But we will find the church — as church. We will find the church negotiating a new world, filled with both danger and opportunity, and doing so with a faith that is bold and a witness that is compelling. We can't think of anything more needed by the church and its leaders today than such a story. It may help us reframe our own story in such a way that this story becomes our own; or better, that this story absorbs our story, giving it new context, meaning, hope, and promise. That is our hope.

STUDY QUESTIONS

1. How would you describe the role Acts plays in your church's ministry? Are its stories and themes central? Ignored? Prized and preached? Whichever description you chose, why do you think that is the case?

2. How would you describe the place of Acts in your own faith journey? Are there particular stories in Acts that are or have been especially important to you? Narrate this chapter of your story.

3. What relationship does Scripture generally have with other sources of your spiritual formation — a faith tradition, community life, mystery, experi-

ence? What are the distinctive hallmarks of your congregation's faith and life?

4. What social and spiritual issues facing the church and/or your campus strike you as the most urgent today? Explain why. To which of these do you expect Acts to make an important contribution? Again, explain why.

2 *Introducing Acts to a Congregation of Faithful Readers*

The Acts of the Apostles is one of the most entertaining and important books of the Christian Bible. It tells the quintessential story of the church's roots, tracing its beginnings to the final days of the risen Jesus and the dramatic arrival of the promised Spirit during the Pentecost festival in Jerusalem to the exemplary story of an imprisoned Paul, undeterred in continuing his gospel ministry to all comers from his rented apartment in downtown Rome. Acts gives us this inspiring story within a theological framework that interprets the progress of God's word from Jerusalem to Rome as the fulfillment of God's redemptive plan according to Israel's Scriptures (Acts 2:17-21; 15:16-18; 28:26-27; cf. Luke 1:1).

Today Acts is used by scholars as an important (though contested) resource of historical information about the "Jesus movement" following the death and departure of its founder and its pioneering leaders, whose New Testament writings continue to fashion Christian faith. Biblical theologians find in this book distinctive contributions to Scripture's witness to the mysterious third person of the Holy Trinity and to patterns and practices of the Christian community. From its first use in the writings of the ancient church until today, especially among Pentecostal communions, Acts has performed a strategic role in defending a particular account of what it means to be a "Spirit-filled" church in the world. Yet one rarely hears readings from Acts in today's pulpits. Other than the obligatory readings during Eastertide and at Pentecost, the Lectionary use of Acts is strangely silent. Moreover, the impression that Acts demands the conversion from one religion to a personal relationship with a living Jesus confounds and even repels many communicants of mainline congregations, whose spirituality is more tolerant of religious diversity and often proffers a more socially alert form of Christian discipleship than one concentrated on a personal relationship with Jesus.

A primary purpose of this book is to be subversive in two ways. Not only will we encourage a more extended and dedicated use of Acts throughout the year, but we will travel the narrative world of Acts to locate its provocative images of a God at work in partnership with a transformed and transforming community in order to help shape a healthy sense of congregational faith and practice for today. With that as our vital aim, there is hardly another more practical book in all of Scripture to use than the Acts of the Apostles, which touches on the variety of problems that continue to face congregations in every place and in every time.

Rules of Healthy Interpretation

First Timothy 4:6 admonishes its readers to follow carefully the "sound teaching" of Paul's gospel, and to reject all others, because it will nourish a more robust faith and produce a life that engages in the "good works" of God. The root word that captures the contemporary preoccupation with good "hygiene" derives from this same word for "sound" *(hygiaino)*. Even as the physical health of individuals depends on hygienic practices, so a healthy congregation is nurtured by the regular practice of biblical teaching. Retrieving God's word from a biblical text is neither magic nor the by-product of some spiritual kind of osmosis superintended by the Spirit. While our approach to a biblical text is worshipful, and our study cooperates with God's Spirit, reading Scripture for theological profit is hard work — "10 percent inspiration and 90 percent perspiration," as my favorite seminary professor used to say.

Most scholars today agree that a "sound" interpretation of Scripture is regulated by careful attention to four exegetical rules that frame different questions asked of the biblical narrative. The theological and practical value in applying any of these four rules varies from reader to reader according to personal interest and immediate purpose. Healthy interpretations of biblical texts, however, are typically fashioned in some combination of these four rules to ensure a meaning that is made for an attentive congregation, who, in hearing God's word more clearly, will be able to respond to it more faithfully.

Among the church fathers, no teacher influenced the way the church interpreted Scripture more keenly than did Origen of Alexandria (ca. 185-255 C.E.). Simply put, Origen argued that the meaning of a biblical text has two "senses": a literal or plain sense and a hidden or theological sense. In a postmodern, postcritical age, Origen's interpretive strategy has been reclaimed, though chastened by a more critical regard for sacred texts. The first task of a careful interpreter is to "exegete" the text's literal sense: in the case of Acts, this means reading the story closely and carefully to understand its plot line, its characters, the importance of its geographical setting and shipping itinerary, its narrator's theological motive, and even the importance of Acts' relationship to other canonical writings in Christian Scripture. This is how the preacher prepares to teach or preach a passage from Acts — by placing it within a multilayered context that includes elements of the storyteller's social world, his or her literary composition and theological convictions, and the church's placement of Acts within the biblical canon.

But this hard work only provides raw materials, the "stuff" of a great sermon, instructive teaching, or programmatic vision — food for a congregation's spiritual diet. Careful exegesis is the means toward sound interpretation; and sound interpretation always aims a biblical text toward God. According to Origen's formula, the "spiritual" meaning of a passage generates a more vital life with God and is thus the aim of Bible study. What Scripture teaches us about our relationship with the living God is the end, while critical exegesis is but the means. If the Bible's true referent is God, and the object of Bible study is learning God, the overarching "rule" of biblical interpretation is the church's "Rule of Faith," which reminds a congregation of those theological agreements that order its life of faith.

St. Irenaeus of Lyons (ca. 115-200 C.E.), among the first of the church fathers to speak of such a Rule of Faith, argued that our beliefs about God and how we behave as disciples of Jesus must be monitored by the core beliefs that the apostles learned directly from the Lord, which they passed on to others through their missionary work and writings. Even before the church formed the Bible, then, its faith was formed and guided by this Rule of Faith. And as the church formed the Bible during a process that took several centuries to complete, it did so in constant dialogue with this Rule, so that the content of teachings found in canonical writings, as well as the interpretation and performance within congregations of faithful readers, was in demonstrable agreement with the church's Rule of Faith. Any healthy use of Scripture for "teaching, reproving, correcting, and training" (2 Tim. 3:16) must agree in both its content and consequence with the core beliefs that all believers have confessed to be true according to the great ecumenical creeds of the "one, holy, catholic, and apostolic church" — formulated in particular by the Apostles', Nicene, and Chalcedon creeds.

Toward this theological aim, then, the interpreter's first business is to determine the "literal sense" of a selected passage from Acts by following four exegetical rules. If raised in chronological order of a text's history, *the first rule invites attention to the book's origins: What circumstances occasioned the writing of Acts?* Most modern preachers are prepped by their seminary faculty to respond to this question; most are interested in a text's "original" meaning. The questions of who wrote Acts, to whom it was written, why it was written, and when it was written guide the investigation into a text's origins. It is axiomatic today that a biblical narrative such as Acts comes to its modern interpreter wrapped in its own particular social world. This world will shed light on the intentions the author had for his first readers and so, presumably, for us many centuries later. Practically speaking, if we can know something of the narrator's intentions for his story, even his current readers will be better able to limit the number of the story's plausible meanings. Stated in terms of modernity's "hermeneutics of suspicion," paying close attention to the storyteller's intentions "polices" the reader's temptation to displace the author's "intended" meaning with his or her own. Nice theory, difficult practice.

Even if the careful student agrees that the work of reconstructing a book's point of origin within the author's own social world is crucial to the interpretive task, she will encounter enormous problems along the way: Acts is an anonymous book that claims to be written for a "most excellent Theophilus" (Acts 1:1; cf. Luke 1:3-4), about whom nothing is known. The date of its composition also remains unknown, as does the place where it was written. In fact, the late date of its initial use by St. Irenaeus (around 170 C.E.) would suggest a late date of composition: perhaps it was written within a very different social world and religious culture than from what the church was experiencing a century or so earlier. Even if we can determine that the narrator uses oral and written sources that reflect a much earlier period, the international scope of Acts' narrative world frustrates any attempt to link the original conversation between its author and his audience to a particular place.

With so little reliable information of a historical kind, most interpreters of Acts consider inferences drawn from the narrative itself to locate the story at its moment of composition. The idiom and craft of the story suggest that the storyteller was a well-educated gentile. His superb knowledge of Israel's Scriptures and keen attention to the church's Jewish legacy, however, implies that he may have been a convert to Judaism (a proselyte) before becoming a Christian. His reference to himself in the second half of Acts, if taken literally, indicates that he had a reliable source close to Paul; perhaps he was at times a traveling companion of Paul (cf. 16:10-17; 20:5-16; 21:1-18; 27:1–28:16), and his Christian theology may have been cultivated by the latter's instruction. Irenaeus's reading of Acts as inspired Scripture assumes that the narrator's (Luke's) "apostolic credentials" are derived from his working relationship with the apostle Paul, which also seems to reflect the sentiment of the ancient church.

Some have speculated that Theophilus's name (Greek for "dear to God") is a metaphor for new converts seeking theological instruction, who are then the intended readers of both Luke's Gospel and the book of Acts. This is unlikely, however, since his identity is carefully qualified by the honorific title "most excellent" (Luke 1:3), which is never used metaphorically by ancient writers. It is more likely that Theophilus is a wealthy patron who has provided the author with sufficient funds for him to write both his story of Jesus and then later the story of his apostolic successors. In the preface to his Gospel, Luke addresses this "most excellent Theophilus" as a new believer who requires a more secure understanding of his faith (1:4). In this sense, then, the patron Theophilus is also one who would have read and reflected on the story of Acts for spiritual insight that might educate an unformed faith and thereby make him more resilient to the threat of unanswered questions, misunderstood doctrine, or moral compromise.

The approximate nature of these "unanswered questions" — and related spiritual imperatives — may be broadly inferred from the narrative's most important themes:

(1) The persistent struggle to maintain Christian unity in the face of intramural conflict (Acts 5:1-11; 6:1-11; 11:1-18; 15:1-29) may suggest that Acts was written to consolidate the faith communions within an increasingly international church. Moreover, when first read within the Roman world, which was riddled with class conflict, the portraits of a faith community

that resolved conflict with "one heart and soul" (4:32) embody an important line of evidence for the unifying power of God's love (4:33; cf. 2:42-47).

(2) The ambivalent depiction of Rome (and of Paul's Roman citizenship) may be intended to define the church's relationship with secular authority as ambivalent at best. While the Paul of Acts is a Roman citizen, his obligations to Rome are secondary, and they never compromise his obedience to God. If Theophilus has political standing in his community, Acts would remind him that his principal loyalty is to God's kingdom rather than to Caesar's Rome.

(3) If Acts was written to secure the fragile faith of a new believer, Luke may have intended his story to provide a catechism by which new converts might learn about God while locating themselves in a religious movement going back to the risen Jesus himself. The illustrations of the community's "resurrection practices" (for example, sharing possessions with the needy, hospitality to strangers, apostolic teaching, "street" evangelism, conflict resolution, and public worship) are formative of a bold counterculture that would have been especially challenging for the church's growing urban middle class of Roman society.

(4) Most importantly, Acts responds to a theological crisis. The rousing success of Paul's urban mission among non-Jews, coupled with the relative lack of success among Jews, may have prompted some believers to wonder whether the church's Jewish legacy had lost its relevance. The story of Acts makes clear that the threat to the church's religious identity in the public square, if not also its covenant relationship with God, comes not from the so-called Judaizers sometimes mentioned in Paul's letters, who contended for a process of gentile conversion more like what would have been found in the synagogue; rather, the threat now comes from a "gentilizing" movement that seeks to rid the church of those resurrection practices, whose form and even motive are indebted to a Jewish legacy.

The stories of conversion and mission in Acts underwrite the essential continuity between Israel and the church, as well as the continuing importance of Jewish traditions, especially of Israel's Scripture (our Old Testament), in cultivating Christian faith and witness. Indeed, the church must become more Jewish in order to become more Christian! The blessings God has promised to Israel according to Scripture are also to be inherited by gentiles, not because they have displaced Jews in God's favor but because they have been grafted into the "rich root" of Israel (cf. Rom. 11:17-24).

A second question one may ask of Acts is: How did the narrator compose the story? Most scholars interested in a literary analysis of Acts begin their work by noting that the plot line of Acts continues the plot line of Luke's Gospel. But Acts is not a Gospel kind of book, nor is it found with the Gospels in the New Testament. In fact, the framers of the biblical canon would seem to commend a reading of Luke's Gospel with the other three, while a reading of Acts has a singular role to perform. (More on this below.) In a literary note, we should observe only that Luke's Gospel is fashioned by conventions more like those of ancient biographical literature, whose story follows an important person's life and career — in this case, Jesus' messianic career. The book of Acts, on the other hand, sketches the origins of a religious movement in a way similar to historical monographs of antiquity: Acts is best read as a species of ancient historiography.

But we make this observation with an important caveat: a biblical narrative such as Acts does not "report" history as an autonomous "event" with significance all its own. The purpose of a biblical narrative such as Acts is to draw the reader's attention to a God who acts within the bounds of history to save the world from humanity's sin and folly. Acts is a theological narrative whose account of historical events frames a particular account of God, whose purpose is to lead its readers toward a more faithful understanding of that God. Of course, this does not mean that Acts is a fiction or that its account of historical events is unreliable. Many scholars conclude that the historical argot of Acts is actually quite reliable, especially when measured by the historiography of ancient Roman historians such as Suetonius, Josephus, and Tacitus. Rather, our caveat calls attention to the very idea of "history" that is embedded in the narrative world of Acts, which defines the historical moment as the crucible within which the promised salvation of God is worked out according to the prophecies of Israel's Scriptures.

Since Luke was not an eyewitness to much of what he recounted, he depended on unnamed sources for his information (cf. Luke 1:1-3). From these sources he selected certain events to craft into a coherent literary composition, which was the literary process of most ancient historians. Acts tells how the promise of God's redemption is realized for "all the families of earth" (Acts 3:21). Jesus' farewell prophecy (1:8) provides something of a narrative template that allows the reader to follow the story's progress, beginning in Jerusalem (Acts 1–7), then moving into the neighboring provinces of Samaria and Judea (Acts 8), and ultimately taking in other nations and peoples beyond Palestine (Acts 9-28).

The many speeches of Acts are especially important for preachers, not the least because they provide effective patterns that continue to guide a contemporary proclamation of God's gospel. Speeches make up roughly one-third of the story and often signal plot movements while providing summaries of Luke's core theological commitments. The most important serve "missionary" ends: Peter's Pentecost sermon (2:14-41), the inaugural sermon of Paul's mission to the nations at Pisidian Antioch (13:16-41), and his sharply stated Socratic retort at the Athenian Areopagus (17:22-31) are good examples of public discourse that serves to persuade readers toward Luke's understanding of the gospel. While not set in missionary settings, Paul's "farewell" (20:17-35) and defense speeches (22:1-21; 24:10-21; 26:2-23; 28:17-20) define his spiritual authority and frame his personal importance for the church's future. For this reason, believers continue to take important lessons from the Pauline letters that follow Acts in the New Testament.

Even though they use different literary conventions to fit different narrative settings, the speeches of Acts draw on a common pool of images and ideas. The result is the continuity of Christian proclamation from the risen Jesus (see 1:3) to the imprisoned Paul (see 28:30-31). Whether serving missionary, apologetic, or simply edifying purposes, the speeches of Acts agree on the non-negotiable content of God's saving word: Jesus performs signs and wonders as God's Messiah; he then suffers and is crucified; and finally he is resurrected and exalted by God to confirm that "there is no other name under heaven by which we must be saved" (4:12). In order that this messianic "event" conforms to the script of God's salvation, Paul and Peter both layer proofs-from-prophecy into their speeches, though Paul does it more subtly when proclaiming to the secular intellectuals at Athens. Scripture's witness is complemented by eyewitness testimony, whether of the risen Jesus (e.g., 2:32; 26:8, 15-16, 26), of personal experience of God's presence (e.g., 15:7-11, 12) or of an exemplary life (e.g., 20:18-21). Religious experience is glossed by Scripture's interpretation to prove the trustworthiness of the gospel's claims about the Lord's messiahship and God's faithfulness to redemptive promises made. Other narrative elements, such as Luke's summaries (see 2:42-47; 4:32-35) and interludes (see 6:1-7), perform roles within Acts similar to the speeches: they emphasize the most important literary themes and provide a retrospective on previous events in preparation for the future.

A third question *suggests yet another critical rule: What does Acts teach us about God?* Both the characterization of God and the plot line of God's activity in Acts express the narrator's core theological convictions as follows:

(1) God the Creator: Even though God is not an evident character within Luke's narrative world in the same way Peter and Paul are, Beverly Roberts Gaventa reminds us that Acts teaches about God not only through the speeches that interpret God (e.g., 7:1-53; 17:22-31) and the prayers offered to God (e.g., 4:23-31) but also by way of the narrated events that occur as a "divine necessity" (1:16; 3:18; 5:38; 13:27; 27:24). We experience God's activities as the fulfillment of biblical prophecy. God is Israel's God (3:13), whose plans are disclosed in Israel's Scripture; however, we often experience the truth about God's way of salvation before we reread Scripture and understand it in that light (cf. 2:1-21; 15:13-21). God is the God of the nations, and God's plans are to save "all the families of the earth," according to the promise made to Abraham (cf. 3:25). And so the plot line orders the redemptive activity of a God who first calls the entire household of Israel through the preaching of the gospel, but then invites gentiles — even those unaffiliated with the synagogue and unfamiliar with Moses — to share in the blessings promised to Israel.

(2) Christ: Jesus is God's Messiah, the one sent by God to fulfill Israel's hopes and to bring to realization God's promise of universal restoration (3:19-21). His divine appointment as the world's Savior is at God's direction (2:22-23, 36; 10:34-43), and it is God's resurrection of Jesus that discloses him as the Lord on whose name all people must call for their salvation (cf. 2:26; 2:21). Israel and the nations divide over Jesus; but even this split decision is prophesied by Israel's Scripture. Ironically, this identifies him as the agent of God's promised salvation.

(3) Holy Spirit: the Spirit supplies the power source that enables those who repent to bear public witness to their risen Lord (1:4-8). However, the powerful influence of the Spirit now extends to all believers and increasingly reflects the characteristics of a personal deity: it speaks (8:29; 10:19; 13:2) and guides (13:4; 15:28; 16:6-7); and people can lie to the Spirit (5:3), test the Spirit (5:9), or resist the Spirit (7:51). The Spirit is not external to those it influences (11:15) but is "poured out" to "fill up" believers (2:4; 4:8, 31; 6:3, 5; 7:55; 9:17; 11:24; 13:9), to empower in them a prophetic ministry that continues what Jesus had begun to say and do (1:1-2).

(4) Church: those who call on the name of Jesus in repentance are baptized into a community of shared goods — material and spiritual (2:38-39). The community's resurrection practices include economic, spiritual, religious, and social actions (2:42). As an economic *koinonia*, the community reorders its possessions so that its generosity toward the needy

reciprocates God's generosity in the gift of salvation (2:44-45; 4:32-35; 4:36–5:11; 6:1-6; 11:27-30). Likewise, the Holy Spirit is shared property among all disciples, so that the Spirit's Pentecostal coming upon repentant Jews is repeated on repentant gentiles (10:44; cf. 11:17; 15:9). The spiritual dimension of the community's solidarity is expressed most profoundly by a prohibition: to "abstain from things polluted by idols" (15:20; 15:29; 21:25), which today might include possessions, careers, television culture, nationalism, or anything else that displaces God as a disciple's central devotion. The concern of Acts is not only the inward, spiritual purification of individual believers (15:9-11) but also the social purity of the entire community's public identity (15:22-29; 21:21-26).

(5) Consummation: the ascension of the risen Jesus and the Pentecostal outpouring of God's Spirit mark the inauguration of the "last days" of salvation's history (2:17): every episode of Acts is understood against this eschatological horizon. Jesus' ascension and his return in like manner (1:10-11) bracket these "last days," during which believers are called by God to live and work according to God's redemptive purposes rather than to count the days until an apocalyptic end to history (1:6-8).

A final interpretive question is: What role does Acts continue to perform within the New Testament? We will return to this question in a concluding reflection on "teaching Acts as Scripture" (chapter 15). A few introductory responses, however, are in order. When St. Irenaeus was the first to use Acts as Scripture toward the end of the second century, he did so on behalf of a faith community that wanted to produce a Christian Bible that would help form that community's distinctive religious identity. The ongoing authority of Israel's Scripture for Christians; the continuity between Jesus, his apostolic successors, and their successors; and the relationship between the fourfold Gospels' "authorized" biography of Jesus and the Epistles written by his apostles, used by some to support "heretical" teachings — all these were contested issues within a deeply divided church. These issues plot the story of how the ancient church added Acts to an emerging biblical canon — a collection of sacred texts — and entitled it "The Acts of the Apostles" as a reflection of its reception and use during the canonical process.

The story of Acts not only confirms the continuity between Jesus and the apostolic traditions of the catholic church; its story also upholds the essential unity between the church's different apostolic traditions and their common agreement with the teaching of Israel's Scripture. If one reads the New Testament sequentially — the four Gospels before Acts and Acts before the Pauline and Catholic Epistles — the importance of Acts' placement after the Gospels and before the Epistle collections becomes more evident to the reader. One can see the parallelism between God's gospel and Acts — and thus the continuity between the "acts of the apostles" and what Jesus "began to say and do" — more readily. The portraits of the apostles in this biblical book not only commend their religious and moral authority but also confirm in advance the importance of their letters for theological understanding. In fact, the relationships among Peter, John, James, and Paul, and their respective missions as depicted in Acts, cue the interpreter on how to manage the ongoing dialogue between their respective New Testament writings. Similarities and dissimilarities in emphasis and theological conception between the different Gospels and the Epistles correspond to and complement the way Acts narrates the internal negotiations between the church's different missions (e.g., 2:42-47; 9:15-16; 11:1-18; 12:17; 15:1-29; 21:17-26).

For this reason, the role this biblical story best performs today is explaining rather than tempering the theological diversity found within the whole New Testament. The church that claims continuity with the apostles should tolerate a rich pluralism, even though it is sometimes accompanied by internal controversy and conflict. What is achieved at the Jerusalem Council (Acts 15; cf. Gal. 2:1-10) is Christian unity rather than theological uniformity. Acts supports the entire biblical canon, Old Testament and New Testament, in forging a dynamic, self-correcting apparatus that prevents its readers from theological myopia and spiritual distortion.

This brief introduction to Acts has now come full circle, from considering the narrative's point of origin many centuries ago as Luke's book for his first reader, Theophilus, to a consideration of his story now canonized as a biblical book that must form a wider, ongoing audience of faithful readers. This shift of perspective from Luke's Acts, with its attendant historical interests, to the Scripture's Acts, with its attendant theological interests, prompts us to draw several conclusions about the way we read Acts for a new day.

1. When the Bible is read sequentially, as it should be, the strategic role of Acts within the biblical canon becomes more apparent. Not only will its many references to Israel's Scripture supply interpretive guidelines for reading the Old Testament as Christian Scripture; its placement between the four Gospels and the following two collections of Epistles implies that it has a bridge-building role in relating the gospel story of Jesus with the

biblical writings of his apostolic successors. According to the Bible's final form, the fourfold Gospel (and not just the third Gospel) is required reading for the study of Acts, even as the book of Acts is required reading for the study of the Epistles that follow (see chapter 15).

2. The contribution Acts makes to the church's understanding of God is now measured as an indispensable part of the entire biblical witness; in fact, it's hard to imagine what a fully biblical witness to God might be if it did not include Acts. What distorted idea of the church's faith, its religious or social identity, or its vocation in the world might result from a conversation with a body of sacred writings that did not include this book? What thin reading of the Pauline letters would result if the interpreter failed to prep herself by first reading the story of the canonical Paul of Acts? Simply put, reading Acts within its biblical setting reminds us that we run the risk of distorting Christian faith and life if we ignore the theological understanding that comes from its witness.

3. One can more keenly understand the enduring importance to the church of Peter, Paul, and James because of their portraits in Acts. At stake is not the historical accuracy of these portraits, which remains contested, or even the important questions concerning their status within earliest Christianity. The more important issues from Scripture's own angle of vision are theological: What do the Peter and the Paul and the James of Acts have to say about the future of the church, and how do their respective stories in Acts orient readers to the Pauline and Catholic Epistles that follow?

4. The church's conflict with the synagogue at the end of the canonical process was no doubt different from Luke's assessment when he wrote his "rough draft" of Acts decades earlier. What began as an intramural "Jewish problem" had become a "Judaism problem" by the third century. Keen competition had developed between two "world religions," made all the more prickly by their common history and theological conception. The scribal emendations to alternative versions of Acts, which include more negative characterizations of unrepentant Jews, may well reflect the church's heightened sensitivity to its relationship with the synagogue. In a different sense, Luke's portrait of Jews who remain divided over Jesus clarifies the real difference between Christianity and Judaism for a later period: the only real issue that divides the two is not based on concerns of ethnicity, race, or national origin, but it is Christological. Thus Acts read as Scripture continues to subvert any "Christian" prejudice against Jews (or other religious groups) on the mistaken presumption that God has re-

neged on promises made according to Israel's Scripture or that God has replaced Jews with Christians in the economy of salvation. God's faithfulness to Israel, properly understood, remains inviolate; today's church must become more Jewish, not less so, in order to be fully Christian in its worship and witness.

5. The "primitivism" of Acts simply reflects the ecclesiastical experience of the earliest church, which fashioned itself after the Diaspora synagogues and other voluntary organizations of the Roman world. Worship consisted of prayer meetings and teaching, with Christian fellowship centered in the homes of middle-class believers. The sociology of the church dramatically changed during the canonical process: these loosely confederated house-congregations became, over time, participants in an emerging church catholic. For this reason, the ongoing interest in the images and ideas of "church" in Acts should be based more squarely on its missional vocation and prophetic message, its resurrection practices, and the nature of spiritual leadership — important claims on any congregation in every age — rather than on replicating outward forms of governance and worship and other time-conditioned practices.

6. In this regard, reading Acts as Scripture seeks to impose its narrative world on the changing "real" worlds of current readers. We discover new layers of meaning that were hitherto hidden whenever we allow the sacred texts to penetrate and interpret the world of its interpreters. For example, contemporary readers will more easily discern the relevance of the Ethiopian eunuch's story (8:26-40) for reflecting on the relationship between the church and its homosexual membership. Or one may see Priscilla in Acts 18, along with other women in Acts, as a role model for prophetic ministry in congregations once reluctant to encourage women in ministry. The vivid snapshots of the community of goods or repeated episodes that depict Paul's relationship with Rome may challenge today's congregations to develop a posture apart from civil religion or the wealth-and-prosperity gospel and toward a more prophetic understanding of a church that is countercultural. By inclining its readers in this direction, Acts provides an important element of a wider "canonical context" in which the faithful community gathers to reflect on those issues that either undermine or underwrite God's presence in today's world.

7. Finally, reading Acts as Scripture cultivates a fresh sense of sacred time and space. The church continues to live in "the last days," between Pentecost and *parousia*, when the Spirit of God empowers Christ's disci-

ples to bear witness to the resurrection throughout the world in anticipation of God's coming triumph and creation's final restoration (see 3:20-21). The continuing authority of the book of Acts concerns the formation of a church that proclaims God's word and embodies a witness to its truth to herald that coming day.

STUDY QUESTIONS

1. What beliefs and practices does your congregation or campus community consider primary in identifying what it means to be a Christian? Does your campus subscribe to a particular religious heritage or statement of faith and/or lifestyle? How does the story of Acts inform (or not) those traditions and practices?

2. How do you think your own "rule of faith" is challenged by what Acts teaches its readers about God as summarized in this chapter?

3. To what theological crisis does Acts respond, and does this same crisis continue to subvert the attitudes and actions of Christians toward Jews/Israel?

4. What are the various ways in which the church engages secular culture? How does Acts define this relationship and the role the church performs within society?

3 Called to Be Church

PART I: INTERPRETING ACTS 1:1-14 AS SCRIPTURE

The opening sentence of Acts (1:1-2), which introduces the reader to the narrative to follow, continues with a brief summary of what Jesus did and said over the forty days between his resurrection and ascension. What the reader finds here recalls the final chapter of Luke's Gospel, where Jesus' activities after Easter are compressed into a single day. In Acts, the risen Lord's appearances to his apostles over a protracted period gives the impression of patient and comprehensive instruction that lends authority to the future work of his chosen successors.

The central moment of the narrative is Jesus' prophecy concerning the Holy Spirit (vv. 4-5), whose arrival in the Holy City portends the restoration of Israel (v. 6) and empowers the mission of the church (vv. 7-8). According to Acts, the hope of Israel's restoration and the mission of the church are integral features of "the last days" of salvation's history soon to be inaugurated by God during Pentecost (see Acts 2). The departure of the glorified Jesus into heaven concludes the first stage of his messianic mission, and it also creates the circumstances that require an apostolic succession. But this succession from Messiah to his apostles is not without problems. The messianic community left behind gathers for prayer (v. 14) to wait for God to act on Jesus' promise of the Spirit. We note that the gathering includes only eleven apostles. Will God's salvation go forward without the requisite twelve "to sit on thrones judging the twelve tribes of Israel" (Luke 22:30)?

Acts begins in the conventional way of second volumes in antiquity (vv. 1-2): Luke begins in the first person by sharply summarizing the content of his first volume for his reader, Theophilus. The latter's identity and role in the production of Acts remain unknown, though his name likely refers to an actual person rather than to a symbolic audience. In a single phrase, Luke reviews the story line of the book (the Gospel of Luke) that he presumes Theophilus has already read: the good news of "all that Jesus did and taught from the beginning." He does not present the Acts of the Apostles, then, as a brand-new story to be read in isolation from what has come before it; rather, Luke is careful to locate Acts within a more expansive narrative that includes his own Gospel's story of Jesus, without which Theophilus would be unprepared for the story that follows. The placement of Acts within the canon of the New Testament presumes that the faithful reader, unlike Theophilus, will have first read the four Gospels, not just Luke's Gospel, as the authorized account of "all that Jesus did and taught from the beginning."

Verse 2 introduces the apostles and in doing so gives three signals that alert the reader to the spiritual crisis that the Lord's departure has brought about: Will the promise of God's salvation, fulfilled by Jesus, continue to unfold in Israel's history in his absence? Luke refers first to Jesus' ascension. This seems redundant since it is later narrated in detail (vv. 9-11), but it introduces the ministry of his apostles, whose vocation is to continue to do what Jesus no longer can because of his departure. The Holy Spirit is "the Spirit of prophecy" who empowers and authorizes a ministry that will ensure continuity with what Jesus has already done. Jesus gives his instructions to the apostles "through the Holy Spirit" because only by the Spirit's power and directions will they fulfill their vocation as prophets-like-Jesus (v. 8; cf. Luke 24:46-49; John 20:21-23).

The word "apostle" derives from the verb "to send," denoting someone who is sent out with something important to give to someone else — in this case a word of salvation to proclaim and a mighty work to perform in Jesus' name. The images conjured up by this concept are similar to those associated with Old Testament stories of Israel's prophets, who are chosen by God as carriers of God's word (e.g., Isa. 6; Jer. 1). The reference to Jesus' selection of the apostles recalls that he chose them with God's provident help (cf. Luke 6:13) to give them special responsibilities and a privileged status within a restored Israel of God (cf. Luke 22:30). The plot line of Luke's second book to Theophilus, then, concerns these apostles, who are chosen and instructed through the Holy Spirit to continue the Lord's ministry in his absence.

Unlike the Gospel narrative, where Luke has recounted the details of Jesus' Easter appearances in the course of a very long and exciting day, Acts simply says that Jesus "appeared" to his disciples over an extended period of "forty days" (v. 3). The time compression of verse 3 presumes that the reader of Acts will have already read the Gospel account of Jesus' resurrection and his teaching about the reign of God. The idiom of Luke's generalized account here of Jesus' final instructions, then, is evocative of the Gospel narrative. Luke uses the phrase "many convincing proofs" *(tekmērion)* to support the real presence of a living Jesus; this is the only place that term is found in the New Testament. In ancient rhetoric this same word is used concerning hard evidence that will convince the skeptic or confirm the authority of the apologist. At the beginning of Acts, such "proofs" confirm what Jesus' resurrection is *not* for those who doubt it (cf. Matt 28:17): it is not propaganda, nor a phantom experience, but testimony that "he was alive" and that the "last days" of God's salvation have dawned.

The resurrection of Jesus is a theme of enormous importance in the book of Acts, which in turn witnesses to its importance for Christian faith. The resurrection is testimony of Jesus' faithfulness to God and confirms him as Lord and Christ (Acts 2:36). The authority of Jesus is deeply rooted in his faithfulness to God as God's servant and his relationship to God as son. Jesus not only understands God's redemptive plans but faithfully interprets Scripture's disclosure of those plans. His "suffering" is the signature of his costly obedience, which was required of the Messiah to complete his faithful service to God. Thus Jesus gives his final instructions with the implicit reminder that faithful discipleship will surely result in a costly suffering (cf. Luke 24:26; Acts 9:15-16; 14:22).

Most interpreters remain unclear about the importance of Luke's reference to "forty days." Some think it is a rhetorical marker that extends the compressed last day of the Gospels' account of Jesus to a more leisurely forty days in Acts. Since the passing of time and the movement from place to place are crucial elements in this narrative world, others think Luke adds "forty days" to fill out the chronology from Easter to Ascension — and then finally on to Pentecost, some ten days later. Contemporaneous Jewish writings, which Luke was aware of, often referred to forty days (or years) as a period of preparation during which God fully instructs people for the work ahead (e.g., Baruch 76:1-5; 4 Ezra 14:23-45; Exod. 24:12-18;

34:28; 1 Kings 19:8). Moses was sent away for forty years before assuming the mantle of Israel's leadership, then climbed Mt. Sinai to spend forty days under God's instruction. Jesus was led by the Spirit into the wilderness for forty days of final examinations (cf. Luke 4:1-13). These "forty days" symbolize an extended period of preparation and examination for the difficult work to which the apostles are called.

Jesus' curriculum concerns the "kingdom of God," which again links Acts with the Gospel story in which Jesus announces the fulfillment of God's promise to restore the kingdom to Israel (Matt. 4:17; Mark 1:15; Luke 4:43; 9:27; 13:29; John 3:3, 5). While not as prominent in the speeches of Acts, it is used here and at the very end of this book to form a literary *inclusio* (see 28:31): the reader of Acts is put on notice that the triumph and experience of God's reign in Israel's history is the subtext of the narrative sandwiched in between. The critical problem for the interpreter of Acts, however, is that no normative definition of this crucial catch phrase is anywhere to be found. Elements of such a definition are carried from the four Gospels into Acts; and Luke's narrative world is stocked with images of God's activity in history. God is not detached from this history but is powerfully present to heal and restore those who trust God, and humanity's only hope remains God's provident care for all creation. Jesus' instructions concerning God's kingdom, bolstered by the fact of his resurrection, are about the fulfillment (and experience) of God's promise to save the world.

Jesus' preparation of his apostles includes more than lessons in theology; he seasons his words with the close fellowship enjoyed over meals (1:4). This seems especially important as a preface to his second instruction, which he gives them in close communion rather than shouting it from a distance: "Don't leave Jerusalem." Here the apostles will forge a community of disciples of common mind and heart in support of the hard tasks they are given to perform. Here in the Holy City, according to Scripture's map, are the roads moving people into God's kingdom to be found. It is a city built with the bricks of prophecy, and the fate of all creation depends on what happens here. This has already proven true for the Messiah, for whom Jerusalem was the city of destiny and now the site of his imminent departure (cf. Luke 9:51). Thus it will be also true of his successors because Jerusalem is the point of their departure into the world as they carry the word of the Lord forth to the "end of the earth" (v. 8; cf. Luke 24:47).

The final instruction is to "wait for the promise of the Father": "You will be baptized with the Holy Spirit." John the Baptist's prophecy of the

Messiah's Spirit-filling, which was unfulfilled in Luke's Gospel, is now recalled and prophesied again by Jesus. He calls the Spirit "the promise of the Father" because the Holy Spirit is God's Spirit, who continues to mediate God's Word not only through Christ but after him as well (2:33). There is continuity between the prophetic ministry of Jesus and his apostolic successors because each is baptized into the realm of this same Spirit of prophecy, who empowers an effective ministry of Word and living witness. Jesus' response to the apostles' provocative question about the restoration of the kingdom of Israel (v. 6) indicates that the role of the Holy Spirit in Acts is functional rather than redemptive: initiation into the realm of the Spirit's work enables the believers to perform the prophetic tasks given them by God in bringing an effective witness of the risen Jesus to the world (vv. 7-8).

Unlike the Pauline emphasis on the Spirit's mediation of God's salvation-creating grace, here the images and ideas of the Spirit's role within the faith community are almost always tied to their mission or to the authority of their apostolic leadership. The kind of interpretive myopia that emphasizes the Pauline idea to the exclusion of Acts, or the reverse, is corrected by reading within canonical context, where these different emphases are brought into a mutually enriching relationship. The Pauline concept of the "spiritual life," which pays close attention to the role the Spirit performs within the community in enabling believers to live in new ways, is complemented by the concept in Acts of the Spirit as the invigorating source of the community's witness in the world.

The living Jesus' instruction regarding God's kingdom (v. 3), combined with his promise of God's Spirit (vv. 4-5), evokes the apostles' reasonable question: "Lord, is this the time when you will restore the kingdom to Israel?" While Jesus' resurrection has convinced them of God's triumph, Jesus has not yet engaged in those purifying actions that would ready Israel for God's reign (cf. Luke 24:21). Why the delay? Was this promised arrival of the Spirit Israel's redemptive moment? If we recall that the minds of these followers of Jesus had been opened by his instruction in Scripture (cf. Luke 24:44-45) over a period of forty days, we will naturally presume that they draw the logical inference from Jesus' prophecy of the Spirit's outpouring: the Spirit's arrival must signal Israel's restoration according to Scripture (see Isa. 32:14-20).

Jesus' response (vv. 7-8) does not set aside their connection between Pentecost and the biblical promise of Israel's restoration; it seeks to clarify the means and timing of its fulfillment. Clearly, God's restoration of Israel cannot be reduced to the forecasts of prophets claiming to be "Spirit-inspired" insiders: "It is not for you to know . . ." (v. 7). The coming Spirit will not reveal special knowledge of God's plans when Israel's Scripture provides a script already. Some scholars suppose that Jesus' firm injunction responds to the early church's painful experience with unrealized predictions of his return: they claim that the historical references of these words and of Paul's similar exhortations to the Thessalonians (1 Thess. 5:1-11) are to Christian prophets who claimed personal insight into the "times and periods" of end-time events and had gathered a cult-like and divisive congregation around themselves. This is doubtful. Jesus does not respond to speculation surrounding what is "not yet" but to a concern that his disciples engage in a mission "right now."

Rather than awaiting his Spirit-fueled return to usher them into some apocalyptic time zone when God would enact Israel's salvation in the "twinkling of an eye," Jesus' instruction to wait for the Spirit's arrival is clarified with a "great commission." His apostles will themselves participate with God's Spirit in bringing God's redemptive plans to realization: "You will receive power when the Holy Spirit has come upon you" (v. 8) — a prediction that loudly echoes Isaiah's prophecy of the Spirit's outpouring to renew Israel's eternal covenant with God (Isa. 32:15). Jesus agrees with the theological subtext of the apostles' query — the Spirit's outpouring does signal Israel's restoration — but adapts it to their vocation. God's kingdom will be restored to God's people as promised, not at an apocalyptic coming from heaven but rather through the church's Spirit-led mission on earth.

The catchword Acts uses for "power" is *dynamis,* which denotes a real force at work in dynamic and demonstrative ways for all to see and feel. The Spirit is the source of power, not in the sense of political authority granted to someone holding an ecclesiastical office, but rather a practical power enabling those who have this Spirit to perform the missional tasks given them. For this reason the Lord stipulates emphatically that this power will reside in *you,* enabling you to "be my witnesses" in continuity with "all that Jesus began to do and teach."

When Jesus turns the expectation of the restoration of Israel from an indeterminate chronology to the means of its realization within the church's missional history, he establishes the theological subtext of Acts. He then provides a geographical index to underwrite this history's irrepressible progress. And so the plot line of Acts follows this same index, beginning "in Jerusalem (Acts 2–7), in all Judea and Samaria (Acts 8), and to the end of the earth (Acts 9–28)."[1] The Spirit's outpouring empowers a global mission as the divinely intended means through which God renews the covenant with a repentant Israel and calls Israel "a light to the nations," so that even repentant gentiles can share in the blessings of Israel's salvation (see 3:19-26; 13:44-47; cf. Luke 2:32).

The account in Acts 1:9-11 of Jesus' ascension is unique in the New Testament outside the Gospels (Mark 16:19-20; Luke 24:51). Its narrative in Acts confirms several important impressions for the reader. Jesus' ascension separates him from his followers both spatially and temporally to forge a powerful sense of the crisis facing his friends left behind: What will they do now that their Lord has departed? Will they put up or shut up?

The ascension further validates Jesus' resurrection and vindicates the church's claim that he is God's Messiah (see 2:21, 36). That is, unlike others who are resuscitated to life — for example, Lazarus — Jesus is brought back to life by God, never to die again. The New Testament Gospels report only the discovery of an empty tomb, followed by various postresurrection epiphanies of the risen Jesus (1:3); but there are no witnesses to the resurrection itself. Perhaps for this reason, the verbs Luke uses in narrating Jesus' departure emphasize its physical availability to eyewitnesses: the followers "were watching" him until he was "out of their sight," continuing to "gaze" at him while two men asked them why they were "looking." The biblical story of Elijah's dramatic departure in a fiery chariot (2 Kings 2:11), the apocryphal retelling of Enoch's ascension in whirlwinds to the very "end of the heavens" (1 Enoch 39:3-4), and also Philo's description of Moses' ascension to God while still proclaiming God's Word (*Life of Moses*, 2:291) — these accounts were probably all known to the Acts storyteller. This story draws on that earlier Jewish tradition of exalting God's prophets to interpret Jesus' departure in prophetic terms: Jesus, powerful in word

---

1. The final phrase of the prophecy, *heōs eschatēs tēs gēs*, is singular: "the end of the earth." It probably echoes Isa. 49:6, a prophecy regarding faithful Israel's vocation as a "light to the nations" (see 13:47). If the reader locates this "end of the earth" within the narrative itself, the address is quite possibly Rome, the very epitome of a gentile neighborhood. This unwritten element would then add to the literary *inclusio* of Acts: even as Jesus teaches the "kingdom of God" to his apostles (1:3) to equip their mission to the "end of the earth," so Paul teaches the "kingdom of God" to his guests at the mythic "end of the earth," Rome (28:31).

and work (cf. Luke 24:19; Acts 7:22), and sent forth by God to announce the arrival of God's salvation and broker it on behalf of the world, now returns to God in triumph.

The ascension also provides the implied religious motive for the apostles' testimony of Jesus (v. 8). While they are not eyewitnesses to his resurrection, the apostles are eyewitnesses to his ascension, lending credibility to their proclamation that he is alive. Significantly, the "cloud" that carries Jesus heavenward (v. 9) recalls the use of a "cloud" to symbolize God's faithful presence among the liberated people in the Old Testament story of Israel's Exodus (see Exod. 16:10; 19:9; 24:15-18). If Luke adds "cloud" to capture this allusion, his further point is this: the apostolic proclamation about the living Jesus further confirms God's commitment to fulfill promises made to Israel (vv. 6-8).

The "two men in white robes" redirect our line of vision from Jesus' past to his future with these words: "This Jesus . . . will come in the same way" (v. 11). Their eschatological commentary on Jesus' ascension makes two different though complementary points. First, their words cultivate the haunting awareness of Jesus' bodily absence from his disciples. Only John's Gospel pays attention to the theological crisis brought on by Jesus' departure, when his farewell speech (John 14–16) encourages his followers to see that his departure will result in the "coming of the Counselor to you" (16:7) to "bear witness to me" (15:26) and to "teach you all things and bring to remembrance what I have said to you" (14:26). Jesus exhorts the disciples to find their way in the world without him and to shoulder the tasks of the messianic movement he has begun. His departure is the formal condition of their succession, even as it is the condition of the Spirit's empowerment; in fact, the instructions Jesus has given over the past forty days become sheer nonsense without his bodily departure.

Yet, the two robed witnesses also predict Jesus' return to complete his messianic vocation (see John 14:3). The eschatological horizon of the church's mission, which continues Jesus' *past*, is motivated by the hope of his *future* (Acts 3:19-21; 10:42). Much has been made of the lack of clear references to Jesus' return in the speeches of Acts. This is certainly all the more remarkable when we compare these speeches to the frequency of references to the Second Coming found in the Epistles and the Gospel traditions. While Luke diminishes the "not yet" of Jesus in favor of the "right now" of the church's mission, this narrative opening, which asserts that "this Jesus . . . will come," frames the entire story with future expectation.

Most interpreters claim that the "two men" symbolize Torah's requirement that two witnesses must confirm an alleged event (Deut. 19:15).
Given the integral connection of ascension and resurrection, we should assume that these "men" are the same two who also appeared to the women
at the empty tomb to confirm his prediction of execution and resurrection
(Luke 24:4-7). Earlier, in Luke's Gospel, however, Elijah and Moses — both
of whom ascended into heaven according to well-known Jewish legends —
appear at Jesus' transfiguration and speak of his "departure" from Jerusalem (cf. Luke 9:30-31). The echoes of the familiar traditions about Elijah
and Moses that reverberate throughout Acts provide good reason to think
that the identity of the "two men" is not angelic but "Jesus' prophetic pre-
decessors who ascended, Moses and Elijah." In either case, they provide
"official" testimony to the Lord's importance that will fund the apostles'
proclamation about him.

With the departure of the Messiah and his "official" succession to the
apostles now complete (vv. 12-14), the community is left to wait for God's
Spirit to empower their mission as Jesus predicted. Whether they are able
to continue their Lord's prophetic mission depends on their own faithfulness to Israel's God. For this reason, Acts is careful to depict them as observant Jews who journey only "a sabbath's day" from Mount Olivet back to
Jerusalem (cf. Exod. 16:27-30); they are also faithful to Jesus, who instructed them to wait in Jerusalem for the Spirit's outpouring (v. 4).

The disciples wait together and "constantly devote[d] themselves to
prayer" (v. 14). It is typical in Acts that true believers gather together for
prayer and worship to wait on God to act graciously and powerfully at critical moments of their history (cf. Acts 1:24-25; 4:24-30; 6:6; 8:15; 9:11; 12:12;
13:3; 14:23; 16:25; 20:36; 28:8). This prayerful waiting on the Lord not only
characterizes the church of Acts; it also underscores the implicit importance of Pentecost, when God will deliver the Holy Spirit to them as promised.

The community's constituency is also noteworthy. The listing of apostles (v. 13) is a literary convention of succession narratives and is expected
at the beginning of Acts: that is, these are the names of those who form the
messianic community's apostolate and provide its leadership in the absence of the Messiah. Because of Judas's betrayal, though, only eleven
apostles are named, thus forming an incomplete apostolate. For this reason, what follows is an account of Judas's death (vv. 15-20a) and the selection of his replacement (vv. 20b-26) according to Scripture's prophecy. The

inclusion of "certain women, including Mary the mother of Jesus," recalls the importance of various women in Jesus' ministry (cf. Luke 8:1-3; 24:1-11; John 4 and 11) and makes it clear that women will continue to play a significant role in the church's mission to the end of the earth (see Acts 18). Finally, Luke's curious reference to Jesus' "brothers" has led some commentators to find here a metaphor of all other disciples that make up the messianic community at Pentecost. This is doubtful. Given the central importance of the resurrection in the opening of Acts and of the role that James will play later on in Acts, this final phrase refers to actual members of Jesus' own family (James and probably also Jude), to whom the risen Jesus appears according to sacred tradition (see 1 Cor. 15:7).

PART II: ENGAGING ACTS 1 FOR TODAY'S CHURCH

Acts 1:1-14 is all about the vocation to be church, the calling and mission of the church. But before the focus shifts there, it is also a "succession narrative," and it is a story about the perils and prospects involved in changing leadership.

Leadership Changes Are Perilous!

Pretty much regardless of what group, body, or institution is considered, changing leadership is fraught with the twin words that have come to define crisis: "danger" and "opportunity." Whether it is a family business that is passing into the hands and leadership of a new generation, a city administrative department getting a new director, a university welcoming a new president, a nation after an election, or a congregation making a change in pastoral leadership — these changes and transitions are always important, often difficult, and frequently challenging.

The first fourteen verses of the Acts of the Apostles narrate key aspects of a change in leadership from Jesus to the apostles. Of course, this leadership transition has features that distinguish it from the other more worldly and perhaps mundane examples cited above. Not very often does a retiring president, for example, actually ascend into heaven (though quite a few do, interestingly, rise aloft in a helicopter as their successor is inaugurated). In some situations and traditions the retiring leaders may have called and trained their successors, as in some sense Jesus did; but such situations may be more the exception than the rule these days in business, politics, and even the church. Finally, of course, no one will truly succeed Jesus, at least not in the sense of taking over his role and calling as the Messiah. The apostles are not new messiahs, nor are they substitute or surrogate messiahs. That job has already been filled, once and for all, something that pastors who labor under a "messiah-complex" may do well to note. Nevertheless, the apostles are Jesus' successors in other crucial ways. They will give leadership to the new community of those who follow Christ, and they will carry on the ministry God has begun in him. They will guide the church as it grows and encounters new realities and challenges. They will be "prophets-like-Jesus." This first chapter of Acts is a "succession narrative."

How does the succession unfold? What light might this first leadership transition in the church shed on subsequent changes? These early verses of Acts suggest five elements of such a transition: (1) remembering the story, (2) preparing the new leader(s), (3) articulating expectations for the new leader(s), (4) a significant and validating religious experience, and (5) the actual departure of the former leader.

Luke begins Acts, as he began his Gospel, by addressing Theophilus and reminding him of what has gone before, the story of "the first book." Readers are to come to this account, as do the apostles themselves, aware of all that Jesus said and did in the third Gospel. But we would suggest that this element of remembering the story extends beyond Luke's Gospel to the fourfold Gospel of Matthew, Mark, Luke, and John. The canonical order of the Bible, the church's book, gives us not just Luke as the remembered story but the entire fourfold Gospel; so in a sense that "first book" is not simply the Gospel of Luke but all four of the Gospels — Matthew, Mark, Luke, and John. Together they form the "first book"; they are the church's story, its primal narrative.

Leadership transitions are an important time to get in touch with the primal narrative or story of whatever body, group, or organization is going through change. Remembering the story reminds us of who we are and whose we are: it reminds us of our purpose by telling of the formative events and experiences in our history. The point is not that we should be held captive to the past but that we should be firmly rooted in our core narrative and convictions. Leadership transitions are an important time for us to remember our story and to remember the story of God.

Beyond that, Jesus takes particular care to prepare the disciples over an extended and significant time period — forty days, to be exact. "Forty days" in which Jesus appeared to the disciples and offered convincing proof that he was not a phantom or an apparition but resurrected and alive. Forty days in which he taught the apostles about the kingdom of God. "Forty days" conjures up many other biblical stories of times of God's people preparing for and encountering God. It's easy to rush on in this early part of Acts and overlook this forty-day period of dwelling in the presence of the risen Lord; but this is a time of particular intimacy and preparation marked by teaching and fellowship (Jesus ate with the apostles as well as teaching them).

By telling us this, Luke once again (as in Luke 24) suggests the Word-and-sacrament pattern that was emerging as the core of the church's life. Breaking bread together and breaking open the bread of life, Scripture, were both crucial elements of Jesus' extended preparation of his apostles. Their preparation may, of course, be understood to have begun much earlier, as early as Jesus' first predictions of his passion. Yet here the preparation is concentrated in this forty-day period of being convinced of the resurrection, of learning of the kingdom, of sharing food and fellowship with the risen Lord. Jesus knew that leadership transition requires careful preparation of new leaders for their work and their role. Too many organizations, including churches, simply throw new leaders into the deep end and bark "swim" without such times of preparation.

Third, the apostles are given an explicit job description in verses 7-8. We will return to this vocational charge in more detail shortly; here it is sufficient to note that preparation is followed by laying out the task and responsibilities in a way that is direct enough to provide guidance yet general enough to allow considerable openness to the demands of a future that is as yet unknown. Still, Jesus clearly articulates expectations and imparts a job description. Organizations, including congregations, run into trouble in times of leadership transition when expectations are assumed but not articulated. Too often it turns out that these assumed but unarticulated expectations vary widely and are even in conflict with one another. Congregations do well, during such transitions, to ask themselves: What are we trying to accomplish for the Lord? What are our goals? And then they need to ask, What kind of leadership do we need to help us, to lead us, in this work? Working to clarify what they expect of leaders can be an important way organizations, institutions, and congregations do important internal work.

Even before giving his charge to the new church and its leaders, however, Jesus has instructed them to return to Jerusalem and await the outpouring of the Holy Spirit. There would be a powerful and numinous religious experience that would mark this leadership transition and confer power on the successors. This serves to remind us of the importance of powerful ritual, symbolic action, and gestures at times of leadership transition. Some may say that all the fuss is not really necessary, but in a way it is. We negotiate powerful changes in social relationships, such as leadership change, through the spoken and unspoken action of ritual. The outpouring of the Spirit on Pentecost was certainly more than this, but it was not less.

Finally, the departing leader does need to actually depart. Jesus ascends in a cloud, disappearing from their sight (v. 9). Too many leadership transitions fail because the outgoing leaders, pastors, CEOs, presidents, or directors do not actually leave. Too often they hang around, which inevitably sends mixed signals about who really is in leadership. Moses did not enter the promised land; the children of Israel entered the promised land without him, led by his successor, Joshua. Elijah was lifted up and away, leaving Elisha to carry on the prophetic ministry. The final act of leadership is to leave.

There are, of course, times and places where the previous leader can and does stay; but he or she must do so with a clear understanding of boundaries, of the definition of his or her new role, and what is required in that new role. Actual physical departure may not always be an imperative, but neither is it a bad idea — at least for a period of time. It allows the people to develop an "emotional availability" to welcome a new leader. Without departure or very clear new boundaries and new roles, the group and its members are less likely to have that crucial emotional availability that is necessary to welcome new leadership. That place in their hearts and souls will already be full.

The first instance of the leadership transition in the church, described in Acts 1:1-14, deserves careful pondering in our times of transition. It offers, if not an exhaustive or prescriptive list, then at the least an illustrative list of some of the tasks of such transitions: remembering the story, preparing the new leaders, a clear set of expectations for new leadership, an appropriately powerful and ritualized moment of transition, and the actual exit of the former leader(s).

Giving Responsibility Back

Jesus had signaled his understanding of the transition by doing something gifted leaders do: he gave responsibility back to the people who made up the body, organization, and community. He did not play the role of an all-knowing expert or authority, the one who has the answer for every question and situation (vv. 6-7). Rather, he gave the work back to the people to whom it belonged. This is a crucial task of leadership.

Ron Heifetz, student and teacher of leadership at Harvard's Kennedy School, is fond of saying, "Leadership is disappointing people at a rate they can stand." That is, leaders are often tempted to try to be and do all: they are tempted to be all-knowing experts who have the answer for every question, the solution for every problem. Here, however, we see that even Jesus, who could walk on water, does in a sense "disappoint people" — but at a rate they can stand.

In this regard, note particularly verses 6-8. In verse 6 the disciples ask Jesus, "Lord, is this the time when you will restore the kingdom to Israel?" It is not an unreasonable question given all that has led up to this moment. In a very real sense, it *is* the restoration of Israel, God's people, that is underway here, though the form of that restoration is unexpected. But in response to the apostles' question about timing, Jesus hedges and possibly — nay, probably — disappoints them: "It is not for you to know the times or periods that the Father has set by his own authority." Their query gives — or tries to give — the responsibility for the work to him; but Jesus gives the responsibility for the work of restoration and carrying on of his great mission back to them, back to the people. "It is not for you to know. . . . But you will receive power . . . and you will be my witnesses."

Though the empowerment is yet to come, at Pentecost, here is a decisive turn. One-time disciples, that is, students of the teacher, followers of the master, are getting a new name, a new job title, and new responsibilities. No longer "disciples," they will be "apostles," those who are sent to proclaim the good news of the gospel. Most churches are — or should be — hard at the work, Sunday by Sunday, of transforming disciples (followers and students) into apostles (teachers and witnesses of God's grace). Of course, Christians are always in some sense both disciples and apostles: we never get over our need to follow the master, to learn from our teacher. But there are risks to staying in the receiver and follower mode.

Here Jesus refuses to take all the responsibility; he gives it back. He sends one-time disciples forth as apostles. Many have said that the very best way to learn anything is to teach it; and in some way, at some time, Christian disciples must be both challenged and given the opportunity to teach what they have learned, to do the ministry in Christ's name and by the Holy Spirit's power. All churches that dedicate themselves to Christian formation and to growing people of faith must find ways for students to become teachers, for disciples to move on and become apostles sent into the world to minister in Christ's name.

Having considered these two directions — leadership transition and giving responsibility back — we are ready to move on to the vocation, the calling to be church. Acts affirms that the church does not so much have a mission as it *is* a mission. Increasingly, North America congregations and their leaders are discovering that every congregation is, at least potentially, a missionary outpost, a sign and beachhead of the new creation in the midst of a culture that is secular, religiously pluralistic, materialistic, and — more than we may wish to acknowledge — toxic.

The Church Does Not Have a Mission — It Is a Mission

Verse 8 of this first chapter, especially, states this missional vocation, this calling of the church: "But you will receive power when the Holy Spirit has come upon you; and you will be my witnesses in Jerusalem, in all Judea and Samaria, and to the ends of the earth." In a sense this verse foreshadows everything that follows in Acts, from the pouring out of the Spirit to the witness in Jerusalem, and then beyond Jerusalem, and finally, in Acts 28, to Rome. The task of the members of faith communities is to be "witnesses" to Jesus. This means more than simply telling one's personal story of faith or transformation, as important as that may be. To be Christ's witnesses is to bring forward into our own time and place the truth of the gospel. Just as Matthew, Mark, Luke, and John each took the words, teachings, deeds, life, death, and resurrection of Jesus and brought it to bear in their particular time and their communities, so the church's essential calling and task is to bear witness to what God has done and is doing in Jesus, to this outpouring of grace and healing, to this victory over the myriad powers of death at work in the world and in us — to witness to the power of Jesus to heal all that distorts, disfigures, and diminishes God's dream for life.

Congregations too often equate "mission" with a particular part of their overall budget, or with a set of programs or ministries, or with a particular department of a congregation's life. While the church's mission is never less than any of these varied expressions, there is a temptation to compartmentalize here. That is, "mission" is a part of the budget, a particular program, the responsibility of a certain staff person or committee. On the contrary! The church is in its nature and its total life a mission and missionary endeavor; in its very essence it seeks to be, and is called to be, Jesus' witness in all its words and deeds, in all its life, whether gathered or scattered. The church does not exist to provide a congenial social experience for its members; nor does it exist to satisfy the ego needs of its leaders. The church exists to bear witness to the new creation in Jesus Christ and to be the beachhead of that new creation in the midst of the old.

The domestication of "mission" to a budget, a committee, or a department of the church reflects the Christendom era, when North Americans came to think that the "mission field" was beyond our national borders, that it was somewhere out there where our Western civilization ended, and that it was generally "overseas." Missionaries and soldiers went forth together to "Christianize" the pagans, to bring an uncritical mix of Western culture and values along with Christian religion. Such was the world — and the alliance — of Christendom, of Christianity and worldly power, or "dominion." Those days, we may be thankful, are over.

There is, of course, work to be done everywhere, including overseas and in cultures other than our own. But the mission field today — that is, after Christendom — is not simply overseas or in different and non-Western cultures. The mission field is all around us. It is in our offices, on our streets, in our schools, in our homes, and in our sanctuaries. Note that the apostles and church were charged to begin their ministry close at hand, in Jerusalem, among God's own people!

All God's people, all baptized Christians, are called to be "my witnesses." This need not mean that one is speaking constantly, and perhaps inappropriately, of Jesus in all settings and at all times. Sometimes that actually hardens hearts and closes ears. The well-chosen word spoken at the right moment is the preferred approach. Furthermore, the witness is in both words and actions: the apostles will not only tell the story and name the name, they will be workers of signs and wonders. Here the point is that the whole church is a missionary outpost, a beachhead in the old world of a new one, a colony of heaven, a foretaste of the fullness of the kingdom. Mission can no longer be relegated or delegated to a committee, to a staff person, or to certain specialized persons called "missionaries." Mission belongs to the whole church. Those of us who are baptized Christians are all missionaries, set down here to be witnesses to God's love and God's dream for a broken and bruised creation.

When Jesus turns to the apostles — that is, to the church — and says, "You will be my witnesses," he speaks to us all, charges us all. Moreover, he enables us to then celebrate that great cloud of witnesses, spoken of in the Epistle to the Hebrews, the long line of saints and martyrs, teachers and prophets, ministers and servants, great and small, ordinary and extraordinary, in which we stand. To become Christian is to "join up," to be a part of the long line of witnesses, members of Christ's body on earth, bearing witness to a love and power that moves the planets and heals hearts. This mission, this purpose, belongs to us all.

There is one further way in which the first chapter of Acts emphasizes this point of the church *as* mission. We see that the apostles are somewhat given to speculations about the future, to wondering about the day, time, and nature of the *eschaton*, the end of the age. In verse 6 they ask about the times and periods; in verses 10-11 they stand staring into the heavens after Jesus' ascension and require prodding by the two men robed in white. Both moments direct the apostles — and direct the church — away from speculations about the future and toward mission and responsibility in the present. Jesus refuses to respond to speculation about the future, about the "not yet." He redirects the apostles and the church to the "right now." The two unidentified messengers react in the same way: "Why do you stand looking into the heavens?" Luke rebukes all such fixating on the future, on trying to predict it, on sky-surfing. He turns the apostles and the church to the work that is before them in the "right now." But before the apostles undertake that work, there is a pause — a time of waiting.

Waiting

One might respond to the charge and vocation Jesus extends to his church by saying, "Boy, great, let's go!" But not so fast. We don't go when *we* are ready — or think we are; we go when God sends us. That is, we don't go in our strength alone; we go in the strength of the Lord. And so we must wait, at least sometimes. Such is the instruction to the apostles. They have been prepared, been given responsibility, and have received a charge. But now they are told to wait: "While staying with them, he ordered them not to leave Jerusalem, but to wait there for the promise of the Father." It's not all up to them, not all in their hands: the promise they are to wait for is the gift of the outpouring of the Spirit.

Waiting is almost always difficult — especially in our activist age, which prizes human power, self-sufficiency, and autonomy. "We know what to do, let's get going," we may say, impatiently, confidently. "Let's do something; I'm tired of waiting." But when we get out there, we need to know that this wasn't just our good idea; we need to know and acknowledge that this was God's idea. "You did not choose me, but I chose you," Jesus declares to his disciples in the Gospel of John. "Our waiting," says William Willimon, "implies that the things that need doing in the world are beyond our ability to accomplish solely by our own effort, our programs and crusades. Some other empowerment is needed; therefore, the church waits and prays."[2]

Several years ago the congregation I served as pastor joined in a partnership with an African-American congregation. Both were large, long-established congregations with reputations for good work in the city. Great things would come of this partnership, we were certain. But we on our end were frustrated and disappointed — at least initially. Our opposite numbers seemed to be moving too slowly, at least for us. We were ready to get busy, to do and to act. But they were not. They suggested that we needed to spend some time together in prayer and in the study of Scripture. They suggested that we needed to wait on the Spirit. Only later did we recognize that our new partners were inviting us into the kind of waiting that preceded the day of Pentecost, which was a waiting characterized by prayer and the study of Scripture. It was born of the understanding that whatever we eventually undertook together in ministry needed to be led and empowered by the Spirit. This was truly a revelation for us powerful, impatient, self-confident white folks! Moreover, it was the first and crucial stage of our partnership with this other congregation — of being the church together. Our common work would emerge naturally, as the gift of the Spirit would come, and not merely from our own plans and ambitions.

At this crucial juncture, the church is reminded that before it is a giver or a doer, it is always a receiver. It is reminded that you cannot give to oth-

2. Willimon, *Acts*, Interpretation (Louisville: Westminster/John Knox, 1998), p. 21.

ers what you have not yourself received. Before the church is an instrument of grace, it is always a receiver of grace. Thus we go into the world and encounter others as persons who have ourselves stood in need of God's grace and of the Spirit's power. This imparts a necessary humility to the task of "being my witnesses."

Note also how the church waits: this waiting is neither passive nor solitary. The church waits together in solidarity with one another, and by being in prayer and the study of Scripture. Our images of waiting are often of passivity; everything will come from elsewhere. But as anyone who worships regularly should know, we can cultivate a receptive heart and spirit through active and expectant waiting. Such waiting, done in community, is quite different from standing in the grocery line, at the bus stop, or in a thousand other experiences of waiting in daily life. This active, expectant waiting is a time of calling on the Lord, anticipating the fulfillment of promises, being confident of God's faithfulness, and resolving to restore and create God's people anew.

Here in the first chapter of Acts we learn of our calling to be God's church, Christ's witnesses in the world. We are called to responsibility and equipped for it in a time of transition. We are invited to be not only disciples but apostles, those who are sent out into the world as witnesses to what God has done and is doing. We are reminded that the mission of the church cannot be reduced to a budget item or a department or program, that all we do is mission. But we are also reminded that the mission is not our own; it is God's mission, which began before us and will continue after us. Therefore, we must await the coming of the Spirit, who will empower us to fulfill our calling to be the church.

STUDY QUESTIONS

1. The Bible should be read sequentially from beginning to end. In this light, what should the reader of Acts know about the principal characteristics of "all Jesus did and taught" (Acts 1:1) according to the four Gospels? Why is this prior knowledge of Luke's Gospel story of Jesus important for a right reading of the story Acts narrates of his successors?

2. How does Jesus' prophecy of the church's mission in 1:7-8 correct a "left behind" vision (or any other you may cite) of the future?

3. Why is the Lord's ascension an important element of the church's "Easter faith"?

4. Recall an experience of "leadership transition" that you have experienced, whether in a congregation or campus setting. How did it go? Of the five elements of leadership transition identified in Acts 1, which came into play in your example, and which did not?

5. Have you experienced pastors or campus leaders who "gave responsibility back." When? How? How did it go?

6. "The church does not so much *have* a mission as it *is* a mission." Does this make sense to you? Why or why not? What implications does this statement have for your congregation?

4 Bold Witness: Preaching as If Something Is at Stake

PART I: INTERPRETING ACTS 2:1-40 AS SCRIPTURE

Almost a third of the book of Acts consists of speeches. Although different in many ways, most of these speeches seek to convince their listeners of the gospel's central claim: God's resurrection of Jesus confirms him as the Messiah, and through him God has acted faithfully to the biblical promise to save the world from sin and death. They are thus "missionary speeches" and form a principal expression of the church's obedience to Jesus' commission (1:8).

The attentive reader of Acts recognizes that Peter's sermon on Pentecost (here in Acts 2), a speech made possible by his being filled by the Holy Spirit (vv. 1-4), is exemplary of the community's testimony to Jesus. Only the fact that he has been filled by God's Spirit has enabled Peter to retrieve God's plan of salvation from Israel's Scripture in a way that confirms that the risen Jesus is God's Messiah (2:22-36). Persuasive preaching is not a matter of being "filled [*mestoō*] with wine" (v. 13), or any other man-made resource, but being "filled [*plēstheis*] with the Holy Spirit" (v. 4).

Like other speeches in Acts that address a Jewish audience, Peter's sermon includes Jewish midrash (or commentary) on Israel's Scripture: he begins by echoing the preceding prophecy and then goes on to provide a persuasive commentary on its messianic meaning (vv. 22-40) in order to address the present crisis, namely, the ignorance of the importance of the present moment in salvation history (i.e., Messiah has come and gone;

49

God's Spirit has come to replace him). Not only are these devout Jews confused by the miracle of Galileans speaking their languages (vv. 5-12); the phenomenon has provoked a mocking retort (vv. 13-15) rather than a faithful response (see v. 41).

The speeches of Acts are also composed by the narrator with attention to well-regarded Greco-Roman rules of persuasive speaking, rules that regulate what is said in terms of the particular audience addressed, the specific crisis that occasions the speech, and the subject matter of the speech. Accordingly, Peter's speech logically reaches its climax in verse 36, where he draws on appropriate evidence to support his claim. Peter is not careless with his evidence: he carefully crafts it into a persuasive speech that deals with the immediate crisis of Israel's skepticism. For this reason, faith is the logical response to Peter's speech. Wesley called gospel preaching an "awakening experience." Good preaching compels listeners toward deeper reflection and courageous action; under the aegis of the Spirit, it can even transform scoffers into believers.

No episode in Acts has received more attention than the one reported in verses 1-4. And that scrutiny is justified because of the clear importance Jesus places on the Pentecost experience in his final instructions to the apostles (1:4-8), because of the speech's highly evocative description, and because various communions today have attached themselves to this passage as Scripture's warrant of their religious experience and theological contribution to the church. Furthermore, this passage continues to frame the church's observance of the "Pentecost season," the time when believers worship together in heightened expectation of being renewed and reborn by the power of God's Spirit.

Yet the church's powerful attraction to the story of Pentecost is surprising for two reasons. Luke, alone among biblical writers, tells the story of the Spirit's arrival: it is his "great theme," without which "there would be no story to tell."[1] To be sure, John's Gospel makes a passing reference to Jesus' bestowing the Father's paraclete on his stunned disciples shortly after the resurrection (John 20:22). The reader is doubly surprised, then, to find in Acts an account of this important moment rendered in a narrative so spare.

But much is admitted by the first four verses of Acts 2. The opening phrase claims that the entire community, not just the apostles (cf. 1:6-8), is

1. J. D. G. Dunn, *The Acts of the Apostles,* Narrative Commentaries (Valley Forge, Pa.: Trnity Press International, 1996), p. 22.

baptized into the realm of the Spirit "when the day of Pentecost had come" to the Holy City. *Pentecost* (literally, the "fiftieth day") is the term used by Diaspora Jews for a day-long harvest festival that was more commonly known as the "Feast of Weeks" (Exod. 23:16; 34:22; Lev. 23:15-21; Num. 28:26; Deut. 16:9-12). Luke's staging of the Spirit's outpouring at Pentecost may explain why he lists the nations in verses 9-10, since that day was one of three pilgrimage feasts during which the entire household of Israel gathered together in Jerusalem — fifty days after Passover in celebration of God's goodness to the nation. The prospect of the church's proclamation of the gospel to all of Israel can thereby be realized.

Some interpreters of the Spirit's arrival hear echoes of the Old Testament narrative of God's appearance on Sinai and the divine revelation of Torah to Israel (Exod. 19:16-19; Deut. 5:4-5). On the basis of this allusion, they claim that Pentecost holds typological significance for Luke's theology of the Holy Spirit: if the giving of the Torah fifty days after Israel's Passover is an act of covenant renewal (Exod. 19:5-6), then the Spirit is given on this Pentecost to renew God's promise of a new covenant (cf. Rom. 8:2). To describe the Spirit's descent, Luke draws his language from a deep pool of Old Testament images used in theophanies (divine appearances) — fire, sound, and tongues. Elsewhere in Acts he links the Spirit and law as integral marks that identify the church as a people belonging to Israel's God: that is, a people in possession of God's Spirit are those who obey God's law (10:14, 28; 15:21; 21:21). In any case, the in-breaking of heaven into human affairs is a meaningful feature of Luke's narrative world. And so the reader of Acts is hardly surprised that the promised Spirit arrives from heaven with special effects: the arrival sounds like a "violent wind" and looks like "tongues of fire."

The community's reception of God's Spirit is public and perceptible, as was true in Luke's portrayal of Jesus at his baptism (Luke 3:21-22). The Spirit of God is not the private property of an enlightened few but belongs to all the people of God, which Luke makes clear with repetition: "they were all together" in a "whole house where all were sitting," when the Spirit came to rest on "each of them" so that "all of them were filled." While the Spirit of Pentecost is generally the Spirit of the Old Testament, who rested only on Israel's covenant mediators — and despite the singular importance of the twelve in Acts (cf. 2:42) — the gift of the Spirit extends to and is shared by every member of the community.

The precise meaning of the phrase "filled with the Holy Spirit" (v. 4) remains contested, mostly because it is set against an unclear background. While the phrase is almost certainly shaped by Luke's firm belief that a sovereign God guides the witnessing community through the Spirit, we can no longer limit the meaning of Spirit-filling to prophetic demeanor, to the boldness or even the persuasive rhetoric of the community's (and especially their apostles') evangelistic crusades. In fact, the Jewish background of this idea in Philo's writings suggests a Spirit that gives "extraordinary insight" to those it fills. The prophet who is filled with God's Spirit sets aside the processes of human intellect, such as conjecture and guesswork, and replaces them with true knowledge, the byproduct of a divinely inspired intellect. The practical result, according to Philo, is that the Spirit-filled prophet is given an enriched capacity to exegete Scripture, to interpret the biblical text according to the mind of God. Surely Luke understands the baptism, or "filling," by the Spirit in this way. Thus the Spirit is not only the power by which Scripture is written by the prophets of old (1:16; 4:25; 28:25), but these same prophecies of the Spirit are rendered accurately and with keen insight into the human (and especially Israel's) condition by this same Spirit through the prophets-like-Jesus it now inspires afresh. Therefore, it is unlikely that Acts ever depicts Spirit-filling that empowers speech disconnected from biblical interpretation or proclamation.

The power of the Spirit brings out something extraordinary: the ability to "speak in other languages," that is, in foreign languages known to the hearers but unknown to the speakers. This miraculous "gift of tongues," called *xenolalia*, should not be confused with the spiritual gift of *glossolalia* ("speaking in tongues"), which divides certain Corinthian congregations and is such a concern to Paul in 1 Corinthians 12–14. The relevant issue when one compares the two phenomena is not their common source or the linguistic structure of each, whether "of men or of angels" (1 Cor. 13:1); nor does Luke distinguish this particular incident of Spirit-filling in Acts 2 from subsequent episodes of other extraordinary speeches in Acts (e.g., 10:45-46; 19:6). The key difference between this narrative in Acts and Paul's letter is their competing purposes. According to Pauline teaching, the gifts of the Spirit are used to empower Christian ministry to other believers for the purpose of Christian formation: thus the Pauline meaning of *glossolalia* denotes a special language given to a few believers by the Spirit (1 Cor. 12:14-30) to edify the entire congregation (1 Cor. 14:5).

The crowd of "devout Jews" (vv. 5-13) hears "this sound," whose source is "Galileans" — notorious for their lack of linguistic talent — "speaking in the native language of each" about "God's deeds of power." This is the first of over fifty references to the "Jews" *(Ioudaioi)* in Acts, and it has paradigmatic value for the reader: "Jews," repentant and unrepentant, occupy center stage in Luke's narrative world, and the reader should be ever alert to the nuances of his use of the word in Acts.

Two elements in particular have considerable value for a clear-headed reading of the story. First, these are "devout Jews," even as the disciples who bear witness to God's mighty deeds are also observant Jews. Gospel proclamation begins with faithful Jews — and for them — according to Isaiah's promise of a restored Israel (1:6-8). Significantly, the catalog of nations (vv. 9-11) indicates that these Jews constitute a global assembly: Luke's hyperbole is "every nation under heaven." In effect, the entire household of Israel, including "both Jews and proselytes" (v. 10, i.e., gentile converts to Judaism), is present to hear the community's witness to God's deeds of power and thus represent the purview of God's faithfulness to Israel. Second, these Jews are "bewildered," "amazed and astonished," and "perplexed" (vv. 6, 7, 12) by this phenomenon. Their astonishment reflects the present crisis facing Israel: while followers of Jesus possess the promised Spirit, those who remain ignorant of Scripture's confirmation that Jesus is God's Messiah do not (see vv. 14-36; 3:17-24).

The short-term consequence of Israel's divided house is that some Jews, even though devout, write off the importance of what they have heard as a case of premature inebriation: "They are filled with new wine." But their confusion leads Peter to interpret the divine audition they have witnessed while he dispels their ignorance about the Messiah. Indeed, it is the task of the prophet-like-Jesus to show Israel the way of the Lord.

Peter heads the apostolic twelve: already following the ascension, and prior to Pentecost, he is the one who continues the Messiah's magisterial office (1:15-20). Perhaps the prosaic phrase "raised his voice and addressed [his audience]" suggests his spiritual authority to do so. But authority over whom? Peter's address boldly circumscribes his audience: "Fellow Jews [or Judeans] and all those living in Jerusalem, let this be known to you [who] listen to what I say." Religious Israel's costly ignorance about the identity of God's Messiah has provoked derision rather than confession. Their future with God is imperiled, and their spiritual predicament can be reversed only by careful listening to the prophet's message.

Listening to God's Word is an important literary theme in Acts and sometimes functions as a narrative marker, preparing the reader for an important next moment in the story's plot line (see 15:13; 28:28). In this case, Luke uses an unusual Septuagint word for "listen" *(enōtizomai)*, which literally means "let me place it [i.e., God's word] into your ears" (cf. Exod. 15:26).[2] Jesus uses a similar expression at a critical point in his public ministry, when he tells his audience that "today" Isaiah's promise of good news for the poor is fulfilled, but only among those "with ears" *(en osin:* 4:21) — that is, those who are responsive to his message.

Peter's immediate purpose, then, is to defend the community's Pentecostal experience against the charge that it must have resulted from a round of drunkenness, and to declare that its real meaning must be taken with utter seriousness. Evidently, in the popular culture of the day, "nine o'clock in the morning" was an hour inhabited only by those who intend no good. Peter's repartee, dripping with comic irony, corrects their misunderstanding, allowing him to move his audience from skepticism to an interpretation of their Scriptures that gives normative meaning to their Pentecostal experience.

Peter puts the orienting concerns of the book of Acts into play with a reference to Joel's prophecy (vv. 16-21). More than a prophecy that explains the community's charismatic experiences, this passage bears witness to the purpose of the community's mission, which is to draw people toward "the Lord," whose name they petition for their salvation. Scripture also supplies the working points developed in Peter's sermon that follows: this stunning Pentecostal experience is prophesied by Joel as the "outpouring of the Spirit" that inaugurates "the last days" of salvation's history, when "everyone who calls on the name of the Lord will be saved." Luke quotes LXX Joel 3:1-5 (English translations generally follow the Hebrew Bible verse divisions, which places this prophecy at Joel 2:28-32.) While the differences between the LXX and Hebrew/Aramaic versions of Joel are actually quite slender, they diverge on one important matter: the LXX translates the Hebrew word for God as "Lord," which allows Peter to adapt Joel's climactic prophecy that "everyone who calls upon the name of the Lord *(kyrios)* shall be saved" (v. 21) as referring to the resurrected Lord Jesus (v. 36). That is, Israel must turn to *Jesus* for its salvation.

This must have been a shocking rendering of Joel's "Day of the Lord" prophecy for an audience of devout Jews. Surely they would have inter-

---

2. The Septuagint, in its various versions, was the Greek translation of the Hebrew Bible, dating from the third century B.C.E. — hereafter noted as LXX.

preted Joel to be predicting God's terrifying vindication of Israel over its national enemies, such as the pagan Romans who now occupied the Holy Land. Israel's nationalistic hope of a restored kingdom necessarily anticipated the political purging of Rome, which perhaps would be the work of the messianic ruler to come. Thus a "Jewish" reading of Joel's "Day of the Lord" speech would have interpreted this Pentecostal outpouring of God's Spirit as the sign of Israel's deliverance from its national enemy. Peter's sermon reframes the meaning of Scripture in the light of Jesus' resurrection. In other words, Israel's future is now.

When quoting the Joel prophecy's opening line, Peter substitutes the familiar New Testament catch phrase "in the last days" for the prophet's "after these things" (v. 16). Especially when read within its wider New Testament context (cf. 1 Tim. 3:1; Heb 1:2; James 5:3; 2 Pet. 3:3), "in the last days" locates the outpouring of the Spirit against a new eschatological horizon. Simply put, the demonstrative coming of God's Spirit makes it clear that Israel has already entered into the final epoch of its history, when decisions made about Jesus take on a redemptive meaning that makes the church's mission all the more urgent (see 1:6-8).

The addition of "God declares" to Joel's prophecy emboldens the premise of all prophetic texts in Acts: events that agree with biblical prophecy are part of God's redemptive plan and are "necessary" occurrences for that reason. And Peter uses an additional phrase, "and they shall prophesy" (v. 18): the community's forward movement toward God's eschatological horizon as a restored Israel is fundamentally a prophetic movement, a movement facilitated by Spirit-empowered and -illumined proclamation. The pouring out of God's Spirit is the distinguishing mark of that forward movement.

In recent years much has been justifiably made of the inclusive sociology for the community that is foreseen by this prophecy: "I will pour out my Spirit on all flesh" (v. 17). Ideally, there is not gender, age, or class discrimination that divides the community; its entire membership receives God's Spirit, who enables them all to speak as prophets. Peter adds "my" here to the Septuagint, which is especially suggestive of the grand reversal wrought at Pentecost, when even household slaves are transformed into "my servants" and given important prophetic tasks to perform for God. This revolutionary feature of the eschatological community depicted by Joel anticipates subsequent episodes in Acts that will draw out its fuller meaning.

The special effects that accompany the outpouring of the Spirit are also noteworthy. In their original prophetic setting, these cosmic disturbances signal the imminent arrival of the "Day of the Lord" in judgment of those nations that had treated Israel shamefully. Not so in Acts. In this new setting, the "signs and wonders" mark the presence and progress of the Spirit, who prepares the way for the church's missionary work (see 2:43; 4:16, 22, 30; 5:12; 6:8; 8:6, 13; 14:3; 15:12). In this setting, then, "the coming of the Lord's great and glorious day" no longer conjures up images of God's imminent retribution but of Pentecost, with its promise of empowered witness and God's salvation.

Typically, the most important idea of a quoted text is found in the last words read. Peter's quote from the Joel passage, "everyone who calls upon the name of the Lord shall be saved" (v. 21), is just such a phrase. Only when readers arrive at the Jerusalem Council in Acts 15 do they understand the full meaning of Joel's prophecy of Israel's salvation — and differently from what Peter originally intended on the day of Pentecost. Then, before the surprising experience of a "gentile Pentecost" (10:44-48) or the equally surprising successes of Paul's mission to the gentiles, the meaning of Joel's "everyone" would have included only repentant Israel. The foreshadowing of being "saved" through the first half of Acts will clearly indicate that at the epicenter of Luke's theological conception of a restored Israel is a God who forgives every person who names Jesus as Lord and confesses him as God's Messiah (see 2:38; cf. 4:12; 7:25; 13:23, 26, 47; 15:11).

Frankly, Acts is much clearer in addressing the questions of what one must do to get saved and of who does the saving than it is in addressing the corollary question of what happens when one does get saved. This passage emphasizes the forgiveness of sins for those who repent and believe, as well as the repentant believer's initiation into life with God's Spirit (see vv. 38-39). Insofar as the community of goods exhibits a distinctive social life, we are also led to believe that salvation results in a new way of living with one another (vv. 42-47). As we will find in the following story, however, divine forgiveness and human healing form an integral whole in Acts: to be saved from sins means to be healed from sickness (see 3:1-8; 4:9-12; 14:8-10). While this connection can be and has been pressed in dangerous directions, the theological note sounded by the various healing and prison-escape episodes in Acts makes clear the close relationship in Luke's mind between Jesus' spiritual and physical rescue of his followers from internal and external threat. Even as his conception of God's salvation is international in scope, it is also holistic in consequence.

Peter presents his commentary on the quoted prophecy from Joel (vv. 22-36) in two parts, linking them together with a pertinent question for his captivated audience: "What should we do?" The first part of his commentary (vv. 22-36) appeals to his Jewish listeners (v. 22a) to consider his witness to "Jesus of Nazareth" in light of the substantial evidence put forward from his eyewitness reflection and from Scripture in support of the gospel's claim that "God has made this Jesus whom you crucified both Lord and Messiah" (v. 36). The speech's second part (v. 38) is the preacher's altar call.

Peter's opening reference to the "signs and wonders" (v. 22) of Jesus recalls Joel's prophecy of the Spirit's "signs and wonders" (v. 19): God's Spirit is first poured out on Jesus, who inaugurates the "last days" of salvation's history in his life. But the implied good news is even more telling: what Jesus began to do and to say has not ended with his departure but continues on in the life and mission of his followers, which is made clear by the miraculous speaking of languages.

Peter's appeal to God's "definite plan and foreknowledge" (v. 23) does not envision a predestinarian notion of divine sovereignty but rather a belief in God's providence deeply rooted in a particular account of Scripture's prophetic authority. That is, if the Spirit's outpouring and the Christ event both follow God's prophesied script, then God must have known about both in advance of their occurrence. The entire matrix of biblical texts from Israel's Psalter cited by Peter in his speech (LXX: Ps. 17:4-6 = 2:24; 15:8-11 = 2:25-28; 132:11 = 2:30; 109:1 = 2:34-35) supplies additional biblical testimony in support of the community's claim that the Jesus event, in all its tragic and glorious aspects, is intended by God as messianic.

Peter's clever rereading of these Psalms assumes first that, as a type of the coming Messiah, King David gives expression to a principal element of Israel's hope through his biblical narrative (v. 25a). At the same time, Peter claims that King David is God's prophet (v. 30; cf. 1:16, 20) and that his psalms carry keen insight into the future of Israel and the identity of the Messiah (see 4:25; 13:33-36). And finally, Peter claims that the prophet David is Israel's patriarch (v. 29), obligating the household of Israel to give proper respect to his voice. Peter makes this last point with considerable irony, because all the patriarchs, even though they were important to Israel's history, remain dead — as their now-famous and oft-visited tombs memorialize. On the other hand, a Messiah, such as Jesus is, is resurrected and is now alive (vv. 31-33)!

The readers of Acts will recognize the powerful logic of Peter's point: while David, Israel's great king-prophet-patriarch, "did not ascend into the heavens" (v. 34), Jesus did. As midrashic commentary, Peter's linked series of citations from Israel's Psalter gives substance to his proclamation about the risen Jesus. His appeal to the "my Lord" of LXX Psalm 109:1 is often used elsewhere in the New Testament to support the Christological claims of different writers (cf. Mark 12:36; 14:62; 16:19; Luke 20:42; Rom. 8:34; 1 Cor. 15:25; Eph. 1:20; Col. 3:1; Heb. 1:3, 13; 8:1; 10:12). Peter uses it to support his climactic point that God has made the risen Jesus to rule over Israel as its "Lord" (v. 36). David's "Lord" is this risen Lord Jesus, on whose name everyone must call for salvation.

Conversion

Peter's call for conversion (vv. 37-38) presumes that the crowd understands the implications of his climactic claim that the crucified Jesus of Nazareth is in fact the risen Christ of God. Luke says: "They were cut to the heart." Perhaps the crowd's emotional response simply recognizes their own guilt in the matter of Jesus' death. The phrase recalls Psalm 109:16, a text that sets forth God's case against the arrogant who are responsible for the death of the defenseless downtrodden.

The crowd's question "What shall we do?" is more than rhetorical: it is a sincere request for instruction that will lead to their forgiveness and restoration. As such, the theological subtext of Israel's question of Peter is this: If we do repent of our part in Rome's execution of our Messiah, will God even forgive and restore us then? The reader rightly hears this subtext in light of Judas' demise, since God apparently did not give that betrayer a second chance (see 1:16-20; cf. 5:1-10). Why does Peter continue beyond verse 36 and its implicit indictment of Israel's guilt in rejecting the Messiah? In canonical context, the reader imagines that this rehabilitated Peter — of all people — knows from personal experience that God gives betrayers second chances (1:15-20; cf. John 21:15-17). The outpouring of God's Spirit at Pentecost is God's second chance to Israel. God has scripted the Jesus and Spirit events as the climactic pieces of the plan to restore Israel, and Peter cannot now turn his back on these Jews who want to know what to do in response.

Thus Peter stipulates the basis on which his audience may be saved

(v. 38) and the anticipated results of their salvation (vv. 39-40). In doing so, he demands nothing different from what John the Baptist demanded prior to Easter and Pentecost (compare Luke 3:10 to Acts 2:37). Of course, the undercurrent of Peter's response is that Easter and Pentecost have since occurred: they provide spiritual resources compelling Israel's conversion that were not present to the Baptist. While Peter's speech at this point echoes his redemptive protocol — "repent and be baptized" — the theological implications of his invitation are very different from what they were before.

In shaping Peter's evangelical appeal, Acts emphasizes a repentant response to the gospel message. Jesus earlier predicted that his successors would preach "repentance in his name" (cf. Luke 24:47). "Repentance" denotes a radical change of mind; spiritual reform is possible only with an intellectual reorientation: how one thinks and what angle of vision one takes when looking at the "real world." After all, the wrong-headed response of religious Israel to Jesus can only be explained by their ignorance of him, ignorance that has now been dispelled by Peter's sermon and their witness to the outpouring of God's Spirit. It is significant that Peter uses "repent" in its plural form, indicating that his demand is addressed to the entire household of Israel, though the second demand, to "be baptized," is stipulated only of those individuals who convert. The baptism of converts makes personal what should be true of all Israel. The interpreter should observe the tension in Acts between national and individual repentance. The promise of Israel's restoration obtains only to those baptized individuals within Israel who repent and turn to Christ in faith. These converts will be the ones who constitute a repentant (i.e., restored) Israel, in whose history the promised blessings of God will be realized.

Baptism

The significance of baptism probably stems from John the Baptist's mission, and its symbolism is simply brought forward with new and greater meaning by the command of Jesus (cf. Matt. 28:19; Mark 16:16). Christian baptism remains a rite of initiation into a new life under a different Lord, with membership in a community of his disciples and the prospect of a future with God. The convert is baptized "in the name of Jesus Christ" as the central symbol of this new orientation (v. 21). No believer goes unbaptized in Acts; this is true simply because every new believer is initiated into the church, and no believer exists outside that community. Yet in this narrative setting, Peter issues his demand for baptism because of Pentecost and the community's experience of the baptism in the Spirit. Baptism, then, is initiation into a missionary community that lives within the powerful realm of God's Spirit. We can clearly see that Christian baptism assumes Spirit baptism in Acts and the readiness of the converted for the work of witness.

Repentance and Christian baptism result in the "forgiveness of your sins" and "the gift of the Holy Spirit" (v. 38). The Greek word for "forgiveness" means pardon, and it is typically combined with "sins" because God forgives, or pardons, our sins. But forgiveness of financial debts can also be interpreted in this phrase and may thus reflect the sociology of God's kingdom: believers are initiated into a community of goods whose members, pardoned by God, now pardon the debts of others (vv. 42-47; cf. Luke 11:1-13). The second phrase, "gift of the Holy Spirit," is exceptional. Peter does not have in mind the gifts of the Spirit that edify a worshiping congregation (1 Cor 12–14); rather, he means a Spirit that enables the performance of the church's missionary vocation (1:8; 2:4). Evidently, the Spirit's presence inspires more than powerful preaching; it also inspires a way of living together that evokes "the good will of all the people" in Jerusalem.

The principal interpretive difficulty in the history of this text is whether Christian baptism is a condition for or a consequence of the forgiveness of sins and thus receiving the gift of the Holy Spirit. The problem turns on the causal use of the preposition *eis* — "for [*eis*] the forgiveness of your sins." But Luke does not use this preposition consistently, nor does he place much value in it in any case. Moreover, he uses a variety of grammatical formulae when joining God's forgiveness and baptism together (see 8:16; 10:44; 19:5; cf. 8:38-39; 18:26). Therefore, Peter's formulation of these different demands in this passage does not establish a theological norm.

More significantly, Peter joins baptism "in the name of Jesus Christ" and "forgiveness of sins" to embellish the meaning of Joel's prophecy, which concludes by linking "the name of the Lord" (i.e., Jesus Christ) with salvation. The saving power of the "name" is not magical but rather metaphorical of Joel's announcement of salvation, which has arrived from God in the form of forgiveness because of Jesus. For this reason, Christian baptism after Pentecost initiates the repentant believers into a new spiritual reality that the Baptist could only predict (Luke 3:16), because neither he nor his baptized followers could participate in it, even though their sins were forgiven (cf. Luke 3:3). In addition, the Baptist's exhortation to do "works in keeping with repentance" is glossed in this new setting as those mission-ary tasks that will be part of the community's vocation.

PART II: ENGAGING ACTS 2 FOR TODAY'S CHURCH

If the first chapter of Acts helps us to challenge the idea that "mission" can be reduced to a department or budget or committee of the church, in favor of helping us see the whole church as mission, the second chapter of Acts can help us reframe preaching and proclamation in our new time. Not long ago, the great preacher Fred Craddock observed that the most fre-quent lament regarding preaching was once that preaching was not "bibli-cal." Today, he continued, the frequent lament is that too much preaching sounds as if "nothing is at stake."

What's at stake when your pastor — or you as a preacher — gets up to preach? Is there something urgent and important about this moment? Or is preaching a series of friendly ideas, good advice, cheerful platitudes, and possibly an encouragement to participate in a useful project or activity? In other words, does preaching help us adjust to the world as it is, or does it give us a whole new world?

Garrison Keillor, the bard of Lake Wobegon, observes: "I've heard a lot of sermons in the past ten years or so that make me want to get up and walk out. They're secular, psychological, self-help sermons. Friendly, but of no use. They didn't make you want to straighten up. They didn't give you anything hard. At some point and in some way, a sermon has to direct peo-ple toward the death of Christ and to the campaign God has waged over the centuries to get our attention." Peter's sermon in Acts 2 would seem to measure up to Keillor's criterion for good preaching. Peter does give the listening congregation something hard, and he does direct their attention to the death of Christ — as well as to the resurrection. But before turning to the sermon itself, a word about what precedes and occasions it.

Signs and Wonders

Luke is not bashful about bringing up the signs and wonders of God. Strange things happen here in the Acts journey — some of them astonishing. Things happen in Acts that disorient people in order that they may be introduced to a new orientation. Two people drop down dead, caught in their lies. Paul is blinded by the light and led around like a little child. Earthquakes rattle the jail cells, and storms at sea intervene. But we may begin with the most notable of signs and wonders in Acts, the events of the day of Pentecost. The apostles and a wider group of disciples (120 in all) were gathered together when suddenly there was something like the rush of a violent wind; tongues, as of flame, divided and came to rest on the heads of each. Before long, they were speaking of the mighty acts of God in many different languages, all the various languages of the pilgrims gathered that day in Jerusalem for the annual Pentecost festival. The pilgrims heard them speaking in their own languages, and they were astounded. "What is this?" they stammered.

The wind and fire hark back to the Old Testament signs of God's presence with Israel in the wilderness: the cloud and the pillar of fire. The wind of the Spirit is not a gently refreshing, balmy breeze but a violent wind of hurricane force. Things are breaking open and the Spirit is breaking in. The 120 disciples are "on fire" with the Spirit.

But what is the role of such signs and wonders in Acts and for Luke? Such signs and wonders do not bring people to faith; miracles do not bring people to faith. "The problem with a faith that is based on miracles," an older pastor once told me, "is that it always requires one more miracle." Faith, as Paul writes elsewhere, comes by hearing, and that is certainly true here in Acts. What the signs and wonders do achieve, it seems, is causing enough perplexity and astonishment to get people opened up and receptive. The signs and wonders create a certain dis-ease and confusion. They shake the foundations of people's known world. Faith begins, at least sometimes, with a disorientation that must precede a new orientation. So the signs and wonders are a disorienting wake-up call: they provoke, evoke, and awaken.

I recently heard an art historian try to explain how art works. Reaching for an analogy, he said, "Falling in love disorganizes a person's life." I thought, That's right: we may experience it as pleasant, but it is also disorganizing. This sign and wonder called "love" causes us to do crazy things, to reorganize our days and our plans. Then the art historian said: "A good work of art is like falling in love — it disorganizes us, disorganizes our life." Much art, he went on to say, gets domesticated, housed in a museum, defined to a period, or assigned a meaning. It loses the capacity it once had to disorganize us. One work of art that is not true of is Igor Stravinsky's famous — and famously jarring — *Rite of Spring:* though I have heard it many times before, it retains some of its capacity to disturb and provoke, something it apparently has done many times over since its premiere in 1913, when audience members either booed or walked out.

So "signs and wonders" provoke and evoke, awaken and disturb. They do not so much bring people to faith as prepare the ground for faith. All preachers know this. When a great cataclysmic event such as 9/11/2001 happens, people stagger into church, shattered and disoriented, looking for meaning. Their foundations have been shaken. But it is not only times of world or national tragedy and horror that do this. It can also be a shattering and disorienting experience when a congregation experiences a fire or loses a family. And individuals certainly experience something of this in events that are both bad and good: a death, a birth, falling in love, divorce, an unexpected gift or blessing, a sudden illness. People are often most open to God and to God's world when something has happened to wake them up, to open them up, to cause them to question the ways they have put the world together and explained life and their identities to themselves.

Sometimes preachers are aided by the signs and wonders, ordinary and extraordinary, that life brings. But sometimes good preaching begins with a provocative word, or with bringing out the provocative element of a particular text. For example, one might begin a sermon on the story of the Prodigal Son by saying, "You know, I don't mind the father forgiving his son, but I do have trouble with him throwing a party for him." Or one might say: "I find this parable of the workers in the vineyard offensive. Often I feel like I've put in a long day's work and, to be honest, I'm not sure how I feel about the Johnny-come-latelies being paid the same as me. No, actually, I am sure. I *know* I don't like it."

To begin with provocation, to note the ways Scripture itself disorganizes life, may be an excellent way to preach. If God doesn't provide the signs and wonders, sometimes preachers have to do it themselves. Acts seems to take these things pretty much in stride. Unlike the truncated world modernity has given us, the world of Acts is more alive, open, and dynamic. It is a world full of signs and wonders, perhaps to suggest that there are more signs and wonders around us than we can see or dare think.

Preaching as Reframing

There is no dearth of interpretive narratives, stories, and schemes abroad in the world. We humans are creatures who make meaning. We may find ourselves provoked or disturbed or disoriented for a time, but we don't stay that way for long. We begin to put a frame around our experiences, to attach meanings to them, to make sense of them. Even after something as horrific as 9/11, most churches reported that attendance was pretty much back to usual levels within a month. It didn't take long to put the experience in a frame, to assign it a meaning.

We see this in other parts of Scripture as well. Job's friends put one frame around Job's experience of suffering: they tell him that punishment is what happens to sinners, reward is what comes to those who lead a virtuous life. That's a certain story by which these "friends" try to give meaning to Job's experience: sin punished, virtue rewarded. Job, while no doubt hungry for meaning and explanation, refuses this handy story offered by his friends. In the face of their insistence that he come clean and own up to his sins, Job insists on his innocence. He insists on a better frame, a more truthful story.

The question for us is: Have we framed our experience, our world, with the gospel story or with some other story? Have we turned to a pseudo-gospel moralism, as Job's friends did? Have we made sense of life with a Darwinian survival-of-the-fittest account? Or have we assuaged our emptiness with the narratives of consumerism and materialism — that having lots of stuff is some form of salvation and meaning. Is the story of American manifest destiny where we find meaning? When Peter gets up to preach, following the outpouring of signs and wonders, he notes some other stories, other explanatory frameworks at work; then he begins to reframe their experience and its meaning in light of the story of Jesus. Note that something is very much at stake: what is at stake here is the truth, and what is at stake is also salvation. This is not a case of, "Okay, here are a couple interesting ideas you might want to think about after your Sunday dinner and before the football game." This is: "Let me tell you what's really going on!"

Peter engages in multiple levels and acts of reframing. We can note the many different kinds of reframing he engages in before we return to examine some in greater detail. He reframes people's perceptions. When some say that the disciples are merely drunk and filled with new wine, Peter says,

"They are filled all right, but with the Holy Spirit." Peter takes his text from the prophet Joel and reframes that well-known text (to which we shall return shortly). In reframing the text, Peter reframes the holy day and festival of Pentecost now underway in Jerusalem. Next Peter reframes the story and narrative of Jesus: one whom they had considered a blasphemer and common criminal is in reality, says Peter, God's anointed one, the Messiah. Peter continues his astounding romp of reframing, moving to David and David's words. Finally, Peter reframes the present moment, casting it as a time for repentance, for turning around and calling on the name of the Lord.

Here we see preaching as transformation — as renaming our experience and thus changing lives. Recall for a moment the story of the disciples on the road to Emmaus, an earlier Lucan story (Luke 24:13-35). There we can see another powerful act of reframing, this one performed by Jesus. The disciples trudge back home, defeated. "We had hoped," they mutter to the seemingly clueless stranger who has fallen in alongside them. But then the stranger begins to take Scripture and reframe what they have just experienced in Jerusalem. He even rebukes them: "Oh foolish ones, slow of heart to believe!" By the time Jesus is finished opening Scripture and breaking bread with them, he has so significantly reframed and reinterpreted their experience and transformed their lives that the disciples reverse course and run all the way back to Jerusalem. Every preacher knows what it is to take such an experience of defeat or disappointment and say, "Well, let's take another look: God's ways aren't always our ways. What the world calls failure, God at least sometimes calls success." Preaching can be a reframing of what we thought we knew, not just helping us adjust to the old and given world but giving us a whole new world.

Preaching as Reframing the Text and the Occasion

Peter takes as his text for this sermon in Acts 2 the words of the prophet in Joel 2:28-32. In its original context this passage from Joel was a prophecy of the deliverance and restoration of Israel. It would have lent itself well to what Pentecost had become, which was something of a nationalistic festival, a time for remembering and giving thanks for God's many blessings to Israel. Moreover, the passage from Joel would have been a welcome word given Israel's current situation — being under the dominance and rule of

Rome. Together, the well-known passage from Joel and the day of Pentecost would have given some comfort and encouragement to an oppressed people. The pilgrims to Jerusalem might have heard that God would "remove the northern army from you, and drive it into a parched and desolate land" (Joel 2:20). They might have rejoiced to hear Joel 3:1: "In those days and at that time, when I restore the fortunes of Judah and Jerusalem. . . ."

In other words, Joel and Pentecost itself had been understood as texts of national deliverance. They were narratives of national triumph, at least until Peter got hold of them. In the hands of preacher Peter, Joel is reframed, given a new context and a new meaning, which is quite often what good preaching does. Good preaching rescues the beloved texts, those passages with which we have become comfortable, and gives them new meaning. As a parallel, consider Jesus' own inaugural sermon at the synagogue in Nazareth (Luke 4:18: "The Spirit of the Lord is upon me, because he has anointed me to preach the gospel to the poor . . ."). He takes a beloved text from Isaiah and finds in it new and challenging meanings: he reframes it into a call to repentance delivered to his own people. Peter manages much the same feat here.

John Calvin said, "Judgment always begins with the house and people of God." Thus Peter takes a passage that had been used to preach God's judgment of other peoples and deliverance for God's people, Israel, and reframes it into a call to repentance directed at Israel itself. Rather than going with the nationalistic interpretation of Joel and of Pentecost itself, Peter seizes on the work of the Spirit swirling around them to say, "No, these are the promised last days, these are times of the outpouring of the Spirit," and these are times for you to repent and call on the name of the Lord. Do not, Peter seems to say, gloat and wrap yourselves in Torah. God is doing a new thing. Can't you perceive it? Turn from your sins and enter God's new age.

In some sense, powerful prophetic preaching will always call us to wake up and turn around. It will never simply or easily comfort us with easy platitudes or cheap moralisms or feel-good projects and activities. It will announce a whole new world and challenge us to let go of our old ways and world and enter, repenting, into the new creation set in motion in Jesus Christ. Such preaching will not exempt us from accountability as the elect and privileged. It will call us to account and to change.

Victims No More!

Given the Roman occupation, it would have been easy for those gathered in Jerusalem to understand themselves as victims. Had Peter gone with the conventional theology that was drawn from Joel and that also characterized Pentecost, he might simply have played on his audience's sense of being victims. In our own time, narratives of victims and oppressors are common. Certainly they are accurate in some — perhaps many — situations. But the interpretation of our experience through this lens also has a consequence and cost: victims are, almost by definition, powerless; others, the victimizers and oppressors, have the power. Victims may have the moral satisfaction of being wronged and seeming innocent, but to the extent that they adopt a "victim mentality," they will remain in that place and in that role.

In the Sermon on the Mount, Jesus addresses those who have been victims, who have suffered at the hands of more powerful and unjust powers and forces; that is, Jesus acknowledges that we cannot always avoid the experience of being victims. Nevertheless, he does not allow those who followed him to adopt a victim mentality. There, in the Sermon on the Mount, he counsels: "If your enemy demands that you walk a mile, go a second mile; if he strikes you on the cheek, turn the other cheek." The point is neither a literal one, nor is it to encourage disciples to be doormats. It is to say: "Exercise your power, surprise them, keep on walking, give them the other cheek." In our own time, both Martin Luther King, Jr., and Mahatma Gandhi understood the power of "victims" and the power of resistance through civil disobedience.

Peter, in his Pentecost sermon, refuses to buy into any sense of a victim mentality that his hearers might have held and in which they might have found some comfort. Rather, he reminds them, in effect, of their power — of the freedom they do have. He urges them to "repent, to call upon the name of the Lord." That is, he sets before them the ways of life and the ways of death (Deut. 30) and urges them to "choose life." You have power, you have choice, and you can act, says Peter.

In our own time, when a dominant narrative framework is one of the victim/oppressor, and when it often seems that the quickest and surest route to the moral high ground is to identify oneself as a victim, Peter's sermon challenges and reframes this narrative as well. Yes, you have suffered, and yes, you do suffer; but that's not all you are. That's not the whole story. Repent, turn around, choose this day whom you shall serve. Take responsibility for your life.

Spirit and Scripture

We should note two other qualities of bold preaching that are evident here in Peter's sermon and throughout Acts. First, this preaching holds Spirit and Scripture together in creative tension. Sometimes one hears preachers who seem to spend little time in the study of Scriptures. They announce their confident reliance on the Spirit: "I just say whatever words the Spirit gives me," some will say, almost as a boast. But frequently one may wish that they had spent a little more time and effort in studying the text! Still other preachers go deep into the text, so deep that it sometimes seems as though they'll never come out again. They confuse proclamation with Bible study. They may carefully exegete the text, but they do not call on the Spirit to enliven proclamation and make it contemporary and urgent. As Harry Emerson Fosdick once noted, "Not many people come to church wondering what happened to the Jebusites!" Biblical study is important, by all means, but it should have the purpose of proclaiming the old story in a new time. So it is crucial for Scripture and Spirit to be properly held together in the preaching and proclaiming of the gospel. Calvin maintained that the Word of God was not simply Scripture per se; rather, the Word of God is an event, an occurrence that takes place when "the Spirit that was present to the one who wrote is also present to those who read and those who preach." The Word of God is a dynamic experience that occurs when Spirit and Scripture interact.

The Person of the Preacher

Finally, consider the person of the preacher — as all preachers must. Consider Peter's own story and journey. He does not proclaim "repent" as one who has never himself known the need or occasion for repentance. This Peter is the same Peter who denied Jesus three times, who on an earlier occasion could not even bear witness to Jesus to a maid in the courtyard outside the palace of the chief priest. In other words, Peter the preacher knows whereof he speaks. He, too, has known the need to turn again and to be healed. He knows failure and forgiveness. He has been encountered by the "God of the second chance." The man who preaches God's grace and forgiveness has experienced the same himself.

The very best preachers do know their own need for grace and for mercy. Moreover, if one imagines a triangle with its three corners marked "preacher," "text," and "congregation" respectively, the best preaching does not find the preacher and text allied over against the congregation; the best preachers do not use the text to beat up on the congregation. The finest preachers stand with the congregation, together under the judging and redeeming word of the text. Peter may signal this in verse 32: "This Jesus, God raised up, and of that all of us are witnesses." "All of us. . . ." As we listen in on the many speeches and sermons in Acts, we cannot hear the words spoken, nor do we look into the preacher's eyes. We don't know how exactly they spoke these words. But it is both my hunch and my hope that Peter spoke with a combination of boldness and humility, knowing both Jesus and himself as he did.

Acts invites us to a new kind of preaching. It is not preaching that is, as Garrison Keillor observed, "friendly but of no use." But neither is it the arrogant proclamation of one who does not know her own need of mercy. The bold preaching of Acts is focused on what God has done and is doing. We are witnesses to that. We tell that story. As we tell that story, we reframe our own stories, we are given a new world, and our lives are changed. In this new time we need preaching that is bold and urgent, honest and humble, daring and provocative. May the tribe of such preachers increase!

STUDY QUESTIONS

1. Discuss together how this passage defines the nature and purpose of a person's actual experience of God's presence. Relate your discussion to the experiences of your congregation or campus.

2. Jesus predicted the Spirit's arrival with "power" in Acts 1:8; and his prophecy is fulfilled soon after, on the Day of Pentecost. What are the "signs and wonders" of the Spirit's baptism according to Acts 2?

3. Read 1 Corinthians 12. How does the prior reading of Acts 2 prepare the reader for a study of Paul's understanding of the Spirit's baptism in 1 Corinthians 12?

4. "Preaching can be a reframing of what we thought we knew." Have you experienced preaching this way, as giving you a fresh look at a text or life ex-

perience? When? How? What difference did it make for you? For your congregation?

5. Robinson and Wall claim that the "Word of God" is an event, a dynamic coming together of Scripture and Spirit. How do you respond to this claim? What implications does it have for your spiritual journey?

6. How would you describe the pattern and purpose of good pedagogy? Relate your responses to those observations made about preaching in this chapter.

5

Christian Community:
Life and Death Together

PART I: INTERPRETING ACTS 4:32–5:11 AS SCRIPTURE

The apostolic leaders have now been singled out by the religious authorities of Jerusalem for special attention: their spiritual authority and prophetic practices have disturbed and challenged powerful people (4:1-2), which has resulted in the arrest of Peter and John and a subsequent hearing before the Sanhedrin court (vv. 5-20). The controversies and conflicts provoked by the church's Jerusalem mission will only increase as the narrative unfolds, even though the reader knows that God has chosen and the Spirit empowers the church's apostles. For this reason, even though the battle lines are drawn, the reader already knows the outcome (see v. 31).

With this passage from Acts 4, the storyteller pauses to reflect once again on the Jerusalem community's inner life, especially its communal practice of members sharing their possessions with one another. Similar to Luke's earlier summary of the community's "resurrection practices" (2:42-47), this text looks back to the "good old days" to retrieve important images of what the church should look like in every age. Luke reminds the reader that the church's internal witness is centered on its sharing of material goods, even as its external witness is centered in the proclamation of God's word. Both are concrete expressions of God's grace and attract favorable responses from "the people" (5:12-16). More than any other activity, the community's care of its poorest members lends support to its bold claim that God resides in its common life through the filling of the Holy Spirit (4:31).

Luke rounds off his second summary of the Jerusalem church's common life (vv. 32-35) with contrasting examples of the community's most distinctive internal practice (4:36–5:11): the redistribution of proceeds among the needy from the voluntary sale of possessions. The people of the community evidently laid the proceeds "at the apostles' feet" (4:35, 37; 5:2) to acknowledge their spiritual authority; the apostles then redistributed these goods to other members according to their financial need, so that "there was not a needy person among them" (v. 34a). Barnabas serves as an exemplar of this practice; but the tragic story of Ananias and Sapphira also serves to illustrate the vital importance of sharing goods as a social marker and spiritual barometer of the entire community (5:1-11).

Acts 4:32-35 turns the reader's mind from the apostles' problems with the Jerusalem authorities back to the faith community by using the well-known rhetorical device called *chiasmus,* which repeats similar narrative themes in reverse order (ABB′A′) in order to showcase a pivotal theme sandwiched in between (C). To follow this story, then, the reader should note the initial description of the community having "all things in common" (A = 4:32) is repeated when concluding that the apostles "distributed to each according to need" (A′ = 4:35b). The reference to the apostles' witness to the Lord's resurrection (B = 4:33a), the essential mark of their religious authority, is then reflected in the act of laying proceeds at their feet (B′ = 4:34b-35a). These two themes then bracket the center of theological gravity in connecting God's "great grace" with the observation that "there was not a needy person among them" (C = 4:33b-34a). Christian unity is never merely a verbal sentiment or heartfelt ideal; it is a social practice that meets real needs wherever they are found.

Luke draws on popular Greek literature for this belief: there the intimacy of close friendship is routinely characterized as sharing "one heart and soul." The combination of "heart and soul" is also found in the Old Testament, notably in the *Shemaʿ* (Deut. 6:5), where the phrase characterizes faithful Israel's singular love for its God, the only God. While the Greek ideal included the practical necessity of reciprocity, Luke's description agrees with Jesus' instruction and indicates that there is no thought of payback: sharing is a spiritual convention that one is obliged to do out of love for a merciful God (cf. Luke 6:20-36).

The wider narrative portrays the spiritual authority of the twelve apostles. Renewed in the Spirit's power (4:29-31), they witness "to the resurrection of the Lord Jesus" (cf. 1:8; 4:2) "with great power [*dynamis*]"

(v. 33a). Indeed, now even the radical economic practices of the community are subject to the apostles' authority: "They laid [the proceeds of what was sold] at the apostles' feet" (vv. 34b-35a). By placing goods at the apostles' feet, which seems to be an element of a liturgy that has formalized the social practice, the believers demonstrate voluntary submission to another person of greater spiritual authority. Later in Acts, Peter dissuades Cornelius, not yet a believer, from falling down at his feet in worship (10:25; cf. 14:13-15). Clearly these two examples of bowing to an apostle's authority clarify Luke's definition: the "great power" of an apostle is not his own but derives from God alone, and thus does not precipitate worship. As an outsider, Cornelius makes an honest rookie mistake, which Peter then gently corrects both by admonition and gospel presentation. But in this scenario, the people place goods at the feet of an apostle not only trusting that they will be justly distributed but also as an expression of God's grace that "was upon them all" (v. 33).

The practice of holding everything in common, which enjoys favorable public reputation at this time (cf. 2:47; 5:11), is now used as evidence of the apostles' increasing grip on the inner life and destiny of all believers. The repetition of "power" in Acts signals their competence to be prophets-like-Jesus, the medium of God's word in the world. Their power does not derive from education or social status; it is not personal (3:12) but is mediated "in the name of Jesus" (4:7). The function of their "great power" is to bear witness to God's "great grace." Given the normative meaning of "power" in Acts, which is mediated by the Spirit to enable the performance of missionary tasks (1:8), the reader resists the temptation to think of the apostles as deities and the gifts placed at their feet the equivalent of the votive offerings that were deposited at the feet of religious shrines by pagan communicants. They are prophets baptized with the Holy Spirit to bear powerful and effective witness to the sovereign Creator (cf. v. 24) — but first to the whole house of Israel.

Luke inserts his theological commentary on the community's internal practices at the center of this vignette to give it principal importance (vv. 33b-34). At this point in Acts, Luke significantly turns his earlier reference that the community enjoyed "favor [*charis*] with all the people" (see 2:47a) toward God's favor: "And [God's] great grace [*charis*] was upon them all" (v. 33b; cf. Exod. 3:21; 33:12-13). Luke's expression "grace upon them all" is similar to Paul's conception of divine grace in that it denotes divine favor and reflects the Holy Spirit's presence within the community. However, there is an important difference between this grace in Acts and in Paul's writings: in Acts, God's grace probably does not effect the personal transformation of believers as it does in Pauline thought. Note that Luke's phrase is not "grace in them" but rather "grace upon them." The effective power of God's grace "upon" the assembly of believers enables it to produce those public behaviors that cultivate good will and interest (i.e., civic "favor") among outsiders. God's grace functions more as an impulse, or a positive influence, "upon" the entire community to move believers in God's direction — an idea that is much closer to the Old Testament than it is to Paul. In any case, Jerusalem's rulers, who were otherwise upset with what the apostles taught in the town square, did not resent the "good deed" of healing the lame man (vv. 9, 16-17).

More crucially, Luke insinuates God's grace into the community's sociology so that "there was not a needy person among them." The practice of landowners selling their property and giving the proceeds over to the apostles for redistribution embodies a sociology of divine grace (v. 34b). This summary recalls an element of Luke's story (in his Gospel) of what Jesus began to teach in his synagogue at Nazareth (cf. Luke 4:16-30). Luke repeats different words for "favor" in that narrative to draw attention to Isaiah's promise of eschatological blessing to the poor: the promise of the Lord's "favorable year" for the poor (cf. Luke 4:18-19; Isa. 61:1-2a) is already underway among those who "hear" (or believe) the Messiah's prophetic announcement of its arrival (cf. Luke 4:21). Before his Nazarene congregation turns against Jesus, they confirm the truth of his prophetic commentary as "words about God's grace." The reader of Acts can now recall the people's ironic response to the Lord's announcement: the gift of the Holy Spirit given at Pentecost effectively mediates God's "great grace upon them all," which reforms and reshapes them into a community of goods.

An early exemplar of this theological principle is Barnabas (4:36-37), who has apparently been influenced by God's "great grace" to sell a field belonging to him and give the proceeds over to the apostles for redistribution (4:37). But first Luke provides three significant features of Barnabas's résumé to give us a fuller understanding of his action. Barnabas is a Levite: according to Scripture, members of the Levitical household were dedicated to the Lord and Israel's spiritual well-being rather than to the stewardship or cultivation of the promised land (Deut. 12:12; Josh. 14:3-4; cf. Josh. 21). Even though the historical record tells us that this stipulation was rarely practiced in Jewish history,[1] the fact that his story is told to illustrate the benefaction of landowners is ironic and may well deepen Luke's sense that an economic reversal has begun with Jesus and Pentecost.

Barnabas is also "a native of Cyprus" (that is, a Jew of the Diaspora) who has become a member of the Jerusalem community. The point certainly continues from Pentecost, when many converts were from the Diaspora. However, this feature of his résumé will become more important later in Acts, when Barnabas defends and then teams up with Paul in their mission to the Diaspora. Barnabas's submission to the twelve (4:37) is a harbinger of his important role as mediator between Paul and the apostles of the Jerusalem church. If Paul is something of a "loose cannon" and always suspect, Barnabas is not, and he adds credibility to Paul's witness in Jerusalem. In this present story as well, he performs the role of a faithful "outsider" — in contrast to Ananias and Sapphira, who are unfaithful "insiders" — and in doing so may anticipate the outward movement of God's word beyond Israel into the nations.

Barnabas is called Joseph, "to whom the apostles gave the name Barnabas (which means 'son of encouragement')." Even though Barnabas does not literally mean "son of encouragement," Luke's purpose is to stipulate the subtext of Joseph's name change to Barnabas: according to Scripture, name changes indicate God's favor (cf. Matt. 16:17-20). Barnabas's obedience to the community's rule of sharing goods embodies God's favor (vv. 33b-34), and so he is given another name to draw the community's attention to his exemplary and grace-filled economic practices.

Ananias and Sapphira

The story of Ananias and Sapphira (5:1-11) survives in ignominy. Many scholars dismiss its historical value because the episode seems factually impossible as described, and it is theologically difficult to explain in any event. Better to dismiss it than to deal with it! Yet, given its narrative context, the story's essential plot line as related to the community's practice of redistributing goods seems more likely than not. A known couple, identified by name, participates in a public practice for which the community is well regarded. They misappropriate ("keep back") funds dedicated for the

---

1. Cf. Josephus, *Life*, 68-83.

community's support. Perhaps they have second thoughts about the amount of their monetary gift (since biblical narratives rarely state the motives for actions, the reader cannot know). In this case, Ananias and Sapphira then compound their original misdeed by attempting to deceive both the apostles and the public (though clearly not God, who justly punishes them for their shameful behavior). Peter's role as the broker of God's verdict seems likely as well, because he is the leader of the Jerusalem community and responsible for their spiritual health and public witness. Finally, the story's conflict and its result agree with Israel's Scriptures, which teach that God curses, even destroys, those who break the community's rule of life (see the story of Achan in Joshua 7). Jerusalem's Jewish community would have retained and kept vivid those memories of members "cursed" by God for covenant-breaking as a reminder that covenants are maintained by obedience to the community's rule of life.

Whether the historical Ananias and Sapphira died by the hand of God as the immediate consequence of their deception is unknown; but it makes perfect sense when one reads Acts as a theological narrative. They are negative "types" whose "hearts" are "filled with Satan" — in sharp contrast to Barnabas, who is filled with the Spirit — as they attempt to subvert the community's common "heart" (4:32) by their deceptive behavior concerning sharing goods. But does the contrast suggest that the redistribution of goods is voluntary or obligatory? Can God's "great grace" be resisted because of human deception, and if so, what are the consequences? Finally, what is the relationship between God's grace and the community's practice? The answers to these important questions are forthcoming in this story.

Ananias and Barnabas belong to the same social class: they are landowners and believers who sell off their property according to the community's practice of common goods and bring the proceeds to the apostles for redistribution (5:1-2). But unlike Barnabas's action — and subversive of the community's common practice (see 4:34b) — Ananias "kept back some of the proceeds," with his wife's consent and knowledge. Aware that a sin has been committed, the reader may want to know whether there exists in this community a protocol for restoring a sinful believer to fellowship (similar to what Jesus provides in Matt. 18:15-17). But Luke's narrative returns only "blanks": we are told nothing of what transpired between verses 2 and 3 — how Peter came to know what was in Ananias's "heart" (5:3; cf. 4:32) or whether Ananias was given a chance to repent and be restored (as was Simon the Samaritan, for instance: 8:18-24). Luke's interests are focused on the nature of Ananias's deception and his tragic end, and what this may teach us about the working of divine grace within the faith community.

Peter's rebuke of Ananias carries the weight of a death sentence (5:5); and here he introduces two elements into Luke's narrative. Assuming that Peter's prophetic insight and his rebuke expresses God's assessment of Ananias's action, we see that Ananias's sin is prompted by his heart's being filled by Satan (5:3) rather than by the Spirit, as was exemplified by Barnabas's generosity. According to its use in Scripture, the "heart" is a metaphor for a person's decision-making apparatus. Satan, who personifies evil in Luke's narrative world, enters the heart to distort a person's capacity to make sound decisions about God. Ananias's divided heart recalls the earlier reference to the community's "one heart" (4:32): his apostate action was not in solidarity with other believers. Acts does not say whether Ananias is a true believer, since only then could Satan have such influence; yet he is a full member of the faith community, which is possible only through repentance.

Suffice it to say that the cosmic struggle between Satan and the Spirit over control of the community's "heart" has a historical precedent here in Ananias's decision to depart from the community's practice, to remove himself out from "under" God's "great grace" (4:33b), and to deceive the apostles and thus the Spirit. Moreover, Ananias is deceived because he remains ignorant of the participatory nature of God's "great grace." Peter tells him that the believer retains ownership of property and the personal freedom to do with it what he wants: if the believer surrenders it to the apostles, it is by voluntary action and the result of an individual choice rather than by apostolic coercion (5:4). Ananias is not charged with failure to sell his property or to place the proceeds at the apostles' feet (cf. 5:1-2). He is charged with deception: he claims more for his action than was justified and as a result "shatters the unity of the church and threatens the prophetic authority of the twelve."[2] But Ananias also engages in a theological deception, similar to that of Adam and Eve in Genesis 3. Peter asks him, "How is it that you have contrived this deed in your heart?" His bid to deceive is, ultimately, not Satan's handiwork but the result of a decision Ananias himself makes: he resists the influence of God's "great grace" (4:33b), without which such promises are impossible to keep.

2. L. T. Johnson, *The Acts of the Apostles*, Sacra Pagina (Collegeville, MN: Liturgical Press, 1992), p. 88.

This Acts narrative does not give reasons for Ananias's resistance of God's grace. However, we may infer reasons from Luke's use of possessions as a narrative theme. Perhaps for pastoral reasons, Luke is deeply concerned to spell out the spiritual pitfalls of trying to juggle the socio-economic values of the "middle class" with a vital piety. Given Luke's interests in this theme, the interpreter may reasonably fill in one of the story's gaps and assume that Ananias falls victim to theological deception and resists the influence of God's grace because he desires to have more money than others in the community. The practices of the common life cannot be obeyed out of a sense of duty or as a requirement of saving grace; compliance results when the believer freely responds to the "light and easy" (Matt. 11:30) prompting of God's grace.

As he hears Peter's verdict, Ananias drops dead, and his body is immediately taken out for burial; and "great fear seized all who heard of it" (5:5; see 2:43). The reader must presume that this is not an accidental or coincidental death: Peter's words are a death sentence, and Ananias's death excommunicates him from the community of goods. The second new element follows the first: three hours after Ananias's death, his unwitting wife, Sapphira, comes before the apostle Peter. The apostle rebukes her as well, and she also dies after hearing it; she is then buried "beside her husband." The second act concludes on the very same note: "Great fear seized the whole church and all who heard about these events" (5:11; cf. 5:5). But the flow of this parallelism is interrupted by Peter's initial question to Sapphira: "Tell me, is this the price you and Ananias got for the land?" At the surface level of the narrative, the reader knows that, even though Sapphira has come to Peter "not knowing" what has happened to her husband (5:7), she has to know his deception full well — because she was in on it from the beginning (5:2). So Peter exposes her as Ananias's accomplice. Yet, at a literal level, Peter's question invites Sapphira to repent and be restored. If she would not have lied in response, his judgment would not have been rendered. Thus Peter's questioning of Sapphira underscores the importance of the believer's choices in determining the outcome of God's provident care of covenant people.

At another level, however, social codes are embedded in the narrative. In this case, Sapphira follows her husband's lead, even though it is dishonest, showing that her fidelity is to him rather than to the Spirit. While such fidelity would have been expected in her culture, in this case it leads to her death. The reversal of the social code that shapes Sapphira's uncritical and tragic submission to Ananias is seen in a later Acts story about another Christian couple, Aquila and Priscilla (Acts 18). Priscilla is characterized as a Spirit-filled "daughter" of Israel who, supported by her husband, leads a misguided but earnest Apollos into the "way of God" and a more effective ministry. Indeed, such a reversal of a woman's status within the community of goods embodies the way of God.

PART II: ENGAGING ACTS 4–5 FOR TODAY'S CHURCH

One of the great strengths of North American culture is its respect for the individual and the way it encourages individuals to realize their aspirations and potential. But every strength or virtue, when pushed too single-mindedly and exclusively, can flip over and become a weakness or a vice. So our North American sense of placing high value in the individual — in many ways a strength — has the flip side of weakening the community, undermining enduring bonds and relationships, disconnecting individuals from structures and networks of meaning, and depriving individual people of their communities of meaning and purpose. The church in North America is also affected by this, as we have noted in the introductory chapter. It is often easier for us to think of "my faith" rather than of "our faith," "my" relationship to Jesus rather than our life together, "my" spirituality rather than our life as a people.

Yet the whole witness of Scripture, from Genesis to Revelation, is bent toward God's intention to form a people, a people who will be a light to the whole world, a blessing to all the other peoples of the earth. Sometimes our emphasis on the individual has blinded us to this social and theological reality: God is in the business of creating a people, building a community, and calling each of us into a new community that is defined by new loyalties and a new story. In Acts we see God at work to create a new people who are not to be defined by the old categories of race, language, gender, or social class, but a people united in witness to the resurrection and in a way of life that embodies what we call "resurrection practices."

Acts 4:32-35 sounds very similar to the book's earlier description of life together in the new community of Christ (2:44-47). Both snapshots of the new community of Christ emphasize unity ("those who believed were of one heart and soul"), the sharing of goods ("everything they owned was held in common"), the great power and grace emanating from the community ("great grace was upon them all"), and the fact that none in the community went without basic necessities ("there was not a needy person among them"). These same qualities — unity, sharing of goods, provision for the needy, and grace and power resting on a people — mark the earlier summary and snapshot in Acts 2. We take note of this because this portrait of a community follows directly on Peter's bold preaching, which led to the repentance and conversion of a great host of people. The point is that conversion leads to new community and, in a very real sense, depends on that community and its life and practices for embodiment and nurture.

Many people have had something they would describe as a "conversion experience" or a "mountaintop moment" or a "breakthrough" of some sort. While we do not wish to doubt or diminish the power of such moments, we should note that in Acts those who are converted move to a new community, namely, the church, which expresses, builds on, and sustains the conversion experience. In other words, conversion experiences — what the Reformers referred to as "justification" — require structures and settings for *sanctification,* for the newly converted to grow in faith and holiness. Conversion and community belong together. It is no accident that Peter's preaching, which has led to repentance in his listeners, is followed directly in Acts 2 by a picture of community. Without community, conversion experiences easily lose plausibility: one can go back to the old world and the old associations, and before long one is living the same old way. Conversion requires communities that support, express, and embody this new faith and life.

Thus Luke consistently emphasizes the community — its life and its formation. Here in these early chapters that are set in Jerusalem, bold witness leads to a growing congregation. Later in Acts, Paul's preaching leads to the formation of congregations — communities that sustain, express, and embody the new way of life in Christ. These are communities that are all about change, about changed and changing lives, about sustaining those changes and inviting others to share in changed life. Being about the work of changing lives and then changing the world would seem to be the core purpose of the church and of Christian community. To what extent would this characterize the life of today's congregations?

Congregations, like all other forms of human gathering and community, tend to lose sight of their core purpose, even if they honor it rhetorically. The core purpose of the church is to be a community that sustains continuous change and transformation as we grow in the likeness of Christ and image of God. But in today's world, this purpose is often lost or displaced by other purposes entirely. The purpose of churches today often seems to be less about changing lives toward the way of Jesus Christ and making disciples than it is about satisfying the members of the congregation — keeping them happy by meeting their social needs and providing comfort and services. There is, of course, nothing wrong with meeting people's needs or with members experiencing happiness; but when satisfying church members takes priority over changing lives and being a community that is engaged in making disciples, then something crucial has been lost.

There are other ways that congregations have lost sight of their essential purpose. As Kirk Hadaway argues in his book *Behold I Do a New Thing*, some congregations are less about satisfying the members than they are about satisfying the leader. Whole churches of the "charismatic leader/follower" type have as their essential purpose satisfying the leader. Still other congregations may work at changing lives, but can confuse the means (the church's programs and ministries) with the ends (changing lives). In those cases, "working the program" may eclipse changing lives.

Our point here is that changing lives may begin with a conversion experience that is evoked by signs and wonders and powerful witness; but sustaining a conversion experience, giving it enduring meaning, and building the kind of community that is salt to the earth and light to the world requires the formation of a people. Acts understands and demonstrates this. Acts is not just about individual experiences of conversion and transformation, as powerful and prominent as such accounts are. Acts is about God's resolve to form a people, to call into being a new community of people who will share life together.

Everything They Owned Was Held in Common

As we have noted in the text exposition part of this chapter, Christian unity is never merely a verbal expression or heartfelt ideal: it is a set of social practices that meet real needs wherever they are found. The rubber hits the road in the church community, where the ideal has practical expression and consequences. This community is characterized by having their wealth and material goods in common; there is generosity in this sharing, both of spirit and of goods.

How is this possible, and what does it mean for the church today? Beginning with the "how" question, it does not appear that this sharing of goods is born out of a command or obligation so much as it is a response to the "great grace upon them all," and to the experience of the living Christ. In other words, our ethics are all about gratitude, as is always true for Christians. "Salvation," as an old aphorism goes, "is all about grace; ethics is all about gratitude." In order for people to let go of anything — but especially money and possessions and the security they represent — they must have taken hold of, or have been taken hold of by, something else. That's the case here in Acts: the sharing of goods occurs within the climate of "great grace upon them all" and the experience of a new community. Generosity is made possible because God has been generous to them. Something else, namely the Spirit, is filling their lives and hearts, thus allowing hands to freely share the goods and possessions that we so often imagine will fill and secure our lives.

Practically speaking, this suggests to us that significant giving and sharing, the practice of generosity, has its roots in transformative worship, bold witness, rich sacrament, and a vital life together. This generosity and sharing of goods is not born of imperatives such as "you should be generous," or "you should care for those in need," so much as it flows from the indicative of what God has done and is doing. To put it negatively, if there is no spirit of generosity alive in our congregations, it may be time to look at what is going on — or not going on — in worship and in our life together as a community. When people's deep hungers are being met, then generosity overflows naturally — or at least responsively.

This is not, of course, generosity or sharing of goods as an end in itself, but with the goal that there "not [be] a needy person among them." When, in Luke 4, Jesus announces that the time has come, the new age has begun, he speaks of "good news preached to the poor, and liberation to the captives." Here this eschatological reality breaks in as the needy in the community are in fact provided for and taken care of. The promise of "blessed are you who hunger now, for you will be filled" (Luke 6:21) becomes a reality, and as such a sign of God's presence and of the new age breaking into the world.

What are congregations today to make of this? The very idea of "all who believed were together and had all things in common" gives rise in some to fears of "communism" or "socialism." Make no mistake, this portrait of the Acts community *is* a challenge to an ownership society, to the way that most of us in twenty-first-century North America not only participate in a capitalist economy but have even internalized capitalism in our hearts and souls. But having said that, we must acknowledge that Acts is not offering a proposal for political policy but a picture of a community and a congregation's life together. It rests on a fundamental insight that may well escape us in our time and place, but which is consistent with the whole witness of Scripture: that is, strong communities create security and abundance. Communities of shared life and shared goods are safe, secure, and abundant. Conversely, where community is diminished, there is impoverishment, if not in plain dollars and cents, then certainly in our overall sense of being secure, valued, and at peace. There is thus a correlation between the strength and generosity of our common life and the peace and well-being of our personal lives. We may accumulate a great deal of wealth as individuals, but a sense of impoverishment and insecurity will continue to dog us, nipping at our heels, so long as our social bonds, our communities, and our relationships are in jeopardy or at risk. Acts is informed by an understanding of this basic relationship between community and security.

We return, then, to the question of what this means in the life of contemporary congregations, noting two implications that we have already touched on: (1) The strength of a congregation's life of worship and sacrament is profoundly significant for its generosity and sharing of goods. (2) Building Christian community, as well as building the fabric of human community beyond the congregation, will contribute to people's sense of security, well-being, and capacity for generosity.

As contemporary Christians weigh the picture of a community of shared goods, we would urge congregations and their leaders not to write off these snapshots as impossible ideals by saying, "We could never do anything like that." Instead, we would urge congregations and their leaders to look for instances in which such sharing of goods is in fact already happening in their communities, and to fan those flames, so to speak. There are people in every congregation who do practice, to a greater or lesser degree, the sharing of goods and providing for the needy. Churches should focus there, highlight that, and build on it rather than emphasizing how far they are from realizing the ideal described in Acts. For even in Acts, as we shall see shortly, it does not work out perfectly. There are those who hoard and deceive (Ananias and Sapphira), and there are innate problems with the just and equitable sharing for those in need (6:1). But congregations and their leaders are almost always better off to work from the "glass half full" perspective than from the "glass half empty."

But we can go beyond that. Part of bold preaching and witness today must meet the challenge of wealth and possessions head on, and must say with Acts, and without equivocation, that discipleship that does not affect our checkbook is no discipleship at all. In an acquisitive and ownership society, this is indeed a countercultural practice. Moreover, it is not "fundraising" nor even "stewardship" in the usual limited sense of those words; it is engaging people in a spiritual practice of generous giving. The paradoxical insight of the gospel about money is that we will never have enough, no matter how much we have; the only way to "have enough" is to give it away. That is, the only way to gain some sort of freedom from the voices that chant relentlessly in our ears and pluck the strings of our anxiety is to be obedient to Christ's call to give and to share.

There is freedom in this obedience. It is the testimony of saints today, and throughout the ages, that "it is in giving that we receive." This is a spiritual practice, a part of the way of life that is core for those who affirm God's victory over death's power in Jesus Christ. Nowhere is death's power more evident in society than in the relentless push to have more, to get more, and to hold more. This will not save us, which is not to say that money and possessions are intrinsically bad; neither Acts nor other parts of Scripture suggest that. Money and possessions are resources that hold within them, as do all of God's created goods, the capacity for right use as well as abuse. They represent promise as well as danger.

Acts and the Problem of Possessions

Among the four canonical Gospels, Luke seems more aware of the danger posed by wealth and possessions than are the other three. Thus it comes as no surprise that the proper use of possessions should continue to loom large in Acts. After Luke's description of the community of shared goods, where all things were held in common and no one was in need, the focus of this passage shifts to three individuals who offer contrasting examples in their use of possessions and wealth. As the exposition has pointed out, Barnabas ("the son of encouragement") is the positive type, while the married couple (Ananias and Sapphira) is the antitype. Both sell land they own in order to bring the proceeds to the apostles, who will then provide for the needy.

Perhaps the skeptical reader may consider this highly unlikely — that individuals would, in response to the gospel, sell a piece of property and give the money to the community for those in need. It may not happen every day, but I can assure you that it does happen, because I have seen it. When a congregation I served began to seek the Lord's will regarding how we might minister to the needs of people with mental illness, members put a host of ideas on the table. One of the ideas was particularly ambitious: the creation of a "house of healing," a residential, spiritual community for mentally ill individuals. The church developed and pursued this idea, ambitious as it was. Before long, we reached a partnership with a large public hospital: the hospital staff would screen potential residents for the House of Healing and provide "case management." The house and its residents would provide family and community, routine, a modest spiritual discipline each day, and the support of a stable and safe place to live.

One day a woman of our congregation came forward. She had listened as the ideas for this project were being developed. Even though the congregation had not yet approved this new ministry, she said that she had a piece of land — quite a valuable piece of land, as it turned out — and she would like to sell it and make the proceeds available to buy or build the first House of Healing. This is pretty close to a modern reenactment of the Barnabas story. Note that the church's ministry had received no official authorization, and no fund-raising had begun. But the Spirit was on the move, getting ahead of the usual ways that we plan and organize. Before the congregation knew it, the House of Healing was well on its way to becoming a reality. Within the next five years, that same congregation had created two more Houses of Healing, providing short-term (up to two years) residence and community to fifteen or more persons who had experienced mental illness at any given time. This is not just a "miraculous Bible story" from the book of Acts. This really happens.

Alas, it also happens that some cling to their money and deceive themselves and others to such an extent that it destroys their lives. Maybe today's stories are not as dramatic as Ananias and Sapphira dropping dead at the apostles' feet; but most observant pastors and others can tell you about people who clung to their money so tightly and with so much anxiety that it killed them — maybe slowly draining their life and relationships away, or maybe with the suddenness of a stress-induced coronary. Pollard, for example, scoffed at the church's idea of ministry to a growing number of immigrant families in their small town. His attitude was: "They don't belong here anyway, so why should we help them?" Pollard's house and property, large and expansive, lay on the edge of town, and Pollard stayed on the edge of the congregation. Despite his scoffing, the ministry went ahead and experienced remarkable and life-giving success. The last time I visited Pollard, what I felt more than anything else was, in the midst of his plenty, his isolation and loneliness. His money had not saved him. His possessions and his clinging to them had in reality isolated him and — in the deepest, most spiritual sense — had killed him. Toward the end I sensed in Pollard a deep regret, a regret that he had not been part of a great thing, a generous thing.

Ananias and Sapphira, like Barnabas, sold a piece of property with the idea and claim that they, too, were laying all the money at the feet of the apostles for the good of needy sisters and brothers in the community. But it turned out that they were not telling the apostles and the community the truth. Their sudden death may seem improbable to us today, but in a real sense their death sentence was already announced in their own decision to cut themselves off from the community by means of greed and deception. The dropping dead part of it was simply making real and outwardly evident their cancerous inner spiritual condition. Furthermore, it reminds us that "we don't have forever," as Pollard said to me in his final days, as though he were surprised to discover that. Death can come at any moment, and when it does, it's too late to change, too late to experience the gifts and blessings of community, including generosity and truthfulness.

STUDY QUESTIONS

1. According to Acts, a congregation's belief in the Lord's resurrection is embodied in the sharing of its possessions. Sharing with others more needy than you is a "resurrection practice." Why does Acts consider this sacred practice — and others performed within a "community of common goods" as catalogued in Acts 2:42 — an appropriate demonstration of the Lord's resurrection?

2. This is a hard passage. To many of us, God seems overly harsh in dispensing the death penalty for an infraction so slight as withholding a portion of one's pledge. Clarify your own responses to this biblical text. How would you translate Peter's questions put to Ananias and Sapphira for today's church, especially in its use of wealth?

3. God's kingdom *is* the real world. What does this passage and its contrast-

ing portraits of Barnabas and Ananias/Sapphira teach us about the economics of God's kingdom?

4. This chapter claims that "in Acts conversion and community go together." What implications do you see for your congregation or campus in this statement?

5. Wall and Robinson argue that the sharing of goods and generosity are first to be viewed in narrative context — a rather idealized setting in which the worshiping community shares an experience of "great grace upon them all." How should this truth influence planning in areas of stewardship, worship, and spirituality in contemporary congregations?

6. If you are a student or a faculty member, how might this story help to give shape to a curriculum and faculty pedagogy?

6   *Conflict Resolution and Decision Making within a Healthy Congregation*

PART I: INTERPRETING ACTS 6:1-15 AS SCRIPTURE

This passage continues Luke's narrative interest in the community's resurrection practices, which embody the "great grace" of God (4:33), the most important of which, the distinctive practice of sharing goods, we have discussed in the preceding chapter. This practice has evidently made a considerable impression on the Jerusalem public, and it is partly responsible for the community's vigorous growth (see 2:45-47). But this very growth, without an infrastructure to support it, has created a problem of supply and demand. One group in particular, the widows from among "the Hellenists," has been negatively affected by this growth spurt, and they blame the community's neglect of their material needs on "the Hebrews." Luke does not give a motive for this accusation; he is interested in the practical — rather than the political — problem, which is the community's ineffective administration of goods that has resulted in unmet needs among its most needy members.

The apostles understand the problem and have a plan to effectively resolve it. Curiously, though, they use the unmet needs of Hellenist widows as an occasion to remind the community that their vocation is to be prophets-like-Jesus rather than waiters-on-tables (v. 2). Thus they define the present threat to the widows' welfare in two ways: on the one hand, needy members are being neglected, and the community's public witness to God's "great grace" is subverted as a result (cf. 4:32-33); on the other

88

hand, since goods are "laid at their feet" for redistribution, the apostles find themselves spending more time managing the growing community's feeding program and are thus distracted from their principal ministry (vv. 4, 7).

To resolve this conflict, the apostles gather "the whole community of disciples" to recommend seven "from among yourselves" who will assume responsibility for food distribution. These seven are commissioned by the twelve, so that "the word of God continued to spread" and new converts were added to the church. The related story of Stephen (6:8–8:3), who is the leader of the seven, illuminates the dominant themes of Luke's narrative of the church's Jerusalem mission. The first narrative panel profiles a powerful Stephen, whose résumé indicates that he is a prophet-like-Jesus and thus provokes public scrutiny similar to what Jesus provoked before him (vv. 8-10). For this reason, the alert reader anticipates that the official response to Stephen and his prophetic ministry will be hostile (vv. 11-15). Although beyond the scope of the present passage, Acts continues to tell Stephen's story. He responds to his accusers in a way appropriate to this book of Acts — with an inspired speech (7:2-53), the longest in Acts and one that the majority of scholars count among the most significant for understanding the primary theological claims that shape Acts. Stephen responds to the false accusation that he opposes "Moses and God" (v. 11) by making God and Moses the two central characters of his biblical retelling of Israel's history. His jury's response to the speech's biting conclusion to an unrepentant Israel prompts a martyred Stephen to repeat Jesus' final words on the cross (7:54–8:3). From beginning to end, this is truly the story of a prophet-like-Jesus.

In Acts, Luke routinely depicts the religious solidarity of believers, their life together as friends, and the authority of the apostles within the community by showing their practice of sharing possessions with those in need. While Luke has already introduced this point in previous narrative summaries and without much qualification, the personal tragedies of Judas and then of Ananias and Sapphira have prepared the reader to recognize that the community's common life and public witness are threatened by the problems some believers have with their possessions. In previous profiles of the community of goods, Luke suggests that it is God (in concert with the apostles) who settles these problems by excommunicating the offending parties. Luke has given very little practical advice, however, about resolving these conflicts in a more constructive manner. The importance of this episode in Acts, then, is that it introduces a pattern for resolving congregational conflict that is repeated later in Acts (see 11:1-18; 14:27–15:29; 21:17-26), which suggests that church unity is a strategic element of the church's mission.

The temporal marker that opens this passage ("Now during those days, when . . .") may signal a new day when changes call for a fresh discernment of God's will. In Acts, the experience of internal conflict results in a process that resets the community's bearings in God's different direction. This conflict is, at its root, the economic disparity that threatens any rapidly growing group, no matter how cohesive in mind and practice: "The disciples were increasing in number," and so their "widows were being neglected in the daily distribution" (6:1). Rapid growth puts the greatest pressure precisely on those points where the material needs of the community's newest or most marginal members are evident. If true in this case, the well-known biblical injunction for Israel to care for its most vulnerable and chronically needy members — widows, orphans, resident aliens, the destitute, and the powerless (cf. Lev. 19; 25; Deut. 16:11; Mal. 3:5; 1 Tim. 5:3-16; James 1:22–2:17) — is in peril. The Hellenist widows of Acts combine two welfare classes: they are both widows and resident aliens, without family and without national support. The prophets make clear that the treatment of such people effectively gauges Israel's relationship with God (Mal. 3:5; Zech. 7:10) and heralds repentant Israel's renewed covenant with God (Isa. 47:8). Therefore, the Hellenists are justified in lodging their complaint.

Even allowing for the importance of this episode in Acts, the reader may still puzzle over several of its details. The first puzzling detail is the identity of the Hellenists and the precise source of their conflict with the Hebrews. We should avoid the kind of pigeonholing that places each group into a rigidly defined social class or ideological camp; there is very little basis in the text or behind it for doing so. The reader should presume that the Hellenists and Hebrews "were of one heart and soul" (see 4:32) and in principle shared equally in the blessings of a restored Israel. The present complaint stems from the realization that, in practice, one group has not yet fully participated in the community of goods according to its rule of faith (see 4:32-35).

The terms "Hellenists" and "Hebrews" are used together only in this passage, and their wider currency in contemporaneous Jewish literature is of little help in further defining their meaning in Acts. Luke's use of the adjectival form of the word "Hebrew," however, suggests that he is using both terms to refer to a spoken language. Paul, for example, speaks in Hebrew to his Palestinian audiences (21:40; 22:2; 26:14). If that is Luke's intent here, the division is between language groups and not theological outlooks: the Hellenists speak mostly Greek, and the Hebrews speak mostly Aramaic. The language barrier between the two groups may explain at least in part why the practice of food distribution was troublesome.

But different languages often delineate other differences as well. Since Diaspora Jews have been an important constituency of the Israel of Acts from Pentecost forward (see 2:5-11), Luke may shift to "Hellenists" here to refer to those Diaspora Jews who have settled in ethnic enclaves around Jerusalem and who maintain their own cultural conventions there. Some have evidently become Christian believers, even establishing Greek-speaking congregations in their neighborhoods, while maintaining the resurrection practices and core beliefs of the twelve. If this is the case, the Hellenists' complaint against the Hebrews may well reflect cultural barriers that have come to exist between different congregations located in different neighborhoods of Jerusalem. Luke's choice of words makes this subtext more clear in that it echoes the Old Testament stories of Israel's murmuring in the wilderness about their material hardships (Num. 11:1), much to God's displeasure. Perhaps Luke wishes simply to call attention to a similar situation that posed a real threat to the community's favorable relations with God. In this sense it needs to be resolved — and quickly!

Another feature of this passage that makes it both puzzling and important is the turn it marks toward a second team of leaders, two of whom (Stephen and Philip) are given prophetic tasks to perform similar to those of the powerful twelve. The previous narrative has settled the public debate over Israel's leadership in favor of the apostles (5:40-42), whose spiritual authority within the faith community is unrivaled (see 4:32–5:16). Their prominence is predicated on two important roles that they effectively perform: the first is as inspired prophets-like-Jesus who proclaim the Word of God and perform the signs and wonders of the Spirit; the second role is administering the internal life of the community, whose membership has placed goods at their feet for disposal to those with material needs. They clearly rank their prophetic tasks (preaching, prayer) ahead of their administrative role; and they are willing to share their spiritual authority — symbolized by the redistribution of goods — with other members of the wider community.

Before this crisis, they have acted only in collaboration with the Holy Spirit; however, the community's growth and ethnic diversity prompts the realization that their performance standards have not been met. This recognition, itself a mark of their spiritual authority, signals a new and dramatic movement of the Spirit to redistribute spiritual authority and prophetic tasks to still others beyond the community's apostolate. Ironically, then, the selection of the seven will substantially qualify how the reader comes to understand the authority of the twelve: even though they have continued to do and teach what Jesus began, their authority to do so extends to different leaders of the next generation and from another constituency of believers.

The reader should note that Luke's use of *diakoneō/diakonia* ("to wait on tables"/"distribution") in this passage follows the Lucan plot line. He states the failure of infrastructure as a breakdown in the daily *diakonia* ("distribution") of food (6:1); and his subsequent use of the verbal form *diakoneō* ("wait on tables") assesses this conflict: food is not being "distributed" to the needy. Finally, the repetition of *diakonia* in verse 4 introduces the resolution of this conflict: the apostles are no longer diverted by administrative tasks and are now fully engaged in their *diakonia* ("ministry") of the Word. Significantly, both "distribution" of food and the "ministry" of the Word are represented by the word *diakonia*.

A final interpretive problem regards the identity and purpose of those who belong to "the whole community of disciples." This is the first use of the word "disciples" in the book of Acts. In the Gospels, of course, a disciple is a follower or student of Jesus, and the same could be true here. But Luke introduces this term into Acts in connection with the Hellenists' complaint; so "disciples" here may well be a term for Greek-speaking believers, many of whom are new to the faith (v. 1) and perhaps also new to Jerusalem. The impression that the translations of this text give is that the twelve called together the "whole of/all of" the disciples — well into the thousands by now — for a discussion of the problem. But it is more likely that this "community of disciples" refers to a smaller representative group of Hellenists who bear tacit responsibility for the care of their widows, perhaps because their spiritual maturity will make conflict resolution more likely.

The Seven

The charge given to the advisory committee that represents the interests of the Hellenists is to "select from among yourselves seven men" (6:3-6). The number seven is not arbitrary but reflects the Jewish practice of choosing seven members to provide oversight to local congregations (Exod. 18:21; LXX Num. 27:18-19). Nor is the process of selecting leadership arbitrary. The verb *epikeptein* ("select") comes from a word-family that is used to indicate critical and prudent judgments: this sort of decision is made only after careful deliberation.

The community is asked to investigate potential leaders on the basis of three personal attributes, which are different from those used to select the twelve (1:21-22) but are deemed most important in meeting the urgent demands of this appointment: they must be members of the community in "good standing, full of the Spirit and of wisdom" (v. 3). Each attribute is not only important for "waiting on tables," but each candidate should also have talent in providing competent oversight within the church. The participle translated "good standing" *(martyroumenos)* suggests a good reputation, which is based on the favorable testimony of others and is a crucial feature of leading others (cf. 15:14, 36). The combination of "full" *(plērēs)* with "Spirit" denotes evidence of a candidate's mature faith and also of his prophetic vocation. The final characteristic of a talented leader is "wisdom," which may refer to a person's organizational talent; but in combination with Spirit, it is probably more essential to one's spiritual authority. Seven from among the Hellenists meet these criteria and are selected by the community. Luke provides the reader with a list of their Greek names, highlighting for future reference the appointments of Stephen as "a man full of faith and the Holy Spirit" (v. 5), and also of Philip (see Acts 8).

There are decisive cues in this story indicating that the purpose of this process is to discern God's will. For instance, the apostles ask that the Hellenists "select seven men" whom the community then "chose" (v. 5). Not only is the number seven a well-known theological symbol of God's will, but Luke uses the word "chose" *(eklegomai)* for God's activity in selecting those with whom to do business (Luke 6:13; Acts 1:2, 24; 15:7). The unwritten motive of this process from start to finish is to find those whom God has authorized for the diaconate.

The apostolic vocation is here defined as devotion "to prayer and to serving the word" (v. 4). Luke uses "word" as an omnibus term for the full range of the prophet's tasks: the Spirit-filled interpretation of Scripture, the persuasive proclamation of the gospel, and the performance of "signs and wonders" that provide the eschatological setting for biblical interpretation and evangelistic preaching in the book of Acts (see 4:31; 6:7; 8:4, 14; 11:1; 12:24; 13:48; 19:20). The petition of apostolic prayers seeks greater power from God to make certain these various prophetic tasks will be boldly and effectively executed.

Commentators have made much of the gesture of the twelve of "laying their hands on" the seven Hellenists who stand before them (v. 6). Similar to the community's ritual of placing possessions at the feet of the apostles, this service of installation indicates their religious authority to govern the community's internal life and sanction its decisions. In a biblical setting, the reader will also recognize that this gesture often signals a succession of authority from one leader to the next (cf. Num. 27:18, 23; Deut. 34:9). It is significant that only the apostles have the authority to transfer their power to others; here they do so to preserve the most distinctive practice of the community of goods and to safeguard their prophetic vocation.

Welfare for All

Luke closes this interlude with an optimistic note: "the number of disciples increased greatly in Jerusalem" (v. 7), thereby assuring the reader that the present problem has been effectively handled so that the Jerusalem mission can move ever forward. This latest notice of the community's success is especially noteworthy for its two curious phrases. The first ("the word of God continued to spread") personifies the apostles' proclamation of the gospel, shifting the reader's focus from the power and authority of those who preach it (the apostles) to the power and authority of what is preached (the Word of God). By leaving open the identity of the prophetic carrier of the Word, the narrator alerts the reader to the diminishing attention Acts will pay to the story of the twelve and the increasing attention it will pay to the progress of the Word of God to the end of earth — no matter who is proclaiming it.

The second intriguing phrase claims that "a great many of the priests became obedient to the faith." Some commentators find Paul's influence in Luke's phrasing here. Paul's similar phrase, used to frame the argument of Romans, is "for an obedience of faith" (Rom. 1:5; 16:26) and reflects the central claim of his gentile mission: the sinner's profession of trust that "Jesus is Lord" (Rom. 10:9). In the context of Acts, however, Luke's phrase summarizes a saving response to the missionaries' "Word of God" that requires the new convert to "repent and be baptized" into the community of goods.

Given the apostles' past grievances with the priestly establishment of Jerusalem, this phrase initially strikes the reader as confirming once and for all the reversal of religious leadership within Israel (5:17-42). But closer attention to the historical referent suggests otherwise. Josephus estimates that upwards of 18,000 priests were living in Jerusalem at that time. Most of them had minimal responsibilities in their service of the temple; and because of low public esteem, many lived close to destitution (*Antiquities of the Jews* 20.181). Their attraction to the Jesus movement indicates that the ministry of the apostles offered nothing that was offensive to traditional Jewish sensibilities; however, they also may have been drawn to the community by the availability of food. This, too, implies the favorable result of the community's welfare program, now administered by the seven.

The Testimony of Stephen

Acts introduces Stephen in a way that alerts readers to his spiritual authority (vv. 8-10): "Stephen [is] a man full of faith and the Holy Spirit" (v. 5), a prophet-like-Jesus among his Hellenist peers. His persona is filled out by the present text, which adds that he is "full of grace and power," with competence to defend the Word of God "with wisdom and the Spirit" and perform "great wonders and signs among the people." These references catalog his prophetic gifts and mark him for a ministry of the Word that continues what Jesus and his apostolic successors had begun in Jerusalem. The repetition of the catch phrase "signs and wonders" in Acts (2:17-22, 43; 4:16, 30; 5:12) recalls Joel's prophecy of the last days and enables the reader to more clearly discern Stephen's identity as a prophet-like-Jesus. Both his wonders and inspired words are instruments of the prophet's toolbox, to be used in the service of an effective witness to the resurrected Lord.

Prophetic ministry is most of all a ministry of the spoken word, and it is ultimately what the prophet says to the people that provokes a protest from unrepentant Jews. They "argued with Stephen" but could not withstand the combination of wisdom and Spirit "with which he spoke" (vv. 9-

10). Jesus predicted that his witnesses would be characterized by "words and wisdom that none of your opponents will be able to withstand" (Luke 21:15), and his prophecy is here fulfilled in Stephen. Luke's point is that public opinion no longer matters: Stephen's ministry, authorized by the apostles with their laying on of hands, is sanctioned by the prophecy of the Lord himself.

Stephen's opponents "belonged to the so-called synagogue of the Freedmen" (v. 9). This reference to "synagogue" is neither to a particular building nor a local institution but to a religious movement within Diaspora Judaism that included vast regions of the Roman Empire, including Asia and Africa. The word translated as "freedmen" is *libertinos,* a transliteration of the Latin word for "former slaves" *(libertinus).* Many Jews who had once been enslaved by Romans have now been set free. A few of these freedmen became Roman citizens and had influence in the Roman politics related to Judaism. Apparently, a substantial number of these freedmen had settled in Jerusalem out of a sense of religious devotion and had founded a local chapter, or "synagogue," of this religious movement.

This is Luke's first reference to the movement, and its use in this passage implies its connection with "the disciples" from among "the Hellenists," who are now led by Stephen and enjoying great success in the Greek-speaking neighborhoods of Jerusalem (v. 7). While biblical narrative pays scant attention to internal motives, this latest round of conflict suggests rival factions among "the Hellenists" that are parallel to the standing rivalry among "the Hebrews" between the Sanhedrin and the twelve.

Since fair debate fails, Stephen's opponents resort to dirty tricks to subvert the influence of his mighty deeds and inspired argument (vv. 11-15). The freedmen do so by means of underhanded rabble-rousing, which characterizes them as unfit leaders of Diaspora Israel. The accusations they level against Stephen are three: (1) he speaks "blasphemous words against Moses and God" (v. 11); (2) he "never stops saying things against this holy place and the law" (v. 13); and (3) he claims that "Jesus of Nazareth will destroy this place and change the customs of Moses" (v. 14).

The initial charge that Stephen's words are "blasphemous against Moses and God" is surprising and revealing. It is surprising because blasphemy against Moses is not illegal, and yet they mention it before charging him with blaspheming God, which is illegal. Luke's phrasing of this twofold accusation is revealing in his intention to let the reader know that the substance of the legal case against Stephen is bogus. By posting a prior concern about what Stephen teaches against Moses, his opponents prepare the reader for two "legitimate" allegations they place before the council for judicial deliberation, which concern "the customs that Moses handed on to us" (v. 14). The real issue at stake, then, is the Mosaic prescriptions concerning the sanctity of the temple rather than with the orthodoxy of Stephen's theology per se. In any case, Stephen will defend his loyalty to both "Moses and God" as the two principal characters of his provocative recital of Israel's history that follows (7:2-53).

Luke shapes his story of Stephen's trial to parallel the gospel story of Jesus' trial. Thus the freedmen's charge of "blasphemy" refers back to a similar accusation leveled against Jesus at his trial (cf. Matt. 26:65; Mark 14:57-58). Furthermore, the deceit of Jesus' accusers is reflected in that of Stephen's accusers: while falsely accusing Stephen of breaking the law that prohibits blasphemy against God (Lev. 24:11-26), they break the ninth commandment of the Decalogue, which forbids bringing false witness against another person (Exod. 20:16). (This characterization of witnesses as "false" is a narrative device — an important addition by this storyteller — since the council could not have known this at the time.) The inference to be drawn from Luke's literary interplay is that Stephen is a prophet-like-Jesus whose vocation is to bring the Word of God to Israel, but whose destiny is rejection and death.

Stephen's accusers bring him before a tribunal that has already threatened and flogged the apostles without just cause so that they can hear the claims of "false" witnesses. The chances of Stephen receiving a fair hearing are slim to none! Both accusations heard by the Sanhedrin are part of the earlier charge that Stephen blasphemes against Israel's Mosaic traditions. In the first offense, his accusers claim that Stephen teaches against "this holy place and the law" (6:13). Since the temple and Torah form an integral pair of Mosaic traditions, what they actually allege is that Stephen's teaching about the role of the temple in God's salvation cuts against the grain of traditional Jewish practice as legislated by the scribal "oral Torah" (traditional *halakha*).

The Pharisees made a distinction between biblical Torah and oral commentary on Torah — what Josephus calls "ancestral rules" (*Jewish War*, 7.10.2), what the Mishnah collects as "sayings of the fathers," and what Acts refers to here as "the customs that Moses handed down" (v. 14). This "oral Torah" is based on case study and reflects the pious attempts of Pharisaic scholars to adapt the biblical Torah to their congregational setting. Of course, there was no unanimity within Pharisaic Judaism over these matters. Other devout Diaspora Jews were living in Jerusalem at the time of Stephen who were not disciples of Jesus and yet would have probably sided with Stephen against the temple hierarchy in order to elevate practical "piety" over temple protocol (8:2).

But the real climax of the court case against Stephen comes in the second accusation: "We heard him say that this Jesus of Nazareth will destroy this place" (v. 14). Significantly, this is the first negative appraisal of Jesus' suffering found in Acts, and it is proffered by these opponents of the church's mission. Up to this point we have heard only from Peter, who accuses unrepentant Israel of participating with Rome in the Messiah's death. The charge against Stephen not only implies a rejection of God's Word but a considered political opinion that the Jewish charge against Jesus (that he taught against the temple and a mainstream rendering of Torah) justly resulted in his Roman execution. In this regard, N. T. Wright has recently argued that Jesus' actions in the temple were motivated by the conviction that his messianic role and authority for Israel had replaced both temple and Torah as the central symbols of a Jewish way of life and faith.[1] According to Jesus, then, God's promise to purify and then restore an eschatological Israel does not include the temple at all but is only fulfilled through his messianic activity.

Against this interpretation of Jesus and his followers, the freedmen seek to maintain the centrality of the temple to Israel's national identity and destiny. While their actions certainly intend to counteract the growing influence of Stephen among their compatriots in the Holy City, the various allusions to the Gospel story of Jesus suggest that the freedmen's hostility toward Stephen is deeply rooted in a historical memory of Jesus' troubling actions in the temple (cf. John 2:13-22) and his prediction of its destruction (cf. Luke 21:20-24). We should note that the Second Temple had been destroyed by the Romans long before Acts was written; and the public debate about rebuilding it as an eschatological sign was a lively one within Diaspora Judaism at the end of the first and into the second century. This historical subtext of the council's accusation against Stephen, then, sounds an unwritten note of his vindication. This may explain why the accusers use the future tense in stating the charge that Jesus "will destroy this place"

---

1. N. T. Wright, *Jesus and the Victory of God* (Minneapolis: Augsburg/Fortress Press, 1996), pp. 405-27.

(6:14), when in fact Jesus' prediction had already come true when Luke wrote the story of this encounter.

If Stephen's proclamation of Jesus included, if only implicitly, a denial of the temple's centrality in Israel's future relations with God, in what sense is this second accusation against Stephen false? Are these "false witnesses" because they never really heard him say what they allege? Is the substance of their accusations false because Stephen never said or practiced what they allege? Or are they "false" witnesses — from the narrator's perspective — because *they* claim that Stephen is blasphemous, while the *narrator* believes he is not? Stephen's speech before the tribunal criticizes neither temple nor Torah but rather an unrepentant Israel whose zeal for the temple prevents them from believing that Jesus is the Messiah. In continuity with the teaching and actions of Jesus, Stephen denies the temple its pivotal role in "the last days" of salvation's history, when Israel's purification and restoration are the results of turning to God's Messiah and not by observing the practices of temple purity (3:17-23; cf. 7:44-50). While these allegations against Stephen may misstate what he actually said about Jesus' troubled relations with the temple and are in that limited sense "false," the hostile witnesses do in fact accurately summarize the essence of Stephen's position. Of course, the testimony of Stephen that the Sanhedrin and freedmen would deem false, the resurrection of Jesus, has proved true: he has replaced the temple as the effective means of Israel's covenanting with God.

Stephen's transfiguration before his accusers, who "saw that his face was like the face of an angel" (v. 15), echoes the Old Testament story of Moses' descent from Mt. Sinai, tablets in hand, when "his face shone because he had been talking with God" (LXX Exod. 34:29; cf. Matt. 17:2; 2 Cor. 3:10). This intertextual echo glosses Stephen's trial with this irony: it is Stephen, accused of blasphemy against Moses, and not the Sanhedrin, who makes up Israel's authorized interpreter of Moses, who appears to us and them as a prophet-like-Moses. We should read his speech in Acts 7 from this angle of vision: it is not a speech in defense of his actions but instead a prophet's inspired midrash (commentary) on the biblical traditions of Moses for "the last days." Thus Stephen is hardly critical of Torah; rather, he is an interpreter of these same "living oracles" (7:38) that can lead those who listen to the Messiah.

PART II: ENGAGING ACTS 6 FOR TODAY'S CHURCH

Just as the young and romantic sometimes imagine that "there will never be any conflict in our marriage," so ecclesiastical romantics may imagine that the true and pure church will be marked by harmony in all things and at all times, and that there will be a complete absence of conflict. But both groups of romantics would be wrong. Every human group, community, institution, or *polis* — including Christian congregations — will experience conflict. And as in marriage, the question is not, Will we have conflict? but rather, How will we deal with conflict when it comes? How will we resolve it? By what patterns, principles, or protocols will we be able to handle the inevitable — even growth-producing — conflict?

Today many congregations experience conflict over a range of matters, some that appear major and others that seem minor or even trivial. There is conflict over ministers and leaders, over search processes, over the allocation of the congregation's resources, and over the choice of hymnals or music. And there is conflict over what color the new carpet will be, the menu for the annual meeting dinner, or whether the rummage sale will be on the fourth Sunday of October, as is customary, or might be moved to the third Sunday because of a conflict with a regional women's conference that younger women in the congregation wish to attend. Often the seemingly minor conflicts become major because congregations have not done well at acknowledging and resolving the major issues.

Today a good many congregations, as well as denominations, even appear to be disabled or paralyzed by conflict. In reality, what is disabling or paralyzing congregations and other church bodies is not conflict per se but their inability to deal with conflict and to resolve it in just and faithful ways. Can Acts and the experience of the early church offer any guidance for the church today and congregations as they face conflict and decision making? We believe that it can — with this caveat: Acts does not provide a three-, five-, or twelve-step solution for dealing with conflict, which if followed will magically fix the situation. Acts does affirm that conflict is part of being a community of faith, and that conflict often comes when change occurs; but it shows that conflict can be resolved faithfully, though seldom without growth, some loss, and even pain. But nobody ever said that new life is easy.

Acts appears to offer guidance to the church and to congregations today in two different ways. On the one hand, we can distinguish in the book of Acts certain patterns or protocols for dealing with conflict in the church. While the various conflicts experienced by the church in Acts vary, it is possible to cull from them, and here from Acts 6, some guidance for addressing conflict in the church. There is a second way in which Acts addresses contemporary conflicts in the church. Here it is not so much by a pattern for dealing with conflict as by looking analogically at actual issues of conflict in Acts and asking the interpretative questions one asks of all Scripture: what in our time and place is analogous to this issue? Can we see in the issue of Acts 6, which had to do with enlarging the leadership group, applications to similar or analogous issues and questions in our own time? Let us begin with the first of these two approaches in Acts to conflict and decision making in the church — that is, Acts as a source of patterns or principles for conflict resolution.

Acts as a Source of Patterns and Principles for Resolving Conflict

The preceding exposition of Acts 6 has indicated the nature of the conflict that developed in the internal life of the growing Christian community in Jerusalem. The needy among the Hellenistic portion of the church were not receiving adequate support and care, or so they thought, while the needy among the Hebrew portion of the church were being fed and tended to sufficiently. The truth is that this conflict is not all that different from many today. For example, in one congregation some may feel the elderly portion of the congregation is being neglected, while in another congregation youth see themselves as a source of major energy in the church, and yet their views are not taken seriously by their elders on key matters, such as calling a new pastor. In some multicultural or multiethnic congregations, one group may feel that they and their needy members are not getting the same priority or attention as members of another cultural, ethnic, or language group.

Before we get too far into this particular case, we should note that provision for the needy was an identity issue, a core matter, for the early church in Jerusalem. The growing Christian movement is known by two things in particular: their bold witness to Jesus and his resurrection, and that no one in their community is in need. Therefore, this situation is one of great moment. Failure to deal with it means a continuing gap between what the community says of itself and what is actually the case.

As congregations and their leaders sort out which conflicts to take seriously and to wade into, Acts suggests a criterion for selection: pay attention to conflicts that go to the community's core values and practices. Those are ones the church must face. In some instances, the leadership's role may even be to tease out or lift up such conflicts, seeing in them important opportunities for growth. Not every conflict is worth bringing to community and public attention, but those that go to the heart of the church's identity certainly are. We cannot sidestep these without encouraging a climate in the congregation that lacks basic integrity. As the exegesis notes, the principle in play here is clear: goods are shared in the Christian community in order that no one will go without adequate provision of basic necessities. This is a sign of the new age inaugurated in Jesus Christ, in which the poor have good news preached to them. But the practice of this new age, as the Hellenists point out, is another thing. In practice, some of the vulnerable widows and orphans among the Hellenists are being overlooked. But note the first principle: in choosing conflicts to engage, give priority to those that go to questions of basic identity and mission.

Framing the Challenge

A second aspect of the way the apostles deal with conflict here in Acts 6 can be seen in their framing or naming of the challenge at hand. They hear and register the distress call ("Our needy are going without!"), which is important. Sometimes leadership simply turns a deaf ear to distress. But the apostles don't simply accept the matter as stated in the complaint; they frame the problem and challenge differently, seeing it not simply as a matter of food distribution but as a deeper matter, a challenge occasioned by the rapid growth of the new community. It may have been the case at one time that the apostles were able to serve the Word *and* serve tables for the needy. But with the growth, the increasing complexity, and the geographic distribution of the community throughout Jerusalem, this is no longer the case. Thus the apostles name the challenge differently: they respond to the community's growth, to sharing leadership, and to focusing on their own primary ministry as apostles.

Most of us have been in meetings or discussions where someone says, "I don't think that's the real issue. The real issue here is. . . ." To frame the "real issue," and to do so more accurately than it has been done, is an act of leadership, whether it is done by designated leaders or by others performing the function of leadership at that moment. Whoever offers a more accurate framing of the challenge is offering important leadership to a congregation and to the process of dealing with conflict. More often than we may imagine, conflicts fester and go unresolved because they have been misdiagnosed or misnamed at the beginning. In fact, frequently the way a group identifies and describes its problem is part of the problem!

As I write, I am working with a congregation that was a new church start not too many years ago, and is now a church that continues to experience challenges. Some have diagnosed the problem in the following way: "We need a building, a church building, of our own." Maybe that is the problem, but maybe not. Maybe the conflict is different and hence should be identified or described differently. Perhaps the challenge could be reframed, for example, as: "We lack a clear sense of identity and mission. We need to get clearer about who we are and why we are here." Leadership serves a community well when it helps to frame the problem, conflict, or challenge accurately.

Guiding Principles

Another role of leadership is to establish some relevant guiding principles for dealing with a particular challenge. Here the apostles offer at least two kinds of guiding principles. First of all, they frame the issue as one having been brought on by growth and change, which occasions both a need for widening the leadership circle and focusing on their own central priorities. The apostles are clear about the latter: their most important calling and service to the community will be provided by prayer and proclamation of the Word of God. They are called to be "servants of the Word." Others will have to be called to the ministry of serving at table and distributing resources to those in need. There is no hierarchy of value here. It is not that serving the Word is better than serving at table. It is simply that the apostles are clear about their calling and must focus on it. This becomes a guiding principle for decision making and conflict resolution.

A second guiding principle, necessitated by the first, is a set of qualifications for the new deacons, those who will handle the food distribution and wait at table. These deacons are to be persons of good reputation, full of the Spirit, and possessed of practical wisdom. Having established this, the apostles now give the work of identifying the seven to the community, including the affected part of the community, the Hellenists. But note what the leaders, the apostles, have done to advance the resolution of the conflict. First, they have framed the issue, and in doing so changed it rather significantly from the initial complaint; second, they have articulated guiding principles for the decision-making and conflict-resolution process.

There are two, or perhaps three, such principles evident here: (1) naming the primary ministry of the apostles; (2) naming the criteria for new leaders; (3) and then empowering the community to engage the issue and come to some decision. If conflict is to be dealt with faithfully and justly in the church, Acts suggests that the issue must be accurately framed and named, and that there are guiding principles to be honored in the decision-making and conflict-resolution process. Absent these key moves, many attempts at conflict resolution flounder.

The Community Engages in Discernment

Having framed the question and established guiding principles, the apostles next give the work to the community, and particularly to those most affected, the Hellenists. The latter choose from among their number seven men who will be presented to the apostles as candidates for the new diaconal office. To come to their choices, the community will need to seek the mind of God. That is, selecting the candidates is not merely a matter of political factions and lobbying. The criteria the apostles have set forth demand that the community seek God's will and wisdom in this matter: "Select from among yourselves seven men of good standing, full of the Spirit and of wisdom, whom we may appoint to this task."

Note that in this particular matter of conflict resolution and decision making, the leaders — that is, the apostles — do lead, and their authority to do so is acknowledged and respected. But note also that these same apostles do not try to control all the power or the entire process. They give the work back to the community, and they do this in several ways. First of all, they are willing to let go of the task of resource distribution and waiting on tables. Perhaps this will strike some contemporary readers as menial or less significant work. But we don't really know that. Who knows, maybe Peter and James really liked this "hands-on" service and saw it as central to their ministry. In point of fact, Jesus had called Peter to "feed my sheep" in John 21. Nevertheless, they are prepared to let go of this core ministry of the church and entrust it to others. Beyond that, the apostles let go of the nominating process and entrust that to the community as well. The point here may be suggested by the phrase "the dance of leadership," which is not so different from the dance of parenting: knowing when to hold on and when to let go. The apostles perform critical leadership tasks to resolve this conflict, but they don't try to do it all, or to hold onto the entire process. They frame the work and trust the community, under the guidance of the Holy Spirit, with the next steps.

Next, the people present the seven nominated deacons to the apostles, who themselves pray over the nominees. They, too, practice discernment. The church community cannot make decisions without seeking God's way and God's will. Too often in the modern church we have forgotten this crucial emphasis. To put it another way, the church is not a democracy: we do not seek the will of the majority when we make decisions. We seek the will of God and the mind of Christ. So both the community and the apostles have engaged in prayerful discernment, the discernment of God's will.

Public Ritual to Ratify the Decision and Resolution

Having concluded the various levels and experiences of discernment, the apostles lay hands on the seven in a public ritual that installs them in their new office. How odd it is that, when the church today has come to a decision over a tough challenge, there is often no public or liturgical ritual honoring that enactment. One might assume that churches especially would understand the significance of this part of making decisions and resolving conflict, that is, the public and symbolic ritual. It appears to be the final step in this process in Acts 6. Let us briefly recapitulate the moves here in this process of conflict adjudication:

1. hearing the distress;
2. framing the problem or challenge;
3. providing guiding principles;
4. giving the work back to the people with the problem;
5. discerning the will of God; and
6. a public ritual to mark the decisions made.

Again, we do not propose these moves by the apostolic church in Acts 6 as a kind of one-size-fits-all formula for resolving conflict. Every situation is specific and has its own context, and we need to note those particularities and heed them. Nevertheless, these six elements deserve our attention as contemporary congregations and leaders seek to resolve conflict in just and faithful ways.

But wait — perhaps there is one more. No sooner has Stephen been prayed over and installed than we find this new deacon doing apostolic ministry. Stephen, "full of grace and power," performs signs and wonders and preaches compellingly. What happened? Why isn't he waiting on tables? While we cannot pretend to know the answer to that question with certainty, the unfolding of Stephen's ministry suggests that decisions made by the church may be overruled, or at least amended, by the living God and the Holy Spirit. The church may have designated Stephen for diaconal ministry, but God has designated Stephen for something else. In the decision-making processes of the church we should not get so fixed or rigid that we cannot be surprised by fresh decisions of God.

One of my seminary professors, Jim Forbes, Jr., senior pastor at Riverside Church in New York, reminded his students of the line that always appeared in the order of worship at the church of his father, James Forbes, Sr.: "This Order of Service may be changed at any time according to the direction of the Holy Spirit!" The church formed and guided by Acts will keep such a reminder handy.

Acts 6 as Analogy

If one way for Acts to guide contemporary congregations is in the pattern of decision making and conflict adjudication that we find here in Acts 6, this and other Acts narratives may also provide guidance for today in quite a different way. That is, can we look at different conflicts and decisions in the book of Acts and find analogies to questions facing the church today? In a sense, this is the way Scripture most often and appropriately functions among us. We ask, "What is this story like?" We do not expect to reenact or reexperience the Exodus literally, but we may find an analogy to the Exodus experience in the twentieth-century struggle against segregation and Jim Crow and for civil rights in the United States. We do not expect to literally redo or reexperience the original events of Pentecost; but we may find in this story an analogy or series of analogies for the church in North America as it engages an increasingly diverse and multicultural society.

What analogies might be suggested to the narrative of Acts 6? We offer the following suggestions as illustrations of this way of using the narratives of conflict in Acts as analogies, and not as an exhaustive or definitive list of their applications. Indeed, so long as the present age continues, and so long as the God we serve is a living God, there can be no definitive catalog of applications or analogies.

Church Leadership and the Ordination of Women

Today a number of churches and denominations ordain women to ministry and leadership in the church, while other families of faith do not. One example of the latter is the Roman Catholic Church. To what extent do the leadership issues facing the Catholic Church today resemble Acts 6? And to what extent can Acts 6 properly be seen as an analogy for the ordination of women?

In the Roman Catholic Church in North America the shortage of priests is not a matter of debate; it is an accepted fact. There simply are not enough priests to fulfill the functions and roles required by Catholic congregations. As the early church grew, and the apostles were not able adequately to perform both service to the Word and service at table, so in the Catholic Church today — and perhaps others — the demand for ordained priests and leaders has far outstripped the supply, at least the supply of male priests. In many parishes women do play significant leadership roles, but they are limited in what they can do.

Is this situation — more work than there are priests to do it — analogous to Acts 6? Can women be compared to the growing group of Hellenists in the Jerusalem church, or would that be stretching the analogy? Does Acts 6 — which shows an enlargement of the leadership circle by the inclusion of kinds of people (ethnically and linguistically) who had not heretofore been in leadership — "fit" the contemporary Catholic dilemma or not? We do not take it as our task here to advocate a particular response to these questions. We do wish to suggest possible analogies. Here is another.

Church Leadership and a Multicultural Society and Church

Since the changes to the immigration laws of the United States in 1965, American society has become steadily more multicultural and multiethnic. The state of California is already a state in which "people of color" are a majority of the population. Such trends are evident in other states and regions of the United States as well. Moreover, countless neighborhoods and congregations that once served a predominantly Anglo constituency (or Americans deriving from western Europe) now find a very different reality. Perhaps the dominant ethnic group in a given congregation has changed from Swedish to Filipino, or from English, Scotch, and Irish to Hispanic. Or maybe the community of the church is simply much more diverse and pluralistic than once was the case. Where it was once a predominantly Anglo community, today it may be a mix: 40 percent Anglo or Caucasian, 23 percent African-American, and 37 percent Asian-American. How are we to be the church in such new situations and new times? Does Acts 6 speak to us in the midst of such changes, and if so, what does it say?

Note the opening words of Acts 6: "Now in those days. . . ." These words implicitly acknowledge that things do change. In Acts 6, the church was growing, and new growth meant new ethnic and language groups, including the Hellenistic and Disapora Jews. "New occasions teach new duties, time makes ancient good uncouth" — so goes the hymn. Here Luke acknowledges as much: times have changed, conditions are different now. Moreover, God is at work in the midst of these changes. Thus, broadening the leadership group and circle is both necessary and faithful.

Note, too, that the seven called to the new leadership roles and tasks are all from among the Hellenistic element of the church. The apostles do not send Hebrews to deal with the food distribution issues among the Hellenists. They would not have known the language, the customs, or the culture. Does this move — empowering leadership from the new ethnic group within the church — instruct the church today as it seeks to foster multicultural congregations? It would seem so. How can we apply Acts 6 to our newly diverse and ethnically pluralistic society and church? Let us suggest one final analogy that is perhaps appropriate to Acts 6.

Generational Diversity and the Church

Not a few congregations today are aware of — and struggling with — the different needs and sensibilities of different generations of believers within the same congregation. While we would resist any attempt to pigeonhole or segregate people in the church by generation, it is clear that different generations share different formative experiences. The generation that experienced the Great Depression has had one experience, the generation of the Vietnam War another, and the generation that came of age on the Internet still another. Different generations in a congregation may feel, at least at times, that they are being overlooked when the figurative bread is distributed. What does Acts 6 suggest for our thinking about such generational diversity and the issues that may arise from it?

Suppose, for example, that an older generation laments the loss of familiar music and hymnody, which has been replaced by contemporary Christian and praise music? Are they Hellenists who are getting left out of the distribution? Or do different texts and images — such as Paul's consideration of the body of Christ (many parts, one body) — seem better and more helpful analogies? Are there other contemporary questions and conflicts to which Acts 6 and its layered issues of distribution of resources, care of the needy, different ethnic and language groups, and widening the leadership circle seem pertinent? Conflict will continue to be with us in the church. But rather than lamenting conflict as a sign of failure, we may find help in Acts to see conflict in other ways — as occasion and opportunity: occasion for "learning the new duties" taught by new circumstances, and opportunity to explore the connections between the biblical story and our own stories so that all may be woven into one fabric of faith.

STUDY QUESTIONS

1. This passage emphasizes the importance of spreading the "Word of God." What does this Word say about God, and why is the proclamation of this word pivotal in getting people saved in Acts?

2. What additional inferences does Acts draw from the characterization of Stephen's life and death (7:51-60), and why does his portrait resemble so closely Luke's portrait of Jesus in the third Gospel (Luke 22–23)?

3. Recall an experience of conflict in a congregation or campus community of

which you are a member. Would the "moves" or "protocols" described in this chapter have been helpful in settling its conflict? Why? Why not?

4. Of the three contemporary analogies to Acts 6 drawn by this chapter — women's ordination, ethnically diverse congregations, generational diversity — which one seems most urgent to your congregation or campus, and why? Are there other analogies that you can draw between Acts 6 and your own social location?

7

The Holy Spirit and the Life of the Church

PART I: INTERPRETING ACTS 8:4-40 AS SCRIPTURE

This passage narrates the beginnings of the church's mission beyond Jerusalem, thereby fulfilling Jesus' prophecy of Acts 1:8. The Holy City remains in the reader's rear-view mirror, always in sight but now left behind. This passage also tells the story of Philip, another charismatic prophet-like-Jesus and the one among the chosen seven (6:5) who has evidently succeeded Stephen as leader of the persecuted Hellenists. It is principally through his prophetic ministry that the word of God goes forward into these new territories and continues to flourish there (see 21:7-14).

If the primary role of this passage is to depict Philip's prophetic ministry beyond Jerusalem, then of equal importance are the surprising converts that are added to the church's membership rolls as a result. Samaritans and Ethiopian eunuchs are certainly marginal Jews, more removed from Israel's promised blessings than their geographical separation from Jerusalem suggests. Samaritans are counted among "the lost sheep of Israel," religious renegades and racially "impure" (according to the norms of more traditional Jews), and complicit in the Roman occupation of the Holy Land. While the second convert is a pious pilgrim, his geographical location in Ethiopia and his sexual condition indicate a religious status that is far removed from the epicenter of Jewish life and faith. In fact, the subtext of his story in Acts is probably Isaiah 56:8 (see Acts 8:27). According to the prophet, God will gather the entire household of Israel, including both

111

"foreigners" and "eunuchs," for worship in celebration of God's faithfulness to God's people. Philip's mission in Samaria and his conversion of the eunuch do not initiate the church's mission beyond Israel; rather, they are the climactic episodes in this narrative of Israel's restoration that began with Jesus' messianic mission to the household of Israel (cf. Matt. 10:5-6).

Philip's Mission to the Samaritans

As is well known and carefully documented, there was considerable antipathy between Samaritans and mainstream Palestinian Jews of the first century. Even though Samaritans worshiped the same God and followed a version of the same Torah, they were outcasts within the household of Israel. Moreover, they were widely viewed as the politically treacherous gatekeepers of the Roman occupation in Palestine, which was headquartered in Samarian Caesarea. For this reason, the familiar features of Philip's mission in Samaria, including his proclamation of the Messiah to them, as well as his performance of the Spirit's "signs" among them, take the unsuspecting reader by surprise. But the alert reader of the New Testament has been prepared for this story in Acts by having read the story of Jesus' Samaritan mission in John 4:1-42.[1]

The various panels of this episode (vv. 4-8) are bracketed by Luke's characteristic use of the Greek phrase *oi men oun* ("Now those who . . ." [v. 4]; "Now after they . . ." [v. 25]), indicating that his story's plot line has turned in a new direction. He makes this new direction emphatic with a doublet that summarizes the church's Samaritan mission: "Those scattered [in Samaria: 8:1b] preached [*euangelizō*] the word" (v. 4); and "Philip went to the city of Samaria and proclaimed [*kērussō*] the Messiah" (v. 5). The people of the city listen carefully ("with one accord") to what Philip says and watch closely what he does. Earlier missionary speeches fill in the gaps of what Philip proclaims and provide meaning of the "signs" he performs (v. 6; see 2:19). This impression is clear: Philip is a prophet-like-Jesus who has come to Samaria to announce the arrival of God's salvation.

Yet Philip proclaims the Word in a different idiom for the citizens of a different city. A new stage of Christian mission is symbolized by a new sign

---

1. See R. W. Wall, "The Acts of the Apostles," in *The New Interpreter's Bible*, vol. 10 (Nashville: Abingdon, 2002), pp. 137-38.

— the exorcism of unclean spirits (v. 7) — which recalls Jesus' ministry of exorcism as an expression of God's triumphant kingdom (Luke 11:14-26). The Samaritans' "joyful" experience of God's salvation (v. 8) is noted for the first time in Acts and is another symbol of the gospel's arrival in a new territory. Philip's success topples the wall of enmity between Samaritans and Jews, and Stephen's strange reference to the tombs of Samarian "Shechem" (7:16) finally makes sense: the patriarchs buried here found an Israel that includes "the lost tribes [i.e., Samaritans] of Israel."

Simon the Great

One of the most interesting characters in Acts, Simon the Great, illustrates this new day (vv. 9-13). Carefully selected elements from his legendary biography are recalled in a brief narrative flashback: once upon a time, Simon "practiced magic" and "amazed Samaritans" of every kind, who "listened eagerly to him" and called him "Power of God," or simply "Great" (v. 9). This résumé echoes Luke's portrait of the crowd of people who respond to Philip by "listening eagerly" (vv. 6, 11) to the gospel he proclaims. In this way, the narrator links Simon and Philip as two brokers of real power — a power that attracts people to them. Unlike Simon's power, however, the source of Philip's prophetic power is the Holy Spirit, and its motive is redemptive rather than political.

The Samaritans believe Philip and are baptized into Christian fellowship in active response to his proclamation of "the kingdom of God and the name of Jesus Christ" (v. 12). Whatever rivalry existed between Simon and Philip is now over, and Simon's concession is aptly stated: "Even Simon himself believed and was baptized" (v. 13a). This Simon, whom the Samaritans have followed everywhere, now "follows Philip everywhere."

But Luke alerts the reader to a spiritual problem on the near horizon: "Simon was amazed at the signs and great miracles that took place." This expression is characteristic in Acts of the unbelievers' response to their experience of the Holy Spirit, and it typically comes prior to their repentance. In Simon's case, the redemptive protocol is reversed: his amazement at the Spirit's "signs" comes after his conversion and not prior to it — or as a precondition of it. He seems more impressed by the spectacular than by the spiritual. This misguided response to the Spirit's presence reflects Simon's theological error, which will later need correction.

Philip's role in the story is now assumed by Peter and John (vv. 14-19), and the plot thickens as a result. Their apostolic house call is an exercise of spiritual authority and should take no reader by surprise. Reading a political motive into their appearance would be unwarranted given prior descriptions of their personae and the internal life of the Jerusalem community they lead. Rather, their reappearance in the narrative world of Acts is a symbol of solidarity and friendship: Peter and John join Philip beyond Jerusalem to put their apostolic powers to use in service of his mission. The demonstration of their spiritual authority is a different species of a familiar practice: the redistribution of the Holy Spirit among Samaritan believers is analogous to the redistribution of goods within the faith community (see 4:32-35). The redistribution of the community's goods, whether material or spiritual, is a function of their apostolic leadership.

The Samaritan believers have not yet been baptized with the Holy Spirit, even though they already have been "baptized in the name of the Lord Jesus" (v. 16). Luke does not give a reason for the delay between these two baptisms, and the timing of Spirit baptism remains quite fluid in Acts (see 2:38-41; 10:44-48; 19:1-6). We can only gather from Jesus' promise of Spirit baptism that believers will be unable to participate fully in the community's missional vocation without being filled with the Spirit (see 1:8; 2:1-4). Thus the aim of the apostles' mission in Samaria is precisely what it was earlier in Jerusalem: to build a community that shares all things in equal measure. Even the practices of "prayer" (v. 15; see 6:4) and "laying their hands on them" (v. 17; see 6:6) recall the role they performed when commissioning the seven to heal the growing rift between the Hellenists and Hebrews within the community of goods.

As dramatic and important as this apostolic visitation is, the narrative's spotlight remains on Simon: "Now when Simon saw . . ." (v. 18) shifts the story's action quickly back to him for his reaction to the apostles' distribution of the Spirit within the community. There is nothing in the text that indicates that Simon has been excluded from the Spirit's power; but his political ambition seeks a different species of "power" that would qualify him to lead the community, a power that Jesus had given only to his apostolic successors (see 1:2). The Greek word for "power" used here (*exousia:* v. 19) does not refer to the Spirit's power (*dynamis;* cf. 1:8) but rather denotes a political authority to make decisions for others. Simon offers the apostles money to buy himself a share of their religious *exousia,* with all the rights and privileges that obtain to their appointment as leaders of the church. His miscalculation is symbolized by this offering of money for something he wants to possess and manipulate to his own ends, without regard for the community's spiritual well-being (see 5:1-10). Clearly, Simon does not know that he is dealing with the real "great power of God."

Simon's spiritual failure gets the pointed attention of Peter, who exclaims, "To hell with you and your money!" The direction and purpose of God's Spirit (v. 20; see 2:38) are divine prerogatives. F. Scott Spencer contends that the implied subject of Peter's severe rebuke is not Simon's salvation but Peter's honor.[2] That is, Peter regards Simon's spiritual insolence as degrading of his apostolic role — the mistaken presumption that membership in the apostolate can be purchased by someone who is so abundantly unqualified (see 1:21-22). The subtext of Peter's retort and Simon's prompt acquiescence is recognition of the apostle's ultimate authority on earth to dictate the terms of any believer's participation in the heavenly experiences of God's salvation (cf. Matt. 16:19).

Thus, again, the practical objective of Peter's leadership in Samaria is redemptive: his exercise of apostolic authority is to save people from the consequences of their sins. We can see this objective more clearly when we recall his earlier speech that associates Israel's ignorance (3:17) with its wickedness (3:26), which prompted his exhortation to "repent and turn to God so that your sins may be wiped out" (3:19). If we read it in this light, Peter's rebuke of Simon — even though dramatic — is considerably less severe than his earlier condemnation of Ananias, and the prognosis for Simon's restoration is seemingly more favorable. Not only does Peter tacitly forgive Simon for being ignorant (or theologically immature), but the reader more clearly understands the motive of Peter's exhortation that Simon "pray to the Lord" (v. 22): that is, Peter holds out hope for God's forgiveness and Simon's restoration (v. 23).

Philip's Judean Mission to the Ethiopian Eunuch

The story begins with Philip preaching the gospel as he departs Jerusalem with other persecuted believers, and it concludes with the apostles

---

2. F. S. Spencer, *Journeying through Acts* (Peabody, MA: Hendrickson, 2004), pp. 88-89.

retracing Philip's evangelistic mission by preaching their way back to Jerusalem. The common phrase that frames this entire episode (v. 4) indicates continuity between the church's missions within and beyond Jerusalem, between Philip and Peter, while at the same time relativizing the real differences between them. The different "signs" of the Spirit performed in Samaria (e.g., the exorcism of demons), the proclamation of the gospel in a new idiom (e.g., preaching the Christ), and even of the time lapse between water and Spirit baptisms are all parts of the same redemptive reality: the restoration of God's kingdom to the whole house of Israel (see 1:6).

Acts combines the narrative of Philip's urban mission in Samaria with his memorable encounter with an Ethiopian eunuch. As a religious person, the Ethiopian symbolizes everything that the Samaritan Simon is not: he is a spiritual pilgrim who has come from a distant land earnestly seeking to understand Scripture's prophecies of God's salvation. But this eunuch shares an outsider status with the Samaritans: the sexuality of this pious proselyte, who seeks only to know God's purposes more fully, excludes him from full membership in the very religious community whose resources would illuminate his quest for theological understanding (see LXX Deut. 23:1: "He who is emasculated . . . shall not enter the assembly of the Lord"; also Lev. 21:17-21).

The resolution of this conflict puts in sharper focus Luke's well-known concern to give narrative expression to God's commitment to save the poor and powerless. The eunuch, however, faces a religious crisis provoked by neither socioeconomic nor spiritual poverty but by his forbidden sexuality. The essential task of the prophet, then, is to clarify whether Israel's membership requirements extend to the likes of a eunuch from Ethiopia even as it had to the Samaritans. His eventual conversion symbolizes the extent to which the eschatological horizon of Israel — "in the last days" — has been recast according to God's redemptive plans.

The following reading of this important passage follows its literary pattern *(chiasmus)* according to which the critical moment of Philip's exchange with the eunuch is located at the intersection of an inverted parallelism.[3] According to the literary shaping of this story, its climax is the question the seeker asks the Lord's prophet, which is about the interpretation of all Israel's Scriptures: "About whom is the prophet talking?" (v. 34):

---

3. G. Krodel, *Acts,* ACNT (Minneapolis: Augsburg, 1986), p. 167.

A (26-27a): Philip "got up and went" from Samaria south to Gaza
  B (27b-28): Ethiopian eunuch worships and reads Scripture (Isa. 53)
    C (29-30a): Philip "runs" according to the Spirit's command
      D (30b-31): Eunuch queries prophet Philip
        E (32-33): Scripture (Isa. 53:7-8) quoted
          F (34): "About whom is the prophet talking?"
        E' (35): Scripture interpreted by Philip
      D' (36-38) Eunuch queries prophet Philip
    C' (39a): Philip snatched away by the Spirit
  B' (39b): Eunuch rejoices
A' (40): Philip passes through "all the towns" from Gaza north to Samaria

The first sentence of the story (A) introduces its principal characters, the Ethiopian eunuch and Philip. The encounter between the God-seeker and the prophet, complete with angelic visitations and chariot-riding, echoes Elijah's Old Testament story (1 Kings 17–2 Kings 3). Jesus also refers to just such an encounter during his inaugural mission in Nazareth (Luke 4:26-27); and many commentators have noted the parallels between this story and Luke's story of Jesus' exchange with the two travelers on the road to Emmaus (Luke 24). These stories provide additional texture to this story, where Philip is a prophet-like-Jesus whose words and deeds continue to lead the church's mission "from place to place" (8:4) beyond Jerusalem.

Rather than conducting his crusade in a particular "city of Samaria," Philip is on the road. In fact, what seems important for the reader to know is his geographical location: he is up north, and he needs to take a southbound route to Gaza: "the road that goes down from Jerusalem to Gaza." The narrator's aside is that this is "a wilderness road" (v. 26), which is puzzling because the road is not in fact a desert route. Spencer suggests that the story's geographical markers locate the prophet and the eunuch in a "liminal zone off the beaten path of regular traffic," where serious theological reflection and personal transformation is more likely.[4] To this end, God's Spirit (v. 29) in the guise of "the angel of the Lord" (v. 26; see 5:19) gives Philip directions to navigate his "wilderness" and makes clear the divine necessity of his visitation with the Ethiopian. These images of heaven's intervention in earth's work could hardly be clearer.

---

4. Spencer, *Acts*, pp. 90-91. While perhaps another indication that Luke's geographical knowledge of Palestine is poor, this could be read as yet another example of Luke's use of geography to cue a theological interest in his story.

The eunuch's résumé is even more interesting and detailed. As with Philip, the narrator carefully locates him in Judea to align this story with Jesus' prophecy (1:8): "He had come to Jerusalem to worship," and he "was returning home" to Ethiopia, presumably through Judea. He is probably a proselyte from the Diaspora who has completed this hard pilgrimage to the Holy City as a mark of his religious devotion. The reference to "worshiping" in Jerusalem is provocative, because eunuchs, as we have seen, were forbidden by Torah from participating in a worshiping community. By juxtaposing "eunuch" and "worship," the narrator perhaps imagines that the Ethiopian's recent worship experience has triggered a theological crisis over his future in the household of Israel. Careful attention to his social class — "a court official of Queen Candace in charge of her treasury" (v. 27a) — only intensifies the impression that he is certainly not materially impoverished but is indeed spiritually hungry.

The final feature of the eunuch's profile is that "he [is] reading the prophet Isaiah." Perhaps he dwells on Isaiah because of the prophet's hopeful references to Ethiopia's eventual participation in blessings promised by Israel's God (Isa. 18:1; 45:15). While the quoted prophecy from Isaiah 53:7-8 provides the prophetic intertext necessary for interpreting the second half of this story, the Ethiopian's personal biography echoes a second Isaiah prophecy (56:3-8; cf. Ps. 68:32), which provides an important subtext that throws light on the encounter between prophet and convert. According to this echoed prophecy, God promises to "gather the outcasts of Israel" (Isa. 56:8), including the "eunuchs and foreigners" who "keep the Sabbath and do not profane it" and come to "my holy mountain/my house of prayer" (vv. 3-7), and to grant them a future with God. This Ethiopian eunuch, who "had come to Jerusalem to worship" (Acts 8:27), represents both of these disenfranchised, disinherited groups of an exiled Israel as the choice recipient of God's promise.

Philip joins the Ethiopian by the instruction of the Spirit of prophecy (vv. 29-30a), and his abrupt question is entirely appropriate to his prophetic vocation: "Do you understand what you are reading?" At first blush, such a question that a stranger asks a literate man seems condescending and offensive: surely this man of high station can understand the literal meaning of a biblical text. But Philip's question presumes that Scripture is more than a literary text; for this man is reading the prophet Isaiah, who conveys information about God's plan of salvation. Moreover, the man's earnest piety suggests that he is likely interested in the text's theological meaning. Thus his response to the Lord's prophet is also appropriate: "How can I unless someone guides me?" (v. 31). This invitation to Philip to join him in the chariot implies spiritual discernment that recognizes this stranger as his theological mentor and one who is authorized by God to provide commentary on this biblical prophecy.

The cited prophecy is from LXX Isaiah 53, whose place in the history of Christianity has exerted profound influence in shaping believers' core convictions about Jesus' death. Its function here in Acts, however, is to define more clearly why an Ethiopian eunuch should be interested in the Christian gospel. Luke quotes the prophecy verbatim from the Septuagint. At first glance, we note that the text mentions only that portion of the prophecy that speaks of the servant's "humiliation" (*tapeinōsis*: v. 33). If the servant's humiliation in this narrative denotes social ostracism, the eunuch's situation is interpreted by Isaiah's Suffering Servant because he, too, is a social outcast.

A simple comparison between most modern translations of the Old Testament will note that this quotation from the LXX Isaiah used in Acts departs from its Hebrew source in several important ways. The most dramatic and important deviation is found in the final phrase: "For his life is taken from the earth" (v. 33). While the Hebrew text claims that the servant is "cut off [*gzr*] from the earth" (i.e., he dies), the Septuagint translation oddly renders *gzr* as "lifted up" [*airo*] from the earth." This verbal shift allows Luke to interpret the servant's humiliation as the means to his exaltation: he is "lifted up from earth" into heaven (see Acts 1:9-11). If Luke takes this phrase to refer to the vindication (or "lifting up") of the humiliated servant, then perhaps the reader should suppose that the eunuch's identification with the humiliated servant might lead him to hope for a different future than the one consigned him by the official laws of Israel.

At the intersection of the two inverted and parallel halves that make up this pericope of Acts is the crucial question that evokes Philip's redemptive response: "About whom, may I ask, does the prophet say this, about himself or about someone else?" Of three possible renderings, the eunuch omits the nationalistic interpretation most common in his day — that the prophet is referring to faithful Israel. Naturally, an outcast and foreigner would be unlikely to include such a reading, no matter how popular in Palestine, since it excludes him. Some contemporaneous sectarian movements within Judaism interpreted this prophecy as pointing to God's eschatological prophet, whom Isaiah "himself" represents. Given the murderous response to Stephen's accusation that Israel persecutes and murders its prophets, including the "Righteous One" (7:52-53; cf. Isa. 53:11), this second rendering is entirely plausible. It would seem, however, that the eunuch holds out for a "someone else" with whom the outcasts and aliens of Israel might more closely identify and then join in God's coming triumph.

"Then Philip began to speak" (v. 35a) translates a biblical expression for divinely inspired speech (*anoixas . . . to stoma autou,* literally "opening his mouth"; cf. Exod. 4:12; Ezek. 3:27; Acts 10:34). In a story that vividly portrays Philip's mission as divinely directed, the reader should not be surprised that Philip's answer is not his to give but God's. Luke's characteristic summary of Philip's response is filled out with elements of the *kerygma* — "the good news about Jesus" — assumed from the other missionary speeches of Acts.

The conversion of the eunuch is recounted elliptically by his request to be baptized (v. 36), which presumes his public confession of faith. Perhaps for this reason, later versions of Acts add the eunuch's declaration: "I believe that Jesus Christ is the Son of God" (NKJV: v. 37; see 2:21, 38-41). In the earlier story of the Samaritan mission, water and Spirit baptism are discrete but integral media of divine grace (8:12-13, 16-17). Perhaps to preserve this pattern of Philip's mission, a few scribes rewrote verse 39 this way: "When they came up out of the water, the Spirit fell upon the eunuch, but an angel carried Philip away." In any case, water baptism initiates new believers into the realm of the Spirit of prophecy, whose filling empowers them for Christian ministry; conversion makes one dependent on God's Spirit to perform the tasks of God's work. The clear and direct participation of the Holy Spirit in this final panel of the story lends support to the importance of this theme in Acts. The reader is left to presume, then, that when Philip and the eunuch go their separate ways, they both engage in Christian mission.

While we know nothing of what becomes of the Ethiopian, except that he continues on his journey "rejoicing," the Spirit deposits Philip in Azotus, where he resumes his mission by going from "place to place" (cf. 8:4). He travels north up the coastline to Caesarea (v. 40), where he establishes a family ministry of lasting importance (see 21:8-10). The insertion of the Spirit's prerogatives into Philip's missionary career reminds readers of the prophets Elijah (1 Kings 18:12; 2 Kings 2:16) and Ezekiel (Ezek. 11:24), whose experiences with the same Spirit of prophecy brought about compliance to God's plans. The same prophetic calculus is applied here to compute the meaning of Philip's dramatic experience of being "snatched up" and relocated to a place where God wanted him to resume his evangelistic mission according to Jesus' commission.

PART II: ENGAGING ACTS 8 FOR TODAY'S CHURCH

There are many chapters in the Acts of the Apostles in which the Holy Spirit plays a prominent role; indeed, the Spirit plays a prominent role in the whole book of Acts. In chapters 2 and 3 the Holy Spirit comes upon the church at Pentecost and is at work in the Jerusalem mission. In chapters 10 and 11 the Spirit is at work in the conversion of Peter, his visit to Cornelius, and the following portion of the gentile mission. In later chapters of Acts the Spirit is at work in Paul's missionary work. One might — and should — consider the role of the Spirit in all of those narratives, but we have chosen to focus our examination of the Holy Spirit on Acts 8, because this passage explores the role and function of the Spirit in ways that are both profoundly engaging and illustrative of the Spirit's role and purpose throughout Acts.

While the Holy Spirit does play a prominent role in some congregations and traditions today, notably the Pentecostal and charismatic churches, the Spirit is considerably less prominent — or paid attention to — in other parts of the church. As one pastor in the mainline tradition put it, one sometimes even gets the feeling that the Trinity is made up of "the Father, the Son, and the other guy"! Furthermore, it seems that when the church does pay attention to the role of the Holy Spirit in the life of the believer and of the congregation, that attention is more frequently informed by other parts of Scripture and the tradition than by the book of Acts. Many turn to Paul's teaching about the gifts and fruits of the Spirit, life in the Spirit, and the role of the Spirit in the body of Christ. Others draw on John's "farewell discourse" and his other teachings about the Spirit as advocate, comforter, and counselor. All of this is, of course, important and legitimate, but so is careful attention to the role and place of the Spirit in Acts.

We may say, as a generalization, that in Acts we find little about the oft-mentioned gifts of the Spirit, such as speaking in tongues. Nor does the

Spirit appear primarily as an agent of individual transformation, solace, intercession, or comfort. Drawing on Paul's and John's teachings has led the church, at least where the Spirit is emphasized, to pay particular attention to those aspects of the Spirit's role. Acts is different: it provides a picture of the Holy Spirit that in some ways confirms contemporary understandings of the Spirit, but just as often challenges them. In Acts the Spirit is closely related to the church's mission and the missionary vocation. The Spirit is instrumental in guiding, advancing, and empowering the widening and often surprising mission of the church.

Perhaps one of the reasons for contemporary ambivalence about the Holy Spirit — part of what makes it powerfully attractive in some quarters and suspect in others — is that the Spirit is often linked to religious experience that is nonrational, emotional, and ecstatic. This is particularly true, of course, of the gift of speaking in tongues. In Acts the Spirit certainly does move in surprising ways that are not always explicable purely on the basis of reason. Nevertheless, the mark of the Spirit in Acts is not the nonrational, emotional, and ecstatic nature of the experience; nor are such qualities of the Spirit's presence ends in themselves, as if the extraordinary nature of events was itself the point. In Acts the point is the mission of the church, the fulfillment of God's promises, the crossing of boundaries and barriers with the good news of the gospel, and the creation of the new community of shared goods where all things are held in common. In Acts the Spirit leads, guides, builds, corrects, teaches, and empowers the church to be the church.

With this general overview of the Holy Spirit and its role in Acts, let's turn to the variety of subjects raised in Acts 8 and their implications for contemporary congregations. These subjects include power and the Holy Spirit, the gift nature of the Spirit, the Spirit as initiator, the Spirit as innovator (particularly in crossing boundaries to the outcast), and the interaction and interrelationship of Scripture and Spirit. After considering these themes, we will return to the important question of discernment that arises when Christians take the Spirit seriously: How do we discern the Holy Spirit from other — possibly unclean or unhealthy — spirits? In a time and culture where spirituality is newly prized, this question has taken on a new urgency.

Power and the Holy Spirit

Not long ago I found myself teaching at a mainline seminary in British Columbia. The course was entitled "Pastoral Leadership and Leading Change in Congregations," and forty pastors were enrolled. Early in the course I invited all participants to complete an exercise designed to reveal their motivations. What got them up and going in the morning? What did they care most about and find most rewarding? What got their engines running?

The intention of the exercise was to locate each participant in one of three dominant motivational groups: the first group was made up of those motivated by affiliation and relational values; the second group, those motivated by achievement or producing results; the third group, those whose dominant motivation was power and influence (these were the people desirous of changing hearts and minds). Of the forty pastors, the great majority (26 of them) identified themselves as "affiliators," those who were motivated by relationships and attention to personal feelings. There were eleven "achievers," those who really wanted to produce results. And then a very small number — two or three — emerged as motivated by "power and influence."

When we looked at the results and I asked for reactions, the initial responses were self-congratulatory. "We care," said several, "about people, not power." The conversation went on along those lines for several minutes, when a thirty-something female pastor raised her hand and said, "You know, I'm not surprised that so few indicated an interest in power and influence. After all, our denomination has been telling us for years, in all sorts of ways, that power is bad!" Moments later another younger pastor, also female, chimed in: "Yes, that's true. Of course, the fact that power is viewed negatively doesn't mean that power or power issues go away. It only means they go underground, and then pop up in all sorts of unhealthy ways in our congregations." Many nodded assent to that observation.

I noted that teaching and political leadership were among the vocations where power and influence were critical motivational factors and, furthermore, that both of these vocations seemed to have become problematic and even troubled in contemporary society. I then concluded by saying that I would be concerned for a church or denomination where only five percent of the pastors were motivated by changing hearts and minds, by influencing people and communities toward greater health and function through the exercise of power.

We are ambivalent about power today. And we are often ambivalent about — even seemingly frightened of — our own God-given power. We are not sure who should have power or how it should be used. We construct elaborate procedural checks on the exercise of power, which is understandable in some ways but lamentable in others. Sometimes it does seem that we've been taught that "all power is bad," as that first student observed. But in Acts the Holy Spirit confers power *(dynamis)* on the apostles, the disciples, and the believers. What does Acts contribute to our understanding of power and our contemporary struggles to use, but not abuse, it in the church and in leadership?

In Acts 8, Philip has gone down to Samaria to preach the gospel. There he encounters a favorable and responsive audience, though it includes Simon the Great, a magician. Philip blows into town exuding and demonstrating power. This changes things for Simon, who up to this point has been a powerful guy in Samaria and "someone great." The power game changes when Philip, in the power of the Holy Spirit, begins to proclaim the good news and to work signs and wonders. Many in Samaria come to believe and are baptized, including Simon.

Subsequently, Simon keeps close company with the new guy in town, studying his movements and their results. But it's not until the apostles Peter and John show up in Samaria to support Philip and learn from what is going on there that Simon's intention in shadowing Philip becomes clear. Simon wants some of this mysterious power, which he calls by a different name *(exousia)*, indicating a different kind of power, power for a different purpose. Simon wants power to promote and secure himself. When he offers to buy the power he has seen in Philip from Peter, the apostle blasts him for his distorted understanding and his evil intent. This power given by the Holy Spirit is not for sale, and it certainly is not for the purposes of personal aggrandizement or benefit. The power of the Holy Spirit is a different kind of power: it is power to fulfill, further, and advance the mission of the church, which is to proclaim God's victory in Christ over the powers of death and to create a new community of shared goods where all things are held in common.

Power for Simon the Great is about making Simon great. Power given by the Holy Spirit is about the great grace of God now being poured out on all who repent and are baptized. This account and these distinctions in the types and nature of power are important and instructive to the church today. Power is not intrinsically evil, nor is it to be avoided at all cost; the results of that, as one wise student observed, can be that it emerges in ugly and distorted ways. Power that is in service to God and the mission of the church is legitimate; power sought for personal and ego ends is not. To be sure, we can make that distinction more easily in theory than in practice. Still, it is important to affirm the legitimacy and proper role of power, both to avoid its abuse and to avoid repressing it in such a way that it does emerge in destructive ways. Luke links Simon and Philip as two brokers of power that attracts people to them; but, unlike Simon's "magical" powers, the source of Philip's prophetic power is the Holy Spirit, and its motive is redemptive rather than political.

There is also a significant pastoral insight in the story of Simon and Philip. Martin Luther observed, "When the Word of God is active, evil spirits are set in motion." The power of God's Word is here active in Philip, setting in motion evil spirits in Simon, who has held "great power" and has been regarded by Samaritans as a somebody for a long time because of his "sorceries." In congregations, the exercise of the power of the Spirit for redemptive and healing purposes will often result in resistance. False or lesser powers are exposed and reduced when the power of the gospel and the Spirit is at work. Not everyone will welcome that.

The Gift of the Spirit

Acts concurs with the Gospel of John (see John 14) that the Holy Spirit is something that is given — that is, it's a gift. The Spirit is not a commodity that we can purchase or acquire and thus control, which is Simon's great misunderstanding of the Spirit's power. Throughout Acts the gift of the Holy Spirit remains a gift. There is no single protocol or way that the Spirit comes or that the Spirit's arrival can be controlled. Sometimes it is part of the experience of water baptism — sometimes not. Sometimes it is associated with the laying on of the apostles' hands — sometimes not. This variance extends the mysterious quality of the Spirit, and it reminds the church that the Spirit is a gift.

This emphasis comes as a corrective to some contemporary understandings of the Holy Spirit, of God's power, and of the nature of spirituality. These are not commodities, products, or lifestyle accessories that one acquires in order to complete or augment one's personality or personal experience. We can't open a little book with four easy steps to "get the Spirit."

We can't send money to a television preacher, who will then send us a product that will produce the Spirit. We cannot seek a spiritual life or a deepened spirituality in order to further our own personal or egocentric goals. The Spirit is a gift, and it brings with it a task, namely, carrying forward the good news of the gospel of God. In addition, the Spirit comes as a gift that provides direction and sometimes more than direction — outright initiative.

The Spirit as Initiator of the Mission of the Church to the Forgotten

The next move in the narrative of Acts 8 is prompted by the Spirit in the guise of an angel of the Lord (v. 26). "Get up and go," says the Spirit to Philip, out to the wilderness road, the road to Gaza, where Philip will encounter an Ethiopian eunuch, who is making his return journey after a pilgrimage to Jerusalem. Note that the missionary outreach to despised Samaritans, and then to the Ethiopian eunuch, is not the result of a careful demographic analysis of where to spot a new-church development or where to engage in the use of membership growth strategies. This mission is driven by the promises of God, particularly the promise to gather the lost remnant of the house of Israel; and it is driven by the Spirit.

Too often today the evangelism and church-growth programs of congregations and denominations are led more by human agendas and wisdom than by God's agenda and the Spirit's wisdom. We analyze patterns of growth, looking for people like us, or for people with resources. In seeking ways to build our church and increase our denomination's membership, we determine who will "fit" our congregation. This is not to say that the Spirit cannot work through such information and strategies; but the Spirit's priorities and modes of operation often seem different from our own. To the extent that we are informed by the Acts view of church and identify with Philip, we are not in charge. The Spirit is doing the directing. Philip's role is almost always described in passive terms: he is told, led, directed, and "taken away." There is a power other than our own, other than human power and human ways, at work here: the Spirit is at work.

Perhaps the Spirit is necessary, because who among us would think of going to Samaritans or Ethiopian eunuchs on our own? In other words, who of us thinks of going to the disinherited and disenfranchised on our own? Left to our own devices, we tend to go to those with whom we are comfortable, with whom we have much in common. The Spirit, it would seem, loves to thrust people out of their comfort zones, to take them to strange places and strange people. We must ask ourselves: Who are the Samaritans for us? Remember who the Samaritans were then: they were religious and ethnic half-breeds, syncretists, and they were caught up with the Romans. Who are the Ethiopian eunuchs for us? The one in this story is a wealthy and powerful man — not an outsider in one sense. But he is powerless for all that: he is sexually deficient and can produce no offspring, and for that reason Hebrew law bars him from full participation in the faith and community of Israel and its temple. Who are the Ethiopian eunuchs today?

In both instances, the Samaritans and the Ethiopian, we are dealing not with complete foreigners and outsiders but — what's probably worse or harder — the strange ones who have some connection, but not enough, to whoever constitutes the in-group or those of acceptable social and religious standing. These are, so to speak, the odd cousins, the weird uncles, the parts of the family tree we would just as soon forget and overlook. They are "the lost sheep of the house of Israel," and God is determined to gather them in. The Spirit is at work here, gathering the lost sheep and causing apostles and disciples to cross boundaries and barriers to the "foreigner within." Are the Samaritans and Ethiopian eunuchs of today those who are racially impure, homosexuals, single parents, New Age types, the elderly poor, the tattoo-covered teens cruising by on their skateboards? Who is "the other" whom we alternately fear and are envious of?

There is no easy answer to such questions as these. For different congregations and communities they will have different faces. But of this there can be no doubt: the Spirit pushes the church across boundaries and borders, both external and internal, to call and create a new community. The Spirit is tied irrevocably to God's promised plan of salvation and to the church's missional vocation.

Earlier in this book I mentioned one congregation's emerging ministry to the homeless mentally ill through "houses of healing." When the moment finally came for the congregation to vote on its approval of this emerging ministry, the person presenting the proposal, a quiet and thoughtful attorney, concluded his presentation with these words: "I hope that you approve this new ministry. But if you don't, I'm not sure what we're going to do, because the Spirit seems to be going ahead, with or without us!" It is remarkable and gratifying to hear such a testimony in the church today, where too often everything is carefully managed and controlled. How wonderful to find the Spirit, as in Acts, thrusting outward, leading where we didn't think to go, pushing across frontiers and fences that had become invisible to us — but were no less real in spite of that. Surely a sign of the church's vitality will be when more and more congregations are urged to get on board because the Spirit seems to be going ahead no matter which way we vote!

Scripture and the Spirit

Down on the Gaza road, the Spirit instructs Philip to approach a moving chariot and climb aboard. Inside this first-century SUV, Philip finds the Ethiopian government official reading aloud and pondering to himself a text from Isaiah: "In his humiliation justice was denied him. Who can describe his generation?" The eunuch, a model student and seeker of faith, invites Philip's help in understanding this text: "About whom, may I ask you, does the prophet say this, about himself or about someone else?" The eunuch's interest in one who speaks of being cut off, humiliated, and without generation is both understandable and moving. It may be the story of the prophet or someone else, but it is also his story. Or at least he wonders if it might be.

In a way that is quite reminiscent of Jesus himself interpreting Scripture to the two disciples on an earlier road of return, the road to Emmaus (Luke 24), Philip "began to speak, and starting with this Scripture, he proclaimed to him the good news about Jesus." Long ago John Calvin noted that the Word of God happens when the same Spirit is present to the one who reads as it was to the one who wrote. The Word of God, according to Calvin's understanding, is a dynamic moment, an event that occurs when the written word of Scripture and the living power of the Spirit intersect and interact. Without Scripture the Spirit lacks grounding, history, story, text, and context; without the Spirit, Scripture may be no more than words on the page, not the living Word of God. It is the interaction of the two that makes the Word come alive and enables Philip to rightly interpret and relate the goods news about Jesus to the eunuch. What a couple of hours it must have been on the road to Gaza that day! Surely, their hearts "burned within them," as had the hearts of the disciples on the Emmaus Road.

Note several additional elements that contribute to this intersection of Spirit and Scripture and the experience of the living Word: (1) Philip is obedient to the prompting of the Spirit; he is a willing vessel and instrument. (2) The eunuch is an equally willing and receptive student, freely and unashamedly seeking direction and instruction. (3) There is an existential urgency, or one might say "presenting issue," namely the eunuch's own faith search and his sexual mutilation. He wants to know what these words mean, whether they mean what he hopes they mean. This is not an idle inquiry on his part; something is definitely at stake. (4) Scripture and Spirit are joined by a third S, Sacrament. Just as in the Emmaus story, after the Word has been opened up, there follows a sacrament — in this case baptism. The Word prepares us for sacramental participation, and a moment of worship and ritual confirms the power and work of the Word.

In many ways, what we have here is nothing short of a description of vital worship. We have earnestly and honestly searching people, people who are "on the way"; we have their urgent issues and questions (i.e., there is something at stake); we have those both trained and empowered by the Spirit to break open the Word of God; there is a listening and receptive congregation of one; and there is celebration of the sacrament, followed by great joy. That's it — but that's enough. Worship can happen almost anywhere, it seems, when these ingredients are present.

Discerning the Spirits

This brings us to a final, urgent question: How can we tell if it is the Holy Spirit, and not some other spirit or spirits that may be dangerous and destructive? Make no mistake about it: discernment, the effort to determine the genuine and the authentic, is absolutely necessary. Many are the chapters in the lives of congregations where people claimed the leading and power of the Spirit. But if the Spirit is known by its fruits, then at least some of these times the fruit has been bitter, sour, and even poisonous. "Test the spirits," urges Paul.

But how and on what basis? We would suggest that the implications of this chapter in Acts suggest some criteria to be used in discernment. For one thing, discernment, as we see it generally in Acts, is a communal function and act: it occurs in the gathered community and not with one person acting alone. Even Philip and the eunuch constitute a small community, one to which the words of Jesus genuinely do apply: "Where two or three are gathered in my name. . . ." Beyond that, the contrasting types and understandings of power in the story of Simon the Great provide further criteria for discerning, or testing, the spirits. Is it about magnifying or securing one's personal or political power over others? Or is its purpose the redemptive mission and vocation of the church? Is it, to put it another way, about me? If it is, chances are good that it is not about the Holy Spirit. It should be discernible as furthering the missional vocation of the church. It is not, to adapt what Paul says in 1 Corinthians, to puff us up; it is to build up the body of Christ, the church.

Judging from the stories of Stephen and Philip, the Spirit will take us where we did not, on our own, plan to go, and will involve us in ministry that costs us something — perhaps even our lives. Ministry directed by the Holy Spirit will not simply further our own already-arrived-at agendas and preconceived plans. The Spirit has a way of surprising us. Moreover, the Spirit can take us out of our own comfort zones and put us in risky places. In contrast to the mantra "nothing that feels this good can be wrong," our mantra might be: "If it's difficult and demanding, then maybe it is of the Spirit." A wise elder in one congregation offered the following counsel for times of discernment: "When the promise is clear and the cost vague, watch out; the evil one may be wooing you. But when the cost is clear and the promise is vague — yet there is something alluring, something that draws you forward — watch out. You may be hearing the voice of God."[5]

Finally, attempts to test and discern the Spirit will be informed by the close tie we see in Acts between Scripture and Spirit. The Spirit will reveal the meaning of Scripture, bringing it forward for a new time; but the Spirit will not disregard or contradict Scripture. To be sure, judgment is still involved and unavoidable. But the Spirit does not replace or discount Scripture — or render it irrelevant. The two work in tandem. Discernment is without any absolute guarantees or complete knowledge, because "we know only in part." But Acts does provide clear indicators and criteria for the discernment and testing of spirits, so that the church may continue to be led by the Holy Spirit — and not by one of a thousand spirits of this age or of the evil one.

---

5. Westerhoff, *Good Fences* (Harrisburg, PA: Morehouse Publishing, 1999), p. 124.

STUDY QUESTIONS

1. Do a simple "word association" with conversion, listing or saying aloud what words come to mind when you hear "conversion." Keep these associations in mind as you review this chapter and read the book's next two.

2. Acts 8 tells the related stories of two converts to Jesus, Simon of Samaria and the anonymous eunuch from Ethiopia. Compare their conversions. What are other patterns of conversions that can be gleaned from Acts and how do these patterns of "getting saved" relate to your faith tradition and experience?

3. Bringing your faith tradition and religious experiences to conversion stories of Acts, what do the stories of this chapter and elsewhere in Acts seem to lack? What does Acts contribute to your traditions about "getting saved"?

4. Discuss Simon's spiritual failure in light of the failure of today's church or campus to influence secular culture in God's direction. How does the Ethiopian's positive response to Philip correct Simon's immature response to Peter?

5. How does this passage portray the variety of ways the Holy Spirit can influence people toward God? What activities seem to provide a setting for the Spirit's work in the world?

6. Identify those who are the Samaritans for us and those who are the Ethiopian eunuchs today. Give contemporary faces to each. How does the teaching of Acts 8 guide the church's or campus's response to those who are religious outcasts among us today?

8 Conversion and Transformation: The Case of Saul

PART I: INTERPRETING ACTS 9:1-31 AS SCRIPTURE

The book of Acts is a literary tapestry that weaves together different narrative strands of the church's mission to the end of the earth. The reader understands that these separate strands are the warp and weft that give texture to the whole cloth of the entire narrative. If Peter's story is the warp, then Paul's is the weft, and both are prophetic agents of God's salvation during the "last days" of salvation's history. They are both carriers of God's word — though to different places. The next two chapters pair these two very different stories of conversion to God's way of salvation, which was a necessary condition of their prophetic calling.

The literary importance and theological complexity of Saul's (Paul's) Damascus Road encounter with the risen Jesus is indicated by the fact that it is recounted three times in the book of Acts: here in Luke the narrator's voice (9:1-31) and twice again in Paul's voice (22:3-16; 26:4-23). The primary problem facing the interpreter of this narrative triad is not to harmonize the discrepancies in the details of the different accounts but to explain how the repetition of the story within Acts gives a more fully nuanced portrait of Paul as a prophet-like-Jesus. While it is impossible to deny the transforming effect that Jesus' visitation has on Saul and on his understanding of God's promises to Israel, his turn toward Jesus is only one element of a pattern of conversion that climaxes with his prophetic calling. In fact, Saul's calling and not his conversion focuses his story in Acts.

The narrator tells this story with simplicity and familiar irony: Saul's wreaking havoc in the early church (8:1-3) has occasioned Philip's successful mission beyond Jerusalem to the north, which prompts Saul to pursue him toward Damascus in chapter 9 (vv. 1-2). This travel reversal prompts the powerful drama of Saul's own "great reversal": he encounters the living Jesus on his way to destroy him, is converted to him instead (vv. 3-9), and then is called as his witness (vv. 10-18). Now converted and commissioned as a prophet-like-Jesus, Saul takes his first two painful steps toward his destiny, first in Damascus (vv. 19-25) and then back in Jerusalem (vv. 26-30), where he preaches the gospel and suffers for it in accordance with Jesus' commission (vv. 15-16; cf. 1:8).

The Conversion and Calling of Saul

The careful reader of Acts will recognize the very moment Saul has been introduced into the Acts narrative: immediately before Stephen's petition for forgiveness at the end of Acts 7. Luke's narrative of Saul's conversion and commission should thus be read as deeply ironic. Even though Saul approaches Damascus "breathing threats and murder against the disciples of the Lord," God's perspective on his destiny is that he is a forgiven man. Perhaps this best accounts for the stunning meeting Saul has with Jesus, which evokes his repentant response. Thus, what takes place on the Great North Road cashes Stephen's promissory note.

Saul's persecution of the believing Hellenists has evidently ended in Jerusalem, and he now desires to continue and extend his hostilities against them northward to Damascus — among the "men and women who belonged to the Way" (v. 2). Apparently, his efforts in this regard continue to be supported by the same religious elites who opposed and executed Stephen and who have apparently regained the upper hand in Jerusalem. The historical circumstances for Saul's solicitation of letters of support from the high priest (probably Caiaphas) remain uncertain; but the council's "legitimate" interest in his mission in the synagogues of Damascus suggests that the membership of "the Way" consists of devout Jewish believers, probably from among the Hellenists, who have attached themselves to congregations of other Diaspora Jews in that city. Damascus was an important Syrian city about 135 miles to the north of Jerusalem; it was known not only for its former glory but because it was at the time a strategic commercial center for the Roman Empire, with several important trade routes passing through it, including the "Great North Road" on which Saul is traveling. Josephus reports that Damascus was also home to a large population of Jews (*Jewish War*, 2.20.2). Saul's mission is to "bind" believers and return them to Jerusalem for trial.

The action of this passage (vv. 3b-9) testifies to Saul's personal transformation. Again, however, the reader of Acts must understand this transformation in vocational terms: Saul's conversion is not from a past of moral morass to a future of virtuous living; but it is toward a future of preaching the gospel about the living Jesus. His change of mind and heart about Jesus begins when he approaches Damascus (v. 3) as a take-charge zealot; and it ends the same day with him being "led by the hand into Damascus," blind and utterly dependent on others for food and drink (vv. 8-9). What happens in between is the stuff of legends.

What kind of "personal" encounter is this between Jesus and Saul that changes his mind? The sudden appearance of "a light from heaven" (cf. 22:6, 9) that was "brighter than the noon-day sun" (26:13; cf. 2 Cor. 4:4-6) and "flashed around him" (cf. Acts 22:6; perhaps surrounding his traveling companions as well; see 26:13) are the special effects of a theophany, or divine appearance, such as when God makes a house call on a prophet in the Old Testament (see Exod. 19:16; Ezek. 1:4, 7, 13, 28; Dan. 10:6). The practical purpose of such heavenly visitations is to get someone's attention, and it works pretty well: people tremble (Exod. 19:16) and run for cover (Dan. 10:7). In a response similar to the prophet Ezekiel's to his vision of God's glory (Ezek. 1:28), Saul "fell to the ground" in preparation to hear Christ speak. Visions of God in Scripture typically include divine auditions (cf. Exod. 3:4-10; Gen. 31:11-13; see Acts 2:5-13): Saul "heard a voice" (v. 4b). These divine auditions disclose the prophet's future. But as with Moses, who first hears of God's plans to deliver Israel in the extraordinary theophany at the burning bush (Exod. 3–4), what Jesus says first to Saul is an introduction of himself, making his acquaintance before he can perform the demanding tasks he is given. Conversion comes before and is the necessary condition of a sacred commission.

Saul does not recognize the voice he hears, so he asks, "Who are you, Lord?" His ironic use of "Lord" is not yet a confession of faith in Jesus; rather, it is the honest query of a biblical Jew who knows the meaning of his situation from having read Scripture. The Lord is making a house call on him, and he must be absolutely attentive to what is said next: "I am Jesus, whom you are persecuting." Saul's brief exchange with Jesus makes clear what constitutes the central claim of the Christian gospel: God made the crucified Jesus alive as Messiah and Lord (see 2:36). The critical evidence of the claim's validity is that a dialogue takes place. Jesus can keep it brief simply because his appearance exposes the politics of Saul's mission to Damascus as bogus: Jesus is not the anti-Christ but the risen Christ! Moreover, his use of personal names makes the appeal to Saul a direct one, thereby defining salvation as an individual turnabout — to the living Jesus, not a conversion from Judaism to Christianity.

The imperative of their meeting is strikingly introduced by the intensive *alla* (but), which normally links sharply contrasting statements. In the case of verse 6, the *alla* makes more emphatic the purpose of this appearance of Christ. The latter is not exchanging business cards with Saul but sending him on a mission: "Get up and enter the city and you will be told what you are *(dei)* to do" (cf. 22:10; 26:14). Luke's use of *dei*, which stipulates what one "must" do according to Scripture, suggests that Saul is converted to Jesus in order to do what God has purposed for him to do.

At the same time, the other witnesses, Paul's companions on this trip, are in shock because they hear this living and powerful Jesus without seeing him (cf. Deut. 4:12; Dan. 10:7). We hear nothing else about them, other than that they must now help their *former* leader into town as the voice has commanded. Saul's "blind obedience" to Jesus' instruction is emphasized by his fast: "For three days . . . he neither ate nor drank" (v. 9). On the one hand, Saul's response is physical confirmation that a vision has occurred: it is the shock to his system that renders him blind and without appetite. On the other hand, the three days of fast especially suggests Saul's conversion to the risen Jesus, so that when he receives his sight back and begins to eat again (vv. 18-19), he will have completed an intense spiritual journey that will fortify him for the work ahead. Though he once was blind, he now can see.

The next narrative panel (vv. 10-18) concerns what Saul is to do — the reason Jesus has bade him go into Damascus (v. 6). Jesus appears to Ananias ("God is merciful") in a visionary mode, which coincides with Saul's vision of a healing visit from that same disciple. The literary convention of a "double vision" is a familiar feature of contemporaneous fictions. Luke uses visions in the book of Acts to clarify God's call; a double vision underscores God's control over the various details of the call. Ananias's initial response to the Lord's bidding is the prompt reply of a prophet,

"Here I am, Lord," which is reminiscent of Samuel's response to God's call (1 Sam. 3:4, 10) and Abraham's obedience to God's call (Gen. 22:1-2). The Lord reveals Saul's name to Ananias and provides him with a specific address where he can find him. He also provides an important biographical detail: Saul is a Diaspora Jew — "a man from Tarsus" (v. 11).

Ananias's protest to the Lord's command is different from Saul's and more similar to Peter's response to his vision in Acts 10:13-16. In both cases the hesitancy is not so much a spiritual failure on the part of the one called as it is a rhetorical device to let the reader know that a radical turn of events in salvation's history has taken place: God intends to offer gentiles an equal share of Israel's promised blessings. The reader recognizes the subtext of Ananias's recapitulation of the present situation: his hesitancy to deliver God's healing grace to Saul is not a concern for his personal welfare but a realization that healing symbolizes salvation in Acts (see 3:1-8). Therefore, Ananias's protest is properly understood as the "hard rationalist's" case against the possibility of Saul's conversion — and by implication the full salvation of gentiles. This underscores the divine power at work that makes an impossibility possible.

The ironic climax of this narrative is Jesus' prophecy of Saul's forthcoming mission, which indexes the plot line of his mission for the reader of Acts. We will note its centrality in Acts by its repetition in Paul's later defense of his mission to others (13:46-47; 20:18-35; 22:14-15; 26:16-18). The most important element of Saul's commission is the first thing stipulated: "He is an instrument whom I have chosen [*eklogē*]." Even as the Lord has "chosen" *(eklegomai)* Israel (13:17), the twelve (1:2), and then the seven (6:5) as instruments of salvation, so now he has chosen Saul to continue his witness to God's salvation. In particular, the Lord has chosen Saul "to bring my name before Gentiles and kings and before the people of Israel" (v. 15). For the first time in Acts, the international scope of the church's witness is made perfectly clear in the formulation of Saul's prophetic vocation: the order of "Gentiles and kings" coming before "the people of Israel" reverses the pattern of Paul's urban mission in Acts, which is typically to Jews first and then to the gentiles connected to the Jewish synagogue. In fact, Acts never depicts his mission as exclusively to gentiles or to Jews. Paul's is an international mission because God promises an international salvation: "Everyone who calls upon the Lord's name will be saved" (see 2:21).

The second part of the Lord's prophecy about Saul makes the connection between his witness and suffering, and thereby continues an important theme of Acts. Significantly, it is stipulated here of Saul as a divine necessity: "I will show him how much he must [*dei*] suffer" (v. 16; see 1:16, 22; 3:21; 4:12). Not only does the prospect of rejection and hardship place Saul in a continuum within Israel's history that includes the Messiah and his successors, it profoundly qualifies Paul's entire narrative in Acts. It forces the kind of "gut check" that turns the reader from a fixation on the heroic and invincible Paul of Christian legend toward a suffering prophet-like-Jesus whose successes are hard won. The *dei* — the "must" of divine necessity — of Saul's suffering reminds the reader that this, too, is an element of God's plan of salvation. Saul suffers to fulfill what God has promised Israel according to Scripture. The repetition of "my name" in both parts of this commissioning prophecy helps to make Luke's point. The phrase recalls Joel's prophecy that in the last days "everyone who calls upon the name of the Lord will be saved" (see 2:21). Both Saul's witness and his suffering will itself witness to God's faithfulness to the prophesied plan of salvation.

The report of Ananias's mission to Straight Street rounds off this initial account of Saul's calling as a prophet-like-Jesus. It is he who tells Saul what he must do, and his initial gesture of "laying his hands on Saul" (v. 17) agrees with the Lord's instruction for his healing (v. 12). Yet when read in context of Acts (see 6:6) and in combination with Ananias's Christian greeting, "Brother Saul" (see 1:15) — and the extraordinary exhortation for Saul "to be filled with the Holy Spirit" — Ananias's gesture connotes the community's confirmation of his salvation and vocation. While Ananias never tells Saul what he is to do, the reader recognizes that his idiom is pregnant with implicit information about Saul's destiny: the immediate restoration of his sight and his baptism in the Holy Spirit symbolize God's confirmation of his salvation and his prophetic vocation.

With his return to normality (v. 19), Saul begins to proclaim Jesus in the synagogues (vv. 19-20). Luke's repeated use of "immediately" (*eutheos*: vv. 18, 20) gives the impression of the urgency of Saul's mission: he is healed and begins his mission immediately. The location of his mission ("in the synagogues") and the substance of what he says there ("Jesus is the Son of God" [v. 20]) are compressed details of a pattern of ministry that will be expanded in considerable detail later in Acts.

The initial summary of Paul's first preaching in Acts, the familiar confession that "Jesus is the Son of God," is difficult to explain. The reader of the New Testament might expect that these first words from a repentant Saul are the précis of his later, more full-bodied speeches in Acts. Not so.

This is its only use in Acts, though it is used both in the Pauline letters (Rom. 1:3; Gal. 2:20) and as part of a biblical citation (Ps. 2:7) that Paul quotes in his inaugural speech (Acts 13:33), where he contends that Jesus is the Davidic Messiah prophesied by Israel's Scriptures. The reader of Acts should anticipate from earlier crowd responses that "all who heard him were amazed" and that he "confounded the Jews" (vv. 21a-22a). Thus the pattern of his later mission is established: Saul's claim that Jesus is Messiah provokes Jewish protest.

The Great Reversal

The ironic telling of Saul's conversion continues: even as the story begins with him on the road to Damascus, "breathing threats and murder against the disciples" on behalf of official Israel, it now concludes with his former cohort seeking his death. The persecutor has become the persecuted, and thus he fulfills Jesus' prophecy that he will suffer for his name (v. 16). We should note in this regard that this entire incident, so briefly narrated, establishes the literary pattern Acts follows in narrating Paul's mission. His proclamation that Jesus is the Messiah, accompanied in the synagogues by a rigorous exegesis of Scripture that will "confound" his opponents, will also attract the hostile attention of the leaders of Diaspora Judaism. They will plot against him, sometimes even seek to kill him (see 23:12-15); but he will inevitably escape with the aid of others — or through God's miraculous intervention — in order to continue the work to which he has been called by the voice on the Damascus Road.

Reversing the northerly route to Damascus that he took as the persecutor (expressing a symbolic geographical metaphor for the turnaround of his repentance), the persecuted Saul now heads south from Damascus to Jerusalem (vv. 26-31). The escalating conflict provoked by his conversion and prophetic calling becomes more graphic and interesting: the conflict experienced in the public square of Damascus moves indoors, where the church members hesitate to embrace their new brother (v. 26). Their suspicion is reasonable, based on the conventional human wisdom that enemies do not become fast friends overnight. But more importantly for readers of Acts, it is a harbinger of the profound difficulty the Jerusalem church will have with Paul's mission — whether to the gentiles (15:4-5) *or* to the Jews (21:17-21). These initial images of Saul at work are profoundly significant and will help guide the reader through Acts' story of Paul. This species of conflict among believers over the nature of God's salvation, especially the inability of the community to accept its revolutionary shape, is a literary theme of great importance in Acts and one that continues to haunt us today.

Barnabas, already known to the reader of Acts for his generous spirit (4:36-37), intervenes on Saul's behalf and provides for the Jerusalem believers the evidence of his conversion and prophetic calling (v. 27). The consecutive use of "so" (*kai:* v. 28) suggests that Barnabas's intercession has been effective, and the twelve confirm Saul's conversion and calling. This freedom, which allows Paul to take a second step of mission in Jerusalem, results in a showdown with nonbelieving "Hellenists" (v. 29; see 6:1, 9-14), who attempt to kill him as they earlier had Stephen. We are left to assume that their problem with Saul is the same problem they had with Stephen: his "bold speaking in the name of the Lord" (cf. 4:29-31) asserts redemption through Jesus Christ over against temple protocol or even Torah purity. Of course, we cannot forget that Paul was once a zealot among the defenders of traditional Judaism, but now has reversed his position to become one of "them." Such great reversals have tremendous public appeal and are bound to get the attention of friends and foes alike. On this occasion — and unlike Stephen — Paul escapes the Hellenists with a little help from his friends (9:30). Only then does peace break out, and the church is left alone to build itself up (9:31).

PART II: ENGAGING ACTS 9 FOR TODAY'S CHURCH

Conversion and the Contemporary Church

Different ecclesiastical traditions and church families hold different understandings and varied responses to the concept and experience of conversion. In significant measure, the mainline Christian denominations moved away from the language and experience of "conversion" as they embraced other understandings of Christian formation, notably Horace Bushnell's famous nineteenth-century concept of Christian nurture. For Bushnell, the ideal was the Christian who never knew him- or herself to be anything other than Christian. Such a person was nurtured steadily, patiently, and wholesomely in the church from the day of his or her birth. Conversion was rendered unnecessary.

Such a turn to gradualism, to "Christian nurture," may have made good sense in the high period of American Christendom, when Christianity was de facto the official religion of American society. When church and culture were woven together in countless mutually reinforcing ways, and few other religious alternatives existed, the turn to Christian nurture — and thus away from conversion — may have made sense. Not just the church but the whole society worked to raise its young not to know a time when they were other than Christian.

Nevertheless, the more evangelical churches and denominations held to a different understanding and emphasis, one that made a personal and dramatic moment of conversion to Jesus Christ much more central — indeed, essential. If Bushnell-influenced liberals imagined congregations made up of those who had never known themselves to be anything other than Christian, evangelicalism continued a different strand of the American religious experience, one marked by the Great Awakenings and shaped by frontier revivalism. The dramatic event of conversion, of turning around, of "great reversal" remained central here.

Both of these approaches to conversion can benefit from a close reading of Acts 9 and 10, with their pivotal yet differing stories of conversion. The more liberal (or mainline) traditions and churches, negotiating the new American post-Christendom era, are finding that they can no longer assume that those who take a place in their pews on Sundays have been adequately nurtured in the faith; nor have they always come to a moment of change of mind and heart and a clear Christian commitment. Mainline congregations and leaders are slowly — and cautiously — rediscovering the language and experience of conversion, of changed lives and of transformation.

If portraits of conversion in the book of Acts have something to offer mainline and liberal congregations, where Christian nurture may no longer be fully adequate, they also may contribute to a broader and more complex understanding of conversion than has characterized the evangelical experience. For example, conversions in Acts are not primarily moral in nature: that is, the subjects are not obviously "bad people" who suddenly turn good. They are not walking the sawdust trail, swearing off the bottle, and vowing an end to philandering in favor of the upright Christian life. In fact, conversion stories in Acts are often, by contrast, the conversion of "good people." Some are good people in the way that Saul was good: righteous and blameless under the law, and therefore somewhat self-righteous. But there are also conversions of truly virtuous people in Acts, such as that of Cornelius the gentile, Lydia the businesswoman of Philippi, and the Ethiopian eunuch. In the sense of their turnarounds, "conversion" means crossing boundaries and barriers and reaching a whole new way of seeing and understanding life. Conversion is more about putting an end to ignorance than to immorality.

Conversion, not conceived of in narrowly moral terms, is rather seen as coming to a new understanding: it is having one's ignorance alleviated — changing one's mind as well as one's heart. Furthermore, conversion in Acts is almost always, as we shall see, connected to call, to specific tasks, and to vocation. Conversion in Acts is less about pulling one's life together — "straightening up and flying right," as my mother put it — than it is about being called and sent to do God's bidding. Acts also complicates contemporary understandings of conversion that limit it to a once-in-a-lifetime transfer from "saved" to "unsaved." In Acts conversion is a continuing process. Acts 9 narrates the conversion of an unbeliever, Saul; Acts 10 tells of the conversion of a believer, Peter. Conversion, at least in Acts, is not the once-in-a-lifetime, finished-and-done experience or event that has been popularized by American revivalism.

Not only was the believer Peter converted anew in Acts 10; but in Acts 9 another believer, Ananias, was converted for the purpose of ministering to Saul/Paul. Ananias was understandably reluctant to put himself in the presence of one who had so recently been putting Christians in chains, in prison, and on trial. But Jesus' message brought about Ananias's conversion and call to go to Saul and help the latter regain his sight. What a moment it must have been when Saul, able to see again, saw the Christian Ananias standing before him as God's instrument of healing! Portraits of conversion in Acts are many and varied.

Thus Acts both underscores the reality of turning around, of changing both mind and heart, but also challenges many long-standing and conventional definitions that emphasize conversion's moral nature, its sole focus on unbelievers, and its once-in-a-lifetime nature. If Acts is to be believed, the focus of conversion is as much on believers and "good Christians" as it is on unbelievers or the morally reprobate. Moreover, conversion is not simply a matter of the heart or the emotions; it has a cognitive content and carries with it a call to service and action. Conversion and vocation are regularly linked in Acts, because a person is converted in order to be of use.

In the next chapter we will look at the conversion stories of Acts 10 more in the context of the church's multicultural turn. Here we will focus on the conversion of Saul/Paul (he is not referred to as Paul until Acts 13:9). There is no conversion narrative in all of Scripture or tradition that is more famous or frequently alluded to in sermons than that of Saul on the Damascus Road. The very words "Damascus Road" have become a kind of shorthand for conversion and all kinds of experiences of change, turning around, reorientation, coming to Christ, and transformation. This is partly due to how frequently Scripture itself tells and retells the story of Paul's conversion. It is recounted twice more in Acts alone (22:6-12 and 26:12-23), and Paul refers to it often in his letters, including Galatians, Philippians, and 1 Corinthians. The sheer frequency of its appearance may account for the way this story has arrested the attention of the church and Christians throughout the ages.

Of course, it is not just the number of references or the frequency of the retelling but the dramatic story itself — and the person whose story it is — that further accounts for the pivotal and celebrated nature of this particular conversion narrative. The story is dramatic both in broad outline and in finer detail. The details are the blinding light, the voice of Jesus, Saul's loss of sight, and his need to be led by the hand, like a little child, into Damascus. In broader outline, this conversion story narrates the most improbable transformation: God chooses a sworn enemy to carry forward God's mission to the gentiles. Ever since its original telling, this story stands as confirmation of Luke's claim that "with God all things are possible" (Luke 1). Finally, the importance of this story is sealed by the fact that it authorizes the ministry of an apostle who, though "untimely born," is arguably more instrumental than anyone else in both the formation and spread of the church. That Paul's Letters account for more of the New Testament than do the writings of any other single author is further witness to his critically important role. No wonder the story of the "Damascus Road" conversion is so well-known and famous.

What happened on that road to Damascus and in Saul's life that make us speak of it as "conversion"? What was the nature of this turning point that has meant so much in Christian history and tradition? What light does it shed on conversion, turning, and transformation in our times, in our lives, and for the church today? Is Saul's conversion to be understood as a kind of normative experience for all Christians, or is it one conversion among many, important to be sure, but not a normative pattern? Can Saul's conversion be understood in such a way that it does provide some broad patterns of conversion, without being turned into a script or template for all to follow?

In his literary study *The Language of Grace*, Peter Hawkins speaks of a "basic pattern of conversion" evident in the work of such Christian writers as Flannery O'Connor and Walker Percy. In this pattern of conversion, "a person is forced by extraordinary circumstances to transcend the self-centered demands of the ego, who comes to see another person as real and full and who can finally see that person without distortions of fantasy or ulterior motive, a person, that is, who can love someone else."[1]

The significant elements of this description, for our purposes, include the transcending of the self-centered demands of the ego and the corollary capacity to see beyond oneself. As he journeyed on the Damascus Road, Saul was a man with one purpose and mission: to round up the followers of Jesus and bring them to trial. No problem with an agenda: Saul was so completely caught up in his own agenda that he could perceive nothing outside it, nothing beyond "the self-centered demands of his ego." Conversion in Saul's case means that the Other, Jesus, intrudes — almost violently — into his life and agenda, driving him to his knees, blinding him with light, terrifying him by calling his name in a voice that only he can hear: "Saul, Saul, why do you persecute me?" That voice breaks in on Saul's self-centered ego.

Hawkins notes that conversion often seems to begin with something that looks like "breakdown." Breakdown precedes and may, in conversion, give way to a "breakthrough." And that certainly seems to be an apt description of Saul's Damascus Road conversion. Saul, an upright man, is driven to his knees — to the ground. Saul, the one who "sees" and "knows," is blinded and confused. Saul, the one who has been in charge, now needs to be led by the hand by others, becoming "like a little child" again. In a very real sense, Saul experiences a breakdown and a period of disorientation before the experience becomes one of breakthrough and yields a new orientation.

Hawkins remarks on the forcible, even violent, quality of conversion particularly in the works of Flannery O'Connor. "Their [O'Connor's char-

1. Peter S. Hawkins, *The Language of Grace* (New York: Seabury Classics, 2004), p. 3.

acters'] egos have elaborate defenses and must, therefore, be forcibly broken into. For this reason the kingdom will often come with weeping and gnashing of teeth, and the intervention of grace appears like a murderous assault, the end of life rather than a beginning." O'Connor herself has remarked: "In my stories I have found that violence is strangely capable of returning my characters to reality and preparing them to accept their moments of grace. Their heads are so hard that almost nothing else will do the work."[2]

O'Connor might just as well have been speaking of Saul there. Saul is not a man adrift and confused, and he is hardly down and out. Rather, he is determined, resolute, and convinced that he is absolutely right to be persecuting the followers of Jesus. He is hardheaded, and his ego is well-defended. But there is a violent intrusion on the Damascus Road, a breakdown that leads to a breakthrough in the end. The self-centered demands of Saul's ego, which force him to fulfill the requirements of the law perfectly and to destroy anyone who threatens that system, are broken into by the intrusion of grace through the Other, the living Jesus.

There is another way to describe this encounter and conversion. Not only does grace break in on the well-defended ego, but there is also here the theme of forgiveness, one that Paul emphasizes even more prominently in his accounts of this experience in his letters. Forgiveness is another way to describe the action of grace in this story and in the nature of the conversion experience. Saul, who not only violently persecuted the followers of Jesus but took part in the murder of Stephen, experiences mercy and forgiveness in this encounter. The enemy of Jesus and Jesus' people, he will be the instrument Jesus chooses to bring his name before the gentiles. No longer will Saul bring suffering on others; he will experience suffering in the service of a Lord and a power beyond himself.

Conversion and the "Triumph of the Therapeutic"

One possible way to frame the meaning and significance of Paul's conversion on the Damascus Road for our own times and context is suggested by those who have called attention to and critiqued what Philip Rieff has called *The Triumph of the Therapeutic* in his seminal work of that title. The "triumph of the therapeutic," as discussed in the works of Rieff and Chris-

---

2. Hawkins, *The Language of Grace*, p. 29.

topher Lasch *(The Culture of Narcissism),* depicts contemporary Americans as "measuring all things according to the measure of man." How does this enhance or benefit me and my life? How does this work for me? How can this make my life better or more comfortable or more meaningful? Does this meet my needs? Such are the questions of the therapeutically shaped and informed. Perhaps it goes without saying that this is not the impulse of serious therapy, which may in fact be able to overcome such narcissism; but it may characterize its pervasive and popularized forms in our culture. The triumph of the therapeutic may mean that there is no reality beyond the self, no larger reality, no Other to whom we are accountable or to whom we may turn for support.

Theologian Andrew Purves, in his recent book *Reconstructing Pastoral Theology,* remarks that in a society that is so heavily influenced by therapeutic values, "pastoral theology and pastoral practice have become concerned largely with questions of meaning rather than truth, acceptable functioning rather than discipleship, and a concern for self-actualization and self-realization rather than salvation."[3] These shifts, not only in language but in emphasis, suggest that the triumph of the therapeutic has invaded the church as well as the culture. The consequence, evident in various degrees and manifestations, is the self-absorbed individual, a consequence very much like Luther's classic definition of sin: "The self curved in upon itself." There is, of course, considerable ambiguity here: appropriate and faithful self-regard does exist, but it differs from self-absorption, just as the strong ego differs from the inflated ego.

While none of these categories (the "therapeutic," "narcissistic," "self-absorbed") may be exactly or completely adequate descriptions of Saul, they do suggest links from the Damascus Road to the roads and people of our own times — and to our own lives. Saul's conversion meant transcending the self-centered demands of the ego and sustaining the intrusion into his life of another reality, another being — the living Jesus. His literal blindness seems, in some ways, a symbol of a more figurative blindness to what was beyond him and outside him. Saul discovered or was discovered by a power and reality beyond himself. Conversion in our own time may likewise entail an intrusion into and deliverance from our self-centered and self-absorbed — if also anxious — constructions of the self.

3. Andrew Purves, *Reconstructing Pastoral Theology* (Louisville: Westminster/John Knox, 2004), pp. xxi-xxii.

It may find expression in a dawning awareness, almost subversive in contemporary North America, that "it's not about me." There is a power, a reality, a mystery, a mercy, and a grace outside and beyond me. "Who are you, Lord?" asks a bewildered Saul on the Damascus Road.

Just as Saul was encountered on the Damascus Road by the Other, by a reality beyond and outside himself, so today conversion may mean just such an encounter. A popular story, a kind of modern parable, seems to illustrate this point. There were two battleships on maneuvers at sea. The weather was bad, so at nightfall the captain of one remained on the bridge to keep watch through the patchy fog. Shortly after dark, the lookout on the wing of the bridge reported: "Light bearing on the starboard bow."

"Is it steady or is it moving astern?" called the captain.

"Steady, captain," said the lookout, which meant that the other boat was on a dangerous collision course with the captain's ship. The captain called out to the signal man:

"Signal that ship: We are on a collision course; advise you change course twenty degrees." A signal came back: "Advisable for you to change course twenty degrees." The captain said, "Send: I'm a captain! Change course twenty degrees."

"I am a second-class seaman, sir," came the reply. "You had better change course twenty degrees." By this time the captain was furious. He spat out, "Send: I'm a battleship. You change course twenty degrees!"

Back came the flashing light: "I'm a lighthouse!"

"Change course twenty degrees," muttered the captain.

Saul's own experience has been like that of the captain of the battleship. Thinking that he is in charge, that he knows it all, he discovers that he isn't and that he doesn't. Then he goes out to spend the rest of his life speaking to others, saying, "There is a lighthouse. It is Jesus Christ. Advise you change course."

This seems to be a parable for our own time. In many ways we have made the self sovereign. And yet, to paraphrase the words of Jesus, seeking to save ourselves, we have not. We have lost ourselves amid the constant swirl of new strategies and technologies, new gimmicks and therapies that are supposed to be for saving our selves. Conversion is to be encountered by the Other, by the living Jesus, and to find ourselves by losing ourselves for his sake and the sake of the gospel. Some have reported something analogous to this pattern of conversion in the experience of becoming a parent. There is an "other," a being outside the self, whom one sees and actually loves. One's self-full life is transformed. Still others have found the pattern of conversion analogous to their ventures into cultures profoundly different from their own. For example, seeing the strange combination of poverty, hospitality, and generosity that characterizes the lives of believers in parts of the world other than North American has opened eyes to see reality more clearly and accurately, and it has provided a capacity for actual love of the other.

Is Saul's conversion story and experience a normative pattern for all Christians? Not in its specifics and details. It would seem foolish to suggest that everyone must experience such a profound and instantaneous break-down to breakthrough, a Damascus Road of their own. It is not presented in Acts in that way (remember, there are multiple accounts of conversion); to make it into a kind of prescriptive pattern and experience would be to diminish the freedom and the grace of God. The impulse of some Christians to make Paul's experience — or their own — into a norm for others is reminiscent of Peter's desire to capture the Transfiguration in three booths: it is a freezing of the moment that is neither possible nor desirable. Many Christians will still come to faith through a process of life-long nurture. Others will experience more than one conversion or transformation experience in which the self-centered ego is broken open and the person is made new. And for some, something like Paul's blinding experience of transformation will be their experience.

Having said that, we must hasten to say that Paul's experience on the Damascus Road does illuminate patterns of conversion in which we believe there is enduring as well as contemporary meaning and significance. Paul's conversion remains a powerful narration of a turning, of an enemy who becomes a friend, of apparent breakdown that really does become a breakthrough. Paul's conversion can inform our own faith walk and experience without itself becoming a normative pattern, something to be achieved in order for our faith to be valid.

Conversion and Calling, Suffering, and Imperative

There are several additional elements of Paul's experience of conversion that characterize other narratives of conversion in Acts and may deepen and challenge our own understandings of conversion and transformation. As we have noted in the exposition of Acts 9, conversion here is linked to call. Paul is not changed and then simply left to contemplate or recount the experience for the rest of his days. His breakdown/breakthrough on the Damascus Road is in the service of God's plan and in the fulfillment of God's promises. Conversion is for the purpose, here and elsewhere in Acts, of calling: "For he (Paul) is an instrument I have chosen to bring my name before Gentiles and kings and before the people of Israel" (v. 15). In this sense, Paul's experience of blinding light has much in common with Moses' encounter with the burning bush. This theophany, the revealing of God, brings with it a task and a calling.

Not only is conversion often linked to calling in Acts, but it is also linked to suffering. The very next words after verse 15 are: "I myself will show him how much he must suffer for the sake of my name." Conversion, at least here, does not deliver one from suffering; still less does it exempt one from suffering. Conversion brings suffering! Sometimes today's accounts of conversion seem to suggest, or say straightforwardly, that conversion to Christ will bring an end to suffering and trouble and will deliver prosperity, success, and status. Many contemporary "conversion" narratives seem to proceed something like this: "My life was a mess; I was doing poorly in my career; my marriage was a disaster; my kids were on drugs, and were an embarrassment to me. Then I found Jesus, and my life has gotten a whole lot better." This is the very stuff of TV evangelism. This is doubtless the experience of some and may very well express authentic aspects of conversion. But even those who narrate such a story may go on, when pressed, to acknowledge that living a Christian life can bring suffering of its own. A disciple may find herself speaking up about unethical practices at work; or a disciple may be at odds with family members who are suspicious of his new faith. Following Christ may mean sacrifice of time and money that is not always easy or understood by others.

This element of "taking up your cross" as a part of conversion is prominent in the Gospel of Luke and in Luke's stories of conversion in Acts: "I myself will show him how much he must suffer for the sake of my name." Saul, who had been inflicting suffering on others, was not about to experience suffering himself. But in this reversal Paul has, of course, been converted to the way of Christ, which is a way of life that may require him to die for his faith, but which does not permit or sanction him to kill for his faith. That is a crucial distinction.

Not only does Saul's conversion — and conversion in Acts in general — entail a calling and suffering, a whole new frame is put around Saul's life, the frame of divine necessity. If conversion means, in shorthand, "it's not about me," then what it is about is God's plan for our lives, and not only our lives but for the healing and redemption of God's world. There are several key word choices in the story of Paul's conversion that emphasize this element of divine necessity (especially evident in v. 6): "But get up and enter the city, and you will be told what you are to do." The force of the original words is not wholly evident in translation, and the reader may wish to refer back to the exposition earlier in this chapter. But here Paul's life is framed by a sense of the divine imperative, of an "I must."

The great preacher of the last generation, Gardner Taylor, wrote eloquently of the "I must" as he considered Jesus' final words in the Gospel of John: "It is finished." "I think," said Taylor, "oh, not in such grand and cosmic terms, but I think that these words may belong to all of us. They come by way of the 'I must.' We will never be able to say, 'It is finished, Father, I give you now my spirit,' until we say, 'I must.' 'I must work the works of him that sent me.' A few more days shall roll and a few more seasons come and in them, 'I must, we must . . . must serve on, must forgive on.' We must go sometimes when we do not feel like going, trying when nobody seems to care. Our work is ours to do. 'I must.'"[4]

STUDY QUESTIONS

1. Another chapter, another conversion story! His is the most famous conversion in Acts: Saul of Tarsus (St. Paul), the Lord's persecutor, becomes his disciple. Given the frequency of testimony we hear or read today about people converting to Jesus, how is the genuineness of a reported conversion to Jesus tested and publicly confirmed as depicted by Acts 9?

2. What does this passage say with respect to the following question: Do you think Paul's conversion turns him away from his Jewish identity and roots? Defend your answer from a study of Acts 9 (see Acts 22, 26).

3. Wall and Robinson contend that Acts narrates the story of Paul's conversion as a call to ministry rather than a spiritual reversal. What is the relationship between conversion and one's sacred calling?

4. Can you think of instances when some "breakdown" led to a "breakthrough" in contemporary fiction, the movies, or in personal experience? Write them down and discuss.

4. Gardner Taylor, *How Shall They Preach* (Progressive Baptist Publishing House, 1977), pp. 147-48.

9   The Gospel in a Multicultural World: The Case of Peter

PART I: INTERPRETING ACTS 10 AS SCRIPTURE

As Saul heads back to Tarsus in preparation for his future (9:31), Peter takes over again as the central character of Acts. At the very moment that his religious authority extends beyond Jerusalem to Lydda, Sharon, and Joppa (9:32-43), Peter's inability to comprehend the vision of nonkosher foods threatens his service to God. Recalling the Old Testament story of the prophet Jonah, God calls Peter from the city of Joppa (10:8; cf. Jonah 1:3) to carry God's word to "unclean" gentiles — not those living in pagan Nineveh but the ones in the home of a Roman soldier, Cornelius (vv. 1-8, 17b-33). As with Jonah before him, Peter is converted to the Lord's way only after God has more clearly revealed God's intention to save nonkosher gentiles who repent. Peter's reluctance to eat "profane and unclean" foods illustrates this new theological problem: just as God's decision angered Jonah, so now the salvation of unclean Cornelius threatens to divide the Jewish church (11:1-18).

Peter's name in Aramaic, "Simon bar Jonah" (Matt. 16:17), may have suggested to both Luke and his readers the parallel of Jonah's story to Peter's here. In any case, Peter's conversion is shaped by the very same theological belief that shaped the Old Testament story of Jonah: "God shows no partiality, but in every nation anyone who fears God and does what is right is acceptable to God" (10:34-35). Peter's proclamation nicely articulates the central theological claim that shapes all of Acts: Jonah's God, the one who desires to save all who repent, is Peter's God.

The Conversion and Calling of Simon Peter

The taxonomy of God's salvation has now reached a watershed moment, when God discloses to Peter the objective to save everyone who calls on the Lord's name. Jesus' commissioning of Saul has already disclosed indications of God's intent to include repentant gentiles within a restored Israel (9:15); but God's initiative is left to the great apostle to enact. In a manner that bears a striking family resemblance to Saul's story, Peter's mind first needs to be changed before he is able to serve God's redemptive interests.

According to his résumé in Acts, Cornelius is "a devout man who feared God . . . gave alms generously . . . and prayed constantly to God" (v. 2; cf. vv. 22, 31). While the church often defines conversion as the dramatic personal transformation of bad to good, Acts does not — as we have seen in the preceding chapter. Typically, those who are converted in Acts are virtuous people like Cornelius, with the moral capacity to distinguish truth from falsehood (cf. 17:11). Moreover, the importance Acts attaches to this gentile "God-fearer" has led many to distinguish the religious motives and practices of those gentiles whom Cornelius represents. The reader is allowed only the strategic distinction between the gentile proselyte who has already converted to Judaism before converting to Christ (Nicolaus in Acts 6:5; cf. 2:10) and the gentile God-fearer who has not (Cornelius here in v. 2). While Luke's emphasis is on Cornelius's piety, not his status, to establish the logical connection between his character and subsequent conversion (vv. 4, 31), the point remains that Cornelius is a religiously unclean — that is, a nonproselyte — gentile who is outside God's covenant with Israel (Gen. 17). The plot of his story in Acts, and of Peter's role in it, depends on the reader's understanding of this point.

Visionary episodes in Acts impart instructions that more clearly define the church's mission. In Cornelius's vision, the "angel of the Lord" delivers God's message that, if followed, will lead to his salvation: "Send men to Joppa" to fetch a certain man who is staying in a particular house (vv. 5-6). His fearful obedience to do God's bidding is the hallmark of readiness to receive God's grace. But it is noteworthy that Cornelius obeys God according to his own military conventions: he "called . . . a devout soldier from the ranks" whose experience is most like Cornelius's (see v. 2), and who would thus be best able to represent his interests to Peter (v. 8).

References to the time of the day typically have theological significance: the pious Cornelius has a vision "one afternoon at about three o'clock" (v. 3; see 3:1), the time of day set aside for religious observance among the faithful of Israel — in the middle of the afternoon for all to see. Once again, Luke uses a "double vision" to get two people on God's page. Earlier, both Saul and Ananias had separate visions about the same future (9:11-12); here Cornelius and "a certain Simon who is called Peter" will also have visionary experiences of the same future, God's future. Cornelius's response to the angel is the same as Saul's to Jesus, "What is it, Lord?" (v. 4), and for the same reason: he lacks understanding, which the vision then supplies.

As the caravan from Cornelius is making its way from Caesarea to Joppa (vv. 9-16), according to instruction — "about noon the next day" — Peter is making his way to the rooftop to pray. His time of prayer takes place while he is hungry, probably from fasting, and provides a natural setting for a vision about food. Peter's heightened spiritual state explains his "trance" *(ekstasis)* and his reluctance to kill and eat unclean foods forbidden by Torah. In his vision, a picnic blanket is spread with various species of animals; it does not distinguish clean from unclean but only comes with the divine command to "get up, kill and eat" without proper concern for their kosher preparation. Reptiles (Lev. 11:29-38) and birds (Lev. 11:13-19) were especially unclean for a pious Jew.

Peter's negative response to the heavenly instruction — "By no means, Lord" — is anticipated by his Jewish piety rather than by his lack of it (v. 14). In fact, the repetition of this message "three times" symbolizes how revolutionary it is: what is "profane and unclean" is now clean and no longer profane. The repetition of the divine message (v. 15) explains the first utterance and provides the essential meaning of the vision; thus the reader does not require any direct address or message for the third instruction. The conflict between God and Peter (and hence God's dramatic response to Peter, "What God has made clean, you must not call profane") does not concern the currency of Peter's ancestral traditions regarding clean and unclean foods but rather the nature of his mission as prophesied by Scripture (see v. 43). Because God has ordained that gentiles share in Abraham's (i.e., Israel's) blessings, Peter's mission must no longer consider them profane and off limits. There is no evidence that Peter resists God's declaration; instead, when Peter comes out of his prophetic trance, he hesitates only because he "puzzles greatly" and ponders the meaning of divine revelation so cryptically given (vv. 17, 19a); its literal meaning is clearly not its "real" meaning. Peter needs more information.

While the meaning of Peter's vision is not immediately clear to him, several more concrete and coincidental "signs" subsequently occur that will gradually lead him to understand its meaning. Cornelius's emissaries arrive from Caesarea and ask to see Peter (vv. 17-18). The clever literary interplay between two Simons — Simon the tanner, at whose home "Simon who was called Peter" is staying — may intend to create the impression of confusion (related to Peter's understanding of the vision) that is then resolved by the Spirit's intervention (v. 19).

The Spirit's word to Peter — "Look, three men are searching for you" — serves both theological and practical ends. Peter is evidently lost in his meditation on the meaning of his vision and does not hear the three men knocking and calling for him at Simon's door. The special intervention of the Spirit cues the reader that those standing at the door will somehow aid Peter in figuring out his vision; further, the instruction to "go with them . . . for I have sent them" (v. 20) indicates that the message these men bring to him is divinely intended.

At first glance, Peter's question to them ("Why have you come?") seems to challenge the Spirit's instruction to "go with them without hesitation" (v. 20). The phrase translated "without hesitation" *(mēden diakrino-menos)* means to act without doubt or without making a critical judgment on one's own. It could be that Peter's question is a literary prompt to provide us with another explanation by God for answering the prayers of an unclean gentile. Cornelius's compatriots reply: "He is a righteous and God-fearing man, who is respected by all the Jewish people" and was "directed by a holy angel" to listen to what Peter says (v. 22). These details comprise a confirmation and expansion of the earlier résumé (vv. 1-4) and reflect an independent appraisal of Cornelius's religious fitness. The language and concerns of this explanation are adapted to an observant Jew such as Peter, so that now these compatriots describe Cornelius as a "righteous man," replacing Luke's earlier "devout man," which commends him as living according to the Torah.

Significantly, Peter now learns that the "holy angel" has charged him to go to the house of the gentile Cornelius and to listen to what he says. The verb *chrēmatizō*, translated as "directed" (NRSV) or even more timidly as "told" (NIV), is a much stronger word that denotes a revealing word from God (cf. Matt. 2:12, 22; Luke 2:26; Heb. 8:5; 11:7). For this reason Peter is responsive to what his visitors tell him. Indeed, the demonstration of his hospitality toward them anticipates those who will be responsive to truth.

The reader must presume that Peter now understands the meaning of his vision and has converted to the prospect of a gentile mission as a feature of God's plan of salvation (see vv. 28-29).

The next act of this conversion drama begins "the next day," when Peter leaves Joppa for Caesarea to carry out his divinely commissioned task. His caravan is joined by "some of the believers from Joppa" (v. 23b) who are members of the Jewish church and will later function as witnesses to Cornelius's unexpected Spirit baptism. Cornelius has already prepared for this apostolic house call and has "called together his relatives and close friends" (v. 24), members of his extended household and roughly analogous in a secular setting to the community of friends in a sacred one (see 4:32-35).

For all his serious piety, Cornelius has not yet repented, and he remains susceptible to theological mistakes: "Cornelius, falling at Peter's feet, worshiped him" (v. 25). On the one hand, Peter's "feet" symbolize his apostolic authority (cf. 4:33, 37; 5:2); and given that the angel has already informed him of Peter's importance, Cornelius's response is perfectly reasonable. Cornelius's honest mistake is in supposing that Peter dispenses salvation rather than simply announcing it. Peter's response testifies to his subordinate role in Cornelius's salvation: "Stand up; I am only a mortal" (v. 26; cf. 14:14-15).

Peter's opening address is a personal testimony of his own recent conversion: "God has shown me that I should not call anyone profane or unclean" (v. 28b; see vv. 14-15). God has not "shown" Peter this great truth in a split second, nor does the latter immediately comprehend the connection between the nonkosher foods of his vision and the nonkosher people he is to evangelize. The story itself points the reader to a process of disclosure by which Peter's understanding of God's plan evolves over time. The real beginning of this process is surely Peter's missionary experiences beyond Jerusalem among both marginal (see 8:25; 9:43) and Diaspora Jews (see 9:32-42). These experiences of conversion and healing beyond Jerusalem, where his prophetic authority is confirmed time and again, he redirects to those of different ethnic groups beyond the boundaries of Israel. God authorizes Peter's gentile mission through the showing of a "double vision": the first given to him by the Spirit three times, but then complemented by a second vision shown to Cornelius and later reported by his three men to Peter. The temporal framework supplied by the narrative itself stipulates that Peter's understanding of his gentile mission unfolds over several days of visions (v. 30), internal reflection (vv. 17, 19), and through the reports of others (v. 22). In any case, what God "shows" him is the clear motive of his apostolic house call, since an observant Jew deems it "unlawful to visit a Gentile," especially "without objection" (vv. 28-29a).

Peter's question, "May I ask why you sent for me?" (v. 29b), followed by Cornelius's response, at first seems redundant (vv. 4-6, 22) and therefore an unnecessary preface to his proclamation of the gospel. Narrative restatements, however, elucidate and clarify important themes. In this instance, Cornelius's comments emphasize that Peter's arrival is due more to God's faithfulness than to his own piety: "God has heard . . . and remembered" (v. 31; cf. v. 4b). His good will toward Peter, and his willingness to "listen to all that the Lord has commanded you to say," not only submits to Peter's prophetic authority but has also corrected his earlier theological miscue of worshiping the messenger rather than listening to his message from God.

Peter has come to Cornelius to preach the gospel at God's bidding, and he presents his gospel to a receptive audience with the shared premonition that a religious revolution is about to begin in Israel. He need not respond to a theological mistake as in past speeches; for this reason the opening formula, "Then Peter began to speak" (literally, "Peter then opened his mouth"), is a literary prompt that what follows is a prophetic oracle, provided by divine revelation and enabled by the Spirit's inspiration.

The implication of Joel's prophecy of Pentecost, which Peter quoted in his own famous Pentecost speech, is only now made clear to him: "I now realize how true it is that God shows no partiality" (v. 34b; see vv. 28-29). The principal lesson Peter has learned is about God, not about the scope of his mission. That God is no respecter of persons is an old biblical lesson (see Deut. 10:17; cf. LXX Ps. 81:2; Lev. 19:15; 2 Chron. 19:7; Rom. 2:10-11; Col. 3:25; James 2:1, 9-10; 1 Pet. 1:17), and it takes on expanded meaning for Peter in this missionary setting. His definition of the principle of divine impartiality carries forward Scripture's critical apparatus as well: while God may not give one group priority over another based on ethnicity or nationality, God does indeed discriminate "in every nation" based on "who fears him and does what is right" (v. 35). It is important for us to see Cornelius as an exemplar of this theological principle: God does not "hear and remember" Cornelius because he is a non-Jew but because his piety and generosity are pleasing to Israel's God (see 10:4-6, 31).

At the core of Peter's speech is a report of "the message [*ho logos*] God sent to the people of Israel," of which "we are witnesses" (v. 39). Although awkwardly stated, the content of this message reviews what readers of Acts already know: God's message is sent first to Israel and arrives in their midst "through Jesus Christ, who is Lord of all" (v. 36); but this is good news only for those who fear God and live a life that pleases God (v. 35; cf. Luke 10:25-28). Peter stipulates the argument for the fairness of God by the geography of his message. Since the biblical promise of peace is made to Israel, the message of its fulfillment must therefore go to Israel first: Messiah is sent to Israel, and "that message [*rhēma* = "event"] spread throughout Judea, beginning with Galilee" (vv. 36-37).[1]

Peter's appeal to Scripture (v. 43) makes sense only because Cornelius is God-fearing and would recognize its authority. There is no explicit citation, which is characteristic of Luke's appeal to the whole tenor of Scripture (cf. 3:18, 24; 7:42; 26:22; 28:23): all Scripture testifies to God's Word disclosed in the Christ event — his suffering, death, and resurrection, and the promise that "everyone who believes in him receives forgiveness of sins through his name." But this refrain loudly echoes Joel's prophecy again ("everyone" and "name"), now joined by various allusions to the Old Testament Jonah (see the beginning of this chapter), as the unwritten and particular witnesses to the truth of Peter's claim. The familiar Pauline phrase "believes in him" appears only in this passage in the whole book of Acts, and here it is still wrapped around the familiar themes of Peter's earlier preaching: "forgiveness of sins" (see 2:38; 3:18-19) and "through his name" (2:38; 3:6; 4:10, etc.).

Although Acts tells us that Peter's speech is interrupted at this point, it stands as a complete presentation of the gospel. Nothing is left out. Why, then, does Luke begin verse 44 with the phrase "while Peter was still speaking these words . . ."? The "interrupted speech" is a literary convention that has been used in Acts before (see 2:36) and will be used again (cf. 17:32; 22:22; 23:7; 26:24), and it is shaped by theological conviction. The Holy Spirit breaks in on Peter's speech to prove that Cornelius's surprising salvation is not the result of Peter's eloquence but is God's gift according to God's timing (1:7-8).

It is more crucial that Peter's witness of a "gentile Pentecost" enables him to interpret the status of gentiles during the "last days" of salvation's

---

1. For an exegesis of these claims about Jesus according to Acts 10:38-43, see my commentary, pp. 166-67.

history (cf. 2:17-21). He witnesses the outpouring of God's Spirit in Jerusalem on the day of Pentecost, in Samaria, and now among unclean but repentant gentiles. Perhaps Luke, for this reason, shapes his narrative of this episode following the sequence of the Spirit's arrival narrated in Acts 2: (1) "the Holy Spirit fell upon all who heard the word" (v. 44; par. 2:4); (2) "the circumcised believers . . . were astounded . . . for they heard them speaking in tongues and extolling God" (vv. 45-46; par. 2:11-12); (3) "then Peter said, 'Can anyone withhold baptism from those who have received the Holy Spirit just as we have?'" (v. 47; par. 2:38); and (4) they were "baptized in the name of Jesus Christ" (v. 48a; par. 2:41).

This literary parallelism makes it more certain that the reader's response to Peter's question "can anyone withhold baptism from these people?" is a resounding No! There is not one thing that should exclude these gentiles from initiation into life in the Spirit and the vocation of this faith community.

The reader of Acts recalls these earlier stories of the Spirit's outpouring with an enlarged understanding that the fulfillment of Joel's prophecy must include gentiles. What was true of the entire household of Israel is now also true of God-fearing gentiles: "Everyone who calls upon the name of the Lord will be saved" (2:21) from their sins and given the gift of the Holy Spirit (see 2:38). But there is a layer of meaning added to this present story that sounds a more cautionary note. The "amazed" response of the Jews at Pentecost to hearing believers speaking in other languages, declaring "God's deeds of power" (2:11-12), cued a theological mistake that Peter then addressed in his first great missionary speech. That is, "astonishment" is another word for stunned unbelief. Thus, while Peter orders that Cornelius and his household be baptized into the fellowship of believers (v. 48a), the reader realizes that other believers who shared this same experience with Peter may not yet fully understand God's plan (see 11:2).

Thus the question remains: what is it about Peter's conversion experience that amazes his Jewish cohort (v. 45; 11:2-3)? Because they have had earlier experiences with this same miracle, it is doubtful that they are astonished about the speaking in tongues. Nor would they be surprised at the event of gentiles converting to Jesus per se (not only because they have heard reports from both Peter and Cornelius of their coincidental "double vision," but also because they are undoubtedly familiar with gentile proselytism within Judaism). The surprising feature of this gentile conversion is that all believers share the same gift of the Holy Spirit equally: in Peter's words, "these people have received the Holy Spirit *just as we have*" (v. 47).

The inference that Peter draws from this common religious experience, in Luke's telling of it, is that gentile believers "belong as fully to the messianic community" as do these stunned "circumcised believers." There is no pecking order within the whole household of God based on ethnicity or nationality, or based on Israel's privilege in God's *ordo salutis*. "To the Jew first" does not warrant a Jewish triumphalism within the church. Therefore, just as a Jewish believer need not become a gentile, gentile believers need not become "Jews" in order to be initiated into their life with God. The reader of Acts will discover, however, that the view that has been overturned by Peter's epiphany is a religious presumption that dies a slow death within the church — even in the face of the hard evidence gathered here by Peter and later by Paul.

PART II: ENGAGING ACTS 10 FOR TODAY'S CHURCH

If one form of conversion in Acts is the conversion of the unbeliever (Saul), another form of conversion, perhaps surprisingly, is the conversion of a believer (Peter). If conversion for Paul meant the dramatic intrusion of the Other on his well-defended ego, Peter's conversion in Acts 10 is God's continuing intrusion. It means the redirection of Peter's life and ministry, but not only that: it means the redirection of the life and ministry of the church. But let's look for a moment at the "conversion of a believer." Conversion is often understood as conversion from no faith to faith, or from one faith to another. Furthermore, conversion is just as often understood to be something that happens just once in a person's life. Peter's experience throws a monkey wrench into those assumptions: as a follower of Jesus, he is converted to a new understanding of the church's faith and mission, one that leads him to step across boundaries and barriers that had, up to this point, seemed impenetrable. Not only as a believer and follower of Christ, but also as an apostle and leader of the church, Peter finds his mind opened and his life redirected. Conversion continues.

Contrary to much Christian theology and practice, this suggests that the field for mission and conversion may not be solely, or even primarily, outside the church doors, or in non-Christian cultures, or among those who have not yet met Christ. Peter's conversion suggests that the mission field may be, equally, inside our sanctuaries, in the life of our own congregations, and in our own land and culture. Conversion and transformation continue — and thus need to continue — in our lives and churches today because God is a living God, because God is still speaking, and because God is doing a new thing (Isa. 43:19). "There is," as John Robinson, pastor to the Pilgrims in the seventeenth century, said, "yet more truth and light to break forth from God's Holy Word."

The shadow side of the embrace of conversion in some traditions is that it creates a false sense of security and assumptions of complacency: "We're saved. We're done. We have become Christians." We are not done — nor are we finished. Even if we were to consider conversion a once-in-a-lifetime experience, what Luther said of baptism applies here as well. "Baptism," said the great Reformer, "is a once-in-a-lifetime experience that takes our whole life to complete."

The need for new conversion, fresh transformation, and deepened faith continues. It may be that the crucial move in renewing congregations today is a new recognition that it is we ourselves — pastors, lay leaders, teachers, and Christian congregants — who need conversion, transformation, healing, changed minds, and changed hearts most of all. If Peter, the lead apostle, the rock upon whom Jesus would found his church, required continuing and even shocking conversion and transformation, who are we to rest on our laurels? Or to spin this in another, possibly more positive way: What prospects for fresh ministry, for conversion to Christ, exist right where we are? The truth is that the congregation that is spiritually alive, where conversion and transformation are ongoing, is likely to be much more inspiring and inviting than the church where the implicit message is, "We've arrived."

In some respects, the whole thrust of this book is to claim just this: the church is ripe for a renewal, for conversion. To recapitulate the themes of earlier chapters, this means understanding that mission is not just a budget or program of the church but everything the church is and does (Acts 1). It means bold preaching and witness in the face of the powers that be (Acts 2). It means authentic, living-and-breathing Christian community, that is, a community of shared goods that embodies a different way of understanding and using wealth and possessions (Acts 4 and 5). It means congregations that are capable of having — and resolving — disagreements (Acts 6). It means churches where the Holy Spirit comes to rest on all believers and where fresh, innovative, and surprising ministries are the result of the Spirit's bidding — even pushing (Acts 8). It means congregations where transformation is happening, where lives and communities are being changed as they experience God's amazing grace (Acts 9). And now, in Acts 10 as well as Acts 15, it means discovering what it means to be the church in a multicultural world and society.

We urge congregations toward a continuing conversion, but with this caveat: conversion in Acts is not first of all something that we humans and believers "do." It is something God does. The "grammar of the gospel" is the grammar of grace and response, the life-changing and life-giving intrusion of God into our midst, our lives, and our communities. This invites and requires a response; but the priority is, throughout biblical faith and in Acts, on God's initiative. Another way to put this is to reiterate that Christianity is not, in the end, a religion of virtue; it is a religion of grace. A religion of virtue, as Desmond Tutu once observed, says: "If you are good, then God will love you." Instead, Christianity says: "God loves you, therefore live as a beloved child of God." Grace comes first, virtue comes second.

When we forget this, which we regularly do, we can no longer speak the gospel. We forget, as Harry Emerson Fosdick pointed out, that the indicative of the gospel always precedes the imperative of human response. That is, the first word is about what God has done, is doing, and will do; the second word is about what we must do in response. The indicative precedes the imperative. When the church begins with the imperative, as often happens, the faith is turned into a religion of virtue at best, or worse, a religion of good works and achievement. When we speak of continuing conversion, then, it is because we believe that in our own day God is doing a new thing. God is breaking down barriers and crossing boundaries. God is creating a new people.

As in Acts, when God led the way and prompted Peter's conversion with disturbing visions and unexpected strangers, so in our time God is leading the way. Our own conversions, whether informed by the stories of Paul, Ananias, Peter, Cornelius, Lydia, or Tabitha, are in response to what God has done, is doing, and will do. Too often our first question is an anxious "What shall we do?" It would be better if our first question were, "What is God doing?" or even "What is going on?" Human beings, as H. Richard Niebuhr claimed, are answerers. We live in a responsive relationship with the one who is Alpha and Omega, the first and the last word.

In Acts, God is a living God, leading the way, though the way is often not what we expect or would ourselves have chosen.

The Gospel in a Multicultural World

We are newly aware in our own time of the movement of North America from a monocultural to a multicultural society. Of course, North America was never as culturally homogeneous as we might have imagined. There have long been pronounced regional differences, as well as different cultures in urban, suburban, and rural areas. But when the reform of the U.S. Immigration Act took place in 1965, our society began a much more rapid and pronounced movement toward cultural, ethnic, racial, and religious diversity and pluralism. The Seattle public school district, for example, is not atypical in this regard: there are now some seventy different language groups among the students of Seattle's schools. California recently became the first U.S. state on the mainland (it was already true in Hawaii) where "people of color" now make up the majority of the population. Other states will follow this trend during the twenty-first century, as the Asian and Hispanic populations of the United States continue to grow. Sometime during the 1990s, the number of Muslims in America came to exceed the number of Presbyterians. In many Roman Catholic parishes across the country there has been a "browning" of the congregations, as once-dominant Irish, Italian, and Eastern European ethnic groups have been eclipsed by growing Hispanic and Asian-American populations.

The churches and the congregations are affected by these changes directly and indirectly. Often in seeking to make sense of our new multiculturalism, the church has turned to sociological, psychological, and political sources for information and analysis — and those sources can, of course, be exceedingly useful. But it has seemed odd that the church has not more readily turned to its own story, to Scripture, for guidance. In reality, the challenges of a multicultural world and a multicultural church are major themes of the entire New Testament — and of the book of Acts in particular. How will the church, which began among repentant Jews, negotiate its way in new and different cultural settings, whether among near neighbors such as Samaria and Syria or within the vast Greco-Roman world and cultures of the gentiles? What is the relationship between culture and the gospel?

Though the very early church's turn to the gentile world is associated with Paul and is foreshadowed in his Damascus Road encounter, it is Peter who initiates the border crossing. And yet it was hardly Peter's idea. It was God's idea, revealed to Peter in a series of visions and experiences concentrated here in Acts 10. The truth of that is brought home by Peter's lack of understanding and even horror at the visions he receives while staying in Caesarea. The lowering of a sheet with a smorgasbord of "unclean" foods, along with the instruction "take and eat," proves profoundly unappetizing and disturbing to Peter, a devout Jew. It is perhaps difficult for most contemporary people to fully appreciate Peter's instinctive revulsion, since the idea of unclean or taboo foods is not common among contemporary Christians. Still, we might get some idea of his emotion if we were to visit China, say, and were offered a dish of roast dog or rat; or if, in Japan, we were invited to eat fish or other sea life that was still alive and wriggling.

But in the end it is not about food: it's about people. Peter, like Paul, finds himself led where he has not thought or chosen to go — in his case, the home of Cornelius, a gentile and a Roman soldier. And like the double conversion of Paul and Ananias in Acts 9, there is one here in Acts 10 as well: Peter is led by the Spirit to a gentile home, and Cornelius and his household are converted. (Also, as the blind Paul has his eyes "opened" by Ananias, the blind Peter has his eyes opened by his experience with Cornelius.) Peter staggers into this gentile household, saying, "You yourselves know that it is unlawful for a Jew to associate with or to visit a Gentile; but God has shown me that I should not call anyone profane or unclean." Having blurted this out, Peter asks for further instruction: "What in the world am I doing here?" Again, though our own culture certainly is not without barriers and boundaries between different strains of people, it is difficult for us to imagine how extraordinary this visit must have been for Peter. Perhaps our only near equivalent to "unclean" as evidenced here would be moral in nature: that is, going to the home of some people whose way of life we considered morally reprehensible for some reason. While some judgments about cultures or ethnicities that are not our own may exist among us, we probably do not for the most part consider others immoral or unclean in a ritual or religious sense, so much as simply finding them strange or different. I remember, as a boy, my first visits to the homes of black people. I was fascinated by the varied shades, textures, and colors of black skin. I wondered if their homes would look, more or less, like my own. And I wondered if I would be safe. I'm sure that black children visiting my home would have had similar questions, fascinations, and apprehensions.

Peter begins his preaching and teaching in the home of Cornelius with the words: "I truly understand that God shows no partiality, but in every nation anyone who fears him and does what is right is acceptable to him." "Now, I get it," Peter is saying. From there he goes on to tell the Jesus story — that is, until he is interrupted by the Holy Spirit coming upon the gentiles. As in Acts 8, where the Spirit directs Philip to the Ethiopian eunuch, so here in Acts 10, the Spirit takes the lead, running in front of the church leadership. Like Philip, who has hardly planned a campaign to reach Ethiopian eunuchs, Peter has certainly not been going to meetings of the evangelism and church growth committee and pondering, "How can we reach the gentiles?" This is God's doing! Even as contemporary congregations and their leaders consider the varied multicultural realities and challenges of our society and how to respond to them, there is also value in allowing ourselves to be led by the Spirit and instructed by those to whom the Spirit sends us. That is, there is value in seeking God's will and direction in these matters. Moreover, there is value in being prepared, as best we can, for the Spirit's intrusions and interruptions.

We should also be prepared for the fact that change of this magnitude will create some heat, which is Peter's experience in the very next chapter: on his return to Jerusalem, believers there ask him what the heck was going on and what he thought he was doing.

The multicultural turn of the first-century church and the multicultural challenges and opportunities of our own time confront us with what one scholar of leadership calls "an adaptive challenge." Ron Heifetz offers a seminal distinction for church leaders confronting and leading change, one that may be useful to pastors and congregations engaging a newly multicultural society. In distinguishing "technical problems" from "adaptive challenges," Heifetz characterizes a technical problem in the following way: the problem itself is clear and known; the solution involves the application of known or existing technique; and finally, the person responsible for dealing with the problem is usually an expert or authority. For example, a technical problem in the church might be the following: We have too many children for our Sunday School classrooms. The solution would be to enlarge the building or get a couple of portables. Who would do the work? Maybe an outside contractor (expert) or the church building and maintenance committee (authority).

It is a different kind of situation and challenge, for example, when, as in many Catholic communities today, large numbers of Spanish-speaking parishioners begin to attend a church that has been made up entirely of Anglos. There are certainly technical aspects to such a shift; but it is much more than that. It is an *adaptive* challenge, and the marks of an adaptive challenge are different from those of a technical problem. Naming an adaptive challenge usually requires learning, change, and possibly loss: "Our church, our community, is changing. We are becoming something different, something new." And the response to the challenge also requires learning, change, and often risk: "We will have to learn new ways of being the church, including placing a new priority on the gift of hospitality and a willingness on our part to learn new ways." From this very brief illustration we can see that the key difference is who does the work, who is responsible for dealing with the challenge. The answer is: the people, the whole community. Responding to such a challenge will not be something "Father" can do for us, or something that can be dealt with by a building contractor. It will require a change of minds, of hearts, and of behaviors for the whole community.

We give this brief illustration of the distinction between technical and adaptive changes because it applies to many of the challenges the church faces in our new time, but particularly because it is an apt characterization of the multicultural turn of the early church. Becoming a community of "Jew and Greek, slave and free, male and female" meant great change in the minds and hearts and behaviors of everyone involved in that first-century church. Leadership was crucial, both from the Holy Spirit and from the apostles and other leaders of the church, as well as from within the gentile communities. But change, then and now, challenges the church to experience loss (of the known), risk (learning new ways), and engagement in response to God's leading and call.

It also requires discernment, especially discernment about what is an earthen vessel (to draw on Paul's distinction in 2 Corinthians) and what is the transcendent power of God? "But we have this treasure in earthen vessels, to show that the transcendent power belongs to God and not to us" (2 Cor. 4:7). It's not ever easy to sort out what is "earthen vessel" and what is "transcendent power." Nor does this mean that our various earthen vessels (church buildings, traditional practices, styles of music, sacramental forms, powerful preaching, or understandings of ministry) are unimportant or without value. But it is true, Paul suggests, that our various earthen vessels are relative and not ultimate goods. The only ultimate good is God and God alone. Such a distinction may allow us carefully to negotiate some sorting out of cultural practice and gospel content, which is a crucial distinction if we are to respond to this particular adaptive challenge and dwell together in multicultural congregations. At the very least, finding ourselves in a newly multicultural society should cause us to be more critically self-aware of our own cultural practices and norms, whatever they may be, and to value them where they are appropriate — without confusing them with God.

Acts 10 and 11 do not settle or complete the matter for the early church. In our next chapter we will continue to find the church struggling with these issues, as well as related ones, occasioned by the mission to the gentiles and their response to the gospel. As we shall see, the solution of the Jerusalem Council involves measured change, change that responds to God's leading and honors cultural practices that have deep — and religious — significance. Our hunch is that, if we in the church today are to negotiate the challenges and receive the blessings of our own multicultural settings, it will be essential for us to embrace some similar capacity for a both/and approach: both gospel inclusion and diversity, and respect for cultural practices and cultural values.

Even so, it is also our hunch that congregations who observe the gospel first and culture second will be the most successful in this new time. In other words, we are correct to place the primary emphasis not on our congregation's greatness, our members' wonderful qualities, our great fellowship, or our terrific mission programs. The emphasis needs to fall, as in Acts, on God and what God is doing through us — and sometimes in spite of us. When the emphasis falls there, when God is the center and focus of our worship and of our life, then we have a point of commonality that transcends cultural differences. It does not mean that we deny or devalue cultural differences; but it does mean, as Peter discovers in this narrative, that it's about what God is doing.

The multicultural challenge and opportunity creates a host of possibilities for the church in North America. We will briefly suggest three. First, starting up and building congregations that are intentionally multicultural and multiracial. While some existing and long-established congregations may be able to make the transition to being multicultural, it is probably more feasible for congregations that are multicultural from the beginning — and who understand that as a crucial part of their identity and ministry — to succeed and thrive as multicultural congregations. We would hope to see an increasing number of church leaders trained particularly for this kind of ministry, and to see denominations put resources into starting new multicultural congregations.

Second, being reminded that the gospel does transcend any human culture, we wonder if there are ways in which we can encourage crossing cultural boundaries and borders in our own lives and communities. Many congregations that are primarily of one ethnic group or another have found their faith and ministry enriched by entering into a partnership with a congregation of a different cultural or ethnic make-up. Church members have learned much from such experiences, and studies are beginning to develop about building such partnerships. Not only can congregations cross cultural boundaries and barriers with such partnerships, but it can encourage individual members of congregations to do their own ministries of "border crossing." Mainliners can visit evangelicals; African-American Christians can pay visits to predominantly Anglo congregations; Asian-American Christians can get a conversation going with Coptic Christians from Ethiopia. There are all sorts of different cultures and boundaries among us — some racial and ethnic, some of social class, and some of theology. We should follow in the footsteps of Peter and go visiting. Who knows, maybe the Holy Spirit will interrupt our conversations!

Third, our multicultural reality reminds us that the church also transcends national boundaries. Particularly in times of war and suspicion between nations, the church can witness to a larger unity and reality by crossing national boundaries. A growing number of congregations today offer some version of the mission-trip experience. The agenda should not always be — or even primarily be — to go and do something for others who are in need and don't have what we have. The reality is, we may not have what *they* have. Sometimes it is the right agenda to simply be there, to be in fellowship, to see what it means to be a Christian in Nicaragua or China or Palestine or in another part of one's state or city. It is important to see the world and the Savior of the world, insofar as it is possible, through the eyes and experience of another.

Finally, there are congregations and communities that will remain racially and culturally homogeneous. That is not wrong. We are not somehow "less than" or deficient if we are mostly Caucasian or mostly Asian or anything else. And this is simply the reality for some congregations. Whoever we are, wherever we are, the point is to be the best church for God that we can be. God will do the rest.

STUDY QUESTIONS

1. Describe the pattern of God's grace that provokes Peter to a better understanding of God's relations with those non-Jews Israel considers unclean and unfit to enjoy a covenant relationship with God.

2. How does this chapter's most important theological claim, that "God shows no partiality" (10:34), square with the conversion story of Cornelius, whose personal manner evidently attracts God's favorable attention (10:1-4)? Does what kind of person one is make a difference in whom God saves? Does character contribute to conversion? Use examples from Scripture, history, or personal experience to illustrate your responses.

3. Christians must get converted too! In this case study, Peter's conversion to a more correct understanding of God and God's purposes for all people continues to unfold as he is led to gentiles. Can you think of an experience of "continuing conversion" in your own life?

4. Imagine that you were part of a new multicultural congregation. What, in your view, would be crucial to making that experience work and grow?

5. How do the conversion stories of Acts confirm or challenge the mental or theological associations you have made with "conversion"? Does Acts suggest that a person must have the experience of conversion in order to be saved? Is a conversion experience reduced to a single kind, when a sinner becomes a saint?

10 The Challenge of Change in the Church

PART I: INTERPRETING ACTS 15:1-29 AS SCRIPTURE

Two internal conflicts regarding Paul's mission to the nations, first in Antioch (15:1-2) and then in Jerusalem (vv. 4-5), occasion a second Jerusalem Council that assesses God's redemptive plans in light of mission reports (vv. 6-12) and biblical teaching (vv. 13-21). The result is a pastoral letter James sends to Antioch that lists the council's general agreements made for the sake of Christian unity (vv. 22-29).

Most interpreters of Acts fail to recognize that the question raised by Pharisaic members of the Jerusalem congregation, which occasions this Jerusalem Council, is by nature *halakhic* (i.e., clarifying the relevance and authority of Israel's biblical laws) and does not concern the legitimacy of gentile salvation. Jewish believers are rightly concerned whether a pagan who has repented but has not completed a purification routine prescribed by Hebrew tradition will contaminate the purity of the entire congregation. Their concern is not only about the possible corrosive effect on its public identity but also on its covenant relationship with God.

The Jerusalem church had earlier rendered a decision regarding the salvation of repentant gentiles (the "unclean") following Cornelius's conversion (11:1-18). For this reason, the decision rendered here by James, while agreeing with Peter that the observance of Jewish traditions regarding the purification of gentile converts does not save (15:10, 19), in fact prohibits a range of pagan religious practices (v. 20). But his reasons for doing so are sociological, not soteriological: they have more to do with fellow-ship between believers than fellowship with God.

In what sense is this episode a watershed for the rest of Acts, especially the following narrative of Paul's mission to the nations? While the council validates what God has already done according to Acts, its verdict offers readers nothing new. Nor does James's "decree" alter Paul's message or the pattern of his mission from what we have already observed in Acts 13–14. The reader of Acts is thus no more or less confident of Paul's authority after Acts 15 than before, where his importance in the history of God's salvation is made clear when fulfilling Jesus' prophecy about him (see 9:15-16). All that is left to tell in Acts is the story of how Paul gets to "the end of the earth"; whether he will do so is never in doubt before or after this Jerusalem Council. Rather than a "watershed," then, Acts 15 is more a moratorium that readies the reader for that end of the story.

The Jerusalem Council here in Acts 15 is a story of conflict resolution. A precise definition of the conflict that is resolved is thus pivotal for the telling of the story. Making that precise definition, though, is more difficult than is sometimes thought because there are actually two conflicts, within two different congregations, that need resolution. The first intramural conflict takes place in Syrian Antioch, where Paul's mission report (14:47-48) apparently provokes a protest from "certain individuals from Judea" who claim to be members of the Jerusalem church (cf. 15:24). Their protest concerns the pattern of gentile conversion — whether circumcision is a required public expression of a pagan's repentance and thus necessary for salvation. Behind this protest stands a long-standing religious conviction that the rite of circumcision is central to Israel's identity as a people who are covenanted with God for future blessing (see Gen. 17). For this reason, when the Syrian occupation had attempted to suppress the practice of circumcision two centuries earlier, they did so knowing its political importance to Jews for maintaining their distinctively national identity. Israel revolted under its Maccabean leadership (cf. 1 Macc. 1:60-61) to assert circumcision as a national priority (1 Macc. 2:46). Therefore, they viewed the defining of Jewish identity in terms other than circumcision as opposition to God and grounds for exclusion from the covenant community (1 Macc. 1:11-15). Naturally, circumcision was expected of every gentile convert to Judaism who expected a share of Israel's promised blessings.

Beyond Palestine, however, the literal observance of this initiatory rite was not usually practiced. By the time of the early church, the purification of a gentile convert has become more a symbolic exercise, a matter more of the heart than of the flesh. The spiritualizing of circumcision (making it more symbolic than literal) may well have upset the conservative Jews of Judea, who believed in a literal circumcision and perhaps now believed that the earlier Syrian apostasy had revisited the church of Syrian Antioch. Of course, the first Jerusalem Council had already given tacit approval to the conversion of the uncircumcised Cornelius (11:18); so these present protesters apparently constitute a small faction within the Jewish church, a group that is acting "without portfolio" from their religious leaders in Jerusalem (v. 24). Even though they have no religious authority, they presume that they are custodians of the church's Jewish legacy, and they foment unrest within the more liberal Antiochene church by declaring, "Unless you are circumcised according to the custom of Moses, you cannot be saved" (v. 1).

Of course, the readers of Acts know they are wrong. As early as the day of Pentecost, Peter quotes the prophet Joel to establish God's normative pattern of salvation during the "last days" of Israel's history: "Everyone who calls upon the name of the Lord will be saved" (2:21) — the very theological moment that foreshadows the whole direction of Acts. Even so, the result of their protest is "no small dissension and debate"; so a delegation is appointed "to discuss this question with the apostles and elders of Jerusalem" (v. 2).

Acts leaves unclear why the "question" concerning the salvation of repentant pagans requiring circumcision remains relevant, since this very question has already been settled. In fact, we are told that on the way to Jerusalem the Antiochene delegation "reports [*ekdiegeomai*] the conversion of the gentiles," which is favorably received (v. 3). The implication of this transition from Antioch to Jerusalem is that the delegation's primary concern is not the salvation of repentant gentiles at all, and even anticipates the tacit dismissal of the original "question" for another.

The pattern of mission report-reaction repeats itself in Jerusalem, though in much softer tones. Paul and Barnabas are welcomed by the whole "church," which hears their mission report of "all that God had done with them [*met' autōn*]" (v. 4; par. 14:27-28). Pharisees are typically the first to complain when religious Jews fail to live within carefully prescribed social and theological boundaries, especially when they are sharing table fellowship with impure sinners. Pharisees are interested in clarifying a Jewish way of life according to the Torah. A firm commitment to the purity of Israel's religious life within a world ruled by pagan Rome is the central plank of their political platform.

For this reason, their perspective on the conversion of repentant pagans is slanted differently from that voiced by Paul's opponents in Syrian Antioch (v. 1). These Pharisees are hardly troublemakers, and they justifiably press for a legal (or *halakhic*) definition of those religious practices required of repentant gentiles: whether they should include circumcision in accordance with Torah and Jewish tradition. The central issue for deliberation, then, is whether the practice of circumcision and Torah observance should remain public symbols of a repentant pagan's solidarity with biblical Israel in shared witness to the risen Christ in the world. The question is no longer whether the uncircumcised gentile is saved from sin; rather, the Pharisees ask for clarification of the sociology of "table fellowship" within a mixed congregation of the kind found in Antioch (cf. 11:19-26) — but presumably not yet in Jerusalem — whether the ritual cleansing of non-proselyte gentiles should be a requirement of membership.

Their claim is introduced by the provocative use of the word *dei:* "It is necessary [*dei*] for [repentant gentiles] to be circumcised." The use of *dei* in Acts as a literary theme marks out those moments that are scripted by God according to biblical prophecy. The subsequent discussion turns on this question: whether "it is necessary" for the purity of repentant gentiles to agree with Israel's Scripture. First Peter (vv. 7-11), then Barnabas and Paul (v. 12), and finally James (vv. 13-21) will respond to this implied question, and the new consensus will shape the plot line of Paul's story in Acts.

The "church," including its Pharisaic constituency (v. 5), is now excused so that their "apostles and elders" can meet in executive session (cf. 6:1-2; 11:1-2). Too much has been made of the politics of this assembly and whether Luke's passing reference to "apostles and elders" says anything about the dynamics of the Jerusalem community in moving from apostolic rule to elders' rule. In fact, the succession to new leadership within Jerusalem has already taken place (see 11:30; 12:17), which is why the apostle Peter merely provides testimony that Pastor James interprets (and even corrects) for the administrative council. The more important phrase is "to consider [literally, to look into] this matter," which suggests that this assembly convenes as a rabbinic court of law to deliberate on a case requiring *halakhic* adjudication.

Scholars often comment that Peter's testimony is cast in Pauline terms, following closely the argument found in Paul's epistle to the Romans (which the narrator Luke probably knew well). Peter's claim that God chose him to carry "the message of the good news" to the gentiles, along with the pairing of their "hearing and believing," loudly echoes Paul's own description of his apostolic vocation (v. 7b; cf. Rom. 1:5). Peter's reference to God's investigation of the human "heart" (v. 8; cf. Rom. 8:27), without partiality (v. 9b; cf. Rom. 2:11; 3:22), according to a person's faith (v. 9a; cf. Rom. 10:8-10) also follows the deep logic of Paul's gospel. Finally, Peter's contrast between the impossibility of carrying out all the law's demands (v. 10; cf. Rom. 2:25-27) and the universal need for God's grace (v. 11) nicely formulates a familiar Pauline teaching (13:38-39; cf. Rom. 3:21-26; also Eph. 2:5-8).

And yet Peter's portrait in Acts stands behind his words: here is the friend of Jesus, his principal apostolic successor, whose powerful prophetic ministry had congregated a restored Israel in fulfillment of biblical prophecy. Here is the Peter whose miraculous escape from prison merely adds the most recent climactic entry to the curriculum vitae of his life's work. Here is the legendary prophet-like-Jesus par excellence whose witness is unimpeachable. He alone — not James or Paul — has the authority to define the terms of Israel's identity in response to the concern of his Pharisee brothers that the community maintain its commitment to Torah purity.

For this reason, then, Peter's reference to himself as God's "choice" (*eklegomai*) to initiate the mission to unclean gentiles recalls other uses of this expression in Acts that refer to a divine initiative in fulfilling God's redemptive purposes in the world (see 1:2, 24-25; 6:5; 13:17). Even more striking is the phrase "the message [*logos*] of the good news," which occurs only here in the New Testament (cf. 20:24). The use of the noun "good news" instead of its verbal form, which Luke uses often, may well refer to the collection of kerygmatic claims the reader will recall Peter proclaimed to Cornelius (see 10:34-43).

From his initial claim that God has chosen him to bring the word of salvation to the gentiles, Peter speaks of the gift of the Holy Spirit as an act of divine testimony to Cornelius (see 10:44-47). Perhaps this reworks the curious timing of the gentile Pentecost, when the Spirit filled Cornelius before Peter had a chance to finish his gospel presentation. There was at the time no outward gesture of belief or "altar-call" experience indicated by Cornelius; yet God, "who knows the human heart" (v. 8), gave them the Holy Spirit as a testimony to what God found there. That this gift of salvation is predicated on inward trust and not outward legal compliance may very well impose a standard of "divine necessity" on this hearing that opposes the Pharisees' requirement of circumcision, an outward (and human) rather than an inward (and divine) testimony of purity.

The final and most important element of Peter's theological reflection repeats in a sharper way the central claim of his initial review of the Cornelius event in Acts 11:17: "God has made no distinction [*diekrinen*] between them [gentiles] and us [Jews]" (v. 9). Significantly, Peter's repetition of "making no distinction" recalls his own conversion to accepting God's embrace of uncircumcised Cornelius, and then also by the Jerusalem church, whose leaders had reacted to the report of Cornelius's conversion with criticism (*diekrinonto;* 11:2). This string of textual connections follows the repetition of *diakrinō* in Acts 10–15, which emphasizes the difficult history of the present debate and also reminds the reader of God's favorable "judgment" of repentant gentiles, even though they were uncircumcised.

Peter's own experience of conversion prompts him to conclude that the hearts of gentiles are "cleansed [*katharaizō*] by faith" rather than by the ritual purification of circumcision. His conclusion is different here from what it was before, when it emphasized the gift of the Holy Spirit as God's signature of approval. For this *halakhic* setting, Peter expresses a definition of purity relevant to repentant pagans.

Having rounded off his theological reflection on the Cornelius event, Peter is now in a position to draw more practical implications apropos of this assembly's objectives. Peter's rhetorical question, "Why are you putting God to the test?" (v. 10), calls the council back to the case study advanced by the Pharisaic believers: whether the circumcision of gentiles is a "divine necessity." Most commentators take Peter's rhetoric as challenging, even polemical. But why should it be? This is a juridical gathering among colleagues who are attempting to render a verdict in a difficult case.

Peter's argument is neither novel nor revolutionary. He draws on Moses himself to warrant his claims: that true circumcision is of the heart rather than of the flesh is attested by several sacred texts in Hebrew Scripture (cf. Lev. 26:41; Deut. 10:16; 30:6; Jer. 4:4; 9:25-26; Ezek. 44:7-9). No doubt the eschatological horizon of this Jewish teaching is Jeremiah's "new covenant," when restored Israel would live in covenant with God forever by virtue of its transformed (and therefore obedient) heart (Jer. 31:33), an eschatological horizon already envisioned by the believer because of Jesus. God's promises to Israel are not revoked — and its true identity is realized — because of him (cf. Rom. 9–11).

The Pharisees' concern for the purity of the church's social identity is misplaced if defined only by external practices, such as circumcision, rather than by God's cleansing of the believer's heart "through the grace of the Lord Jesus." In a striking way, Peter addresses the Pharisees' concern about Jewish identity in continuity with the community of goods, the community "who believed with one heart and soul" under the aegis of God's "great grace" (see 4:32-33).

Barnabas and Paul's final mission report of what "God had done" continues and climaxes the theme of Peter's original Pentecost speech (see 2:22): God's election of Peter to carry the gospel to the gentiles and God's testimony to them in the "gentile Pentecost" is now consummated by Barnabas and Paul's prophetic work among the gentiles. According to Luke's telling, God's work through these prophets-like-Jesus is "scripted" by Scripture as the fulfillment of biblical prophecy; thus the catch phrase "signs and wonders" is added to cue up Joel's prophecy, which in turn underwrites this final mission report.

Having heard all the relevant evidence from the mission field, James, the new leader of the Jerusalem church, is prepared to render a verdict. The theological method used by James considers first the religious experience testified to by both Peter (vv. 6-11) and then Barnabas and Paul (v. 12). Their missionary experience indicates God's intention of calling out of the nations "a people for his name" (vv. 13-15). Such experiences of gentile conversions, however, must finally be "read" by Scripture. Thus James turns from a summary of religious experiences to Israel's Scripture, citing a prophecy from Amos that provides a prophetic co-text that thickens the meaning of the oral arguments presented to the council.

In due consideration of Peter, Barnabas, and Paul, James addresses the council only "after they finished speaking," and he summarizes the previous testimony: "Simon has related how God looked favorably on the Gentiles" (v. 14). James's use of Peter's Aramaic name is not the result of the narrator's love of sounding archaic to suggest the past, or else we should expect it reflected elsewhere in Acts — which is not the case. Luke's use of Peter's "other" name is a strategic ploy to cue the reader to a shift of narrative theme. And thus, following his brief summary of the case against circumcising repentant gentiles, James moves on to a more relevant *halakhic* matter that will plot the action of the rest of Acts.

While religious experience establishes the theological precedent that challenges religious tradition, such precedents must necessarily align with "the words of the prophets," which script the redemptive plans of God. James's use of the plural "prophets" is perplexing in view of the fact that he quotes only Amos. It's more likely that this formulation pertains to a consensual prophecy and follows the sense of the formula's earlier uses in Acts, when the speaker invokes the testimony of "all the prophets" even though referring to a single prophetic witness (see 3:24; 10:43). In this sense, the prophecy from Amos that James cites will speak for "all the prophets" in clarifying this robust evidence in favor of a circumcision-free mission to the gentiles.

The quoted prophecy and James's subsequent commentary on it has become a storm center of criticism on the Acts of the Apostles. There are two textual issues that face the careful reader. The significant changes made when translating the Amos prophecy from Hebrew into Greek (LXX) allow James to use the Septuagint version of Amos in responding to the issue and expanding on the problem of including repentant pagans in a faith community founded on a Jewish legacy. According to the Hebrew version, the promise of Israel's restoration is coupled with the promise that Israel would reclaim the lands of Edom and all the other nations as well; the Greek (LXX) version promises only that Israel's restoration will make it possible for "all other peoples to seek the Lord." By using LXX Amos, James is able to confirm that Peter's earlier witness, supported by Barnabas and Paul's report, agrees with God's prophesied script: God allows "all other peoples" (i.e., uncircumcised gentiles) to share in Israel's blessings (i.e., forgiveness of sins, gift of the Spirit, eternal life) without first becoming proselyte Jews.

The second problem is trying to understand the role Amos's prophecy performs in Acts: why is it quoted at length and at this pivotal moment? Richard Bauckham has observed that the prophecy belongs to a collection of well-known prophecies (Isa. 45:21; Jer. 12:16; Zech. 2:11-15) that predict the rebuilding of a "third" temple, which Amos predicts as the rebuilt "tent of David." According to rabbinic interpretation, this temple would provide the centerpiece of a restored nation and hence be a gathering point for the eschatological conversion of the nations (see Acts 3:23-25). This reading of Amos is glossed by the earlier Stephen story, where the latter's "false" accusations regarding the Lord's prophecy of the temple's destruction led to his execution. In responding, Stephen argued that Jerusalem's temple plays no role in Israel's restoration since the Messiah alone is the exclusive means of purifying and restoring Israel's covenant with God.

A second resonance is even more important because it gives expression to James's own reticence concerning the question of gentile purification. The very prohibitions that James catalogs in verse 20 (cf. 15:29; 21:25) are linked to religious practices of pagan temples and the object of Israel's outrage. The prophecy's subtext, then, may be this: while Messiah has replaced the temple as the means of Israel's purification, there remain the practices associated with pagan temples — "pollutions of idols," for example — that challenge the sovereignty of Israel's God. If Israel's blessings are extended to repentant gentiles, their response to Israel's God must then embrace the "rules of polite company" set out in Leviticus 17–18. According to this legislation, the conduct of "resident aliens" living or traveling in Israel must respect the holy land and Israel's God. By analogy, the perceived risk of Paul's mission to the nations is that, if pagans are set free from the requirements of Jewish proselytism and left to retain their former religious practices — idols, sexual immorality, food regulations — they will defile repentant Jews who are members of their congregations (cf. 1 Cor. 8–10). That is, the worshiping community is "holy land" in the Diaspora, and repentant gentiles are the "resident aliens" among its Jewish membership and must behave as such.

James begins his commentary on the Amos prophecy with an earnest "I have reached a decision [*krinō*]." This is not a personal opinion but the judgment *(krinō)* of someone of prominence who is in a position to render a verdict for the council. The "therefore" *(dio)* presumes a strong connection between James's verdict and the evidence that includes both personal testimony and Scripture and — from the reader's perspective — all of Acts up to this point. This evidence argues that "we should not trouble those Gentiles who are turning to God." The force of the verb "trouble" *(parenochlein)* denotes pestering someone against his will. In light of Peter's earlier admonition that requiring circumcision of converted gentiles "puts God to the test" (see v. 10), James may assume that to do so unduly "pesters" God against God's will. James's *halakha* is as straightforward as the evidence in hand: God's intention is to purify the hearts of gentiles who are not also Jewish proselytes.

The "but" *(alla)* signals a proviso to the religious liberty of repentant gentiles: James is unwilling to grant them carte blanche. The importance of this text within Acts should not be underestimated and requires the reader's careful attention. James is clearly not convinced by Peter's definition of purity that is only a matter of the heart by faith (15:9). For this reason he expands Peter's definition to include abstinence from four unclean public practices: (1) idolatry, (2) sexual immorality, (3) eating strangled food or (4) food with blood. As argued above, these prohibitions are adapted from Leviticus 17–18, originally written to legislate the behaviors of "resident aliens" living in the holy land among Jews. James adapts them here to guide the public practices of repentant gentiles within the Christian congregations of the Diaspora where Torah is read every sabbath (v. 21). James's *halakha* proffers moral guidelines to ensure that fellowship in a mixed congregation will nurture faith rather than corrupt it: that is, a lack of sensitivity to the traditional requirements of spiritual growth in Jewish believers would have an adverse effect on them (cf. 1 Cor. 8–10; Rom. 14).

The implied contrast between the consecrated conduct found in a place where "Moses has been preached" and the profane behaviors found in the pagan temple adds another layer of meaning to this catalog of prohibitions. To abstain from "things polluted by idols" refers to the food offered in pagan temples, which is contaminated by contact with idol worship (cf. LXX Mal. 1:7). The second behavior, "fornication" *(porneia)*, has broad moral currency in Greco-Roman moral thought but may here refer simply to temple prostitution. The other two impurities from which the gentile convert must abstain fall into the category of food laws: do not eat "strangled food" or "food with blood." The Levitical injunctions regarding table fellowship extend not only to certain kinds of foods but also to food preparation.

We can understand James's concerns more fully if we view them within the more complete context of Acts. The meeting places of believers gather together those "with one heart and soul" (4:32) for instruction, fellowship, breaking bread, and worship (see 2:42-47). It is a society whose structure remains profoundly sensitive to the selfless awareness of the needs of others, without which there will be internal strife at the cost of external witness. But his concern is now understood in the context of Leviticus, where contact between the circumcised and uncircumcised poses a threat to God's relations with both. Even so, James supposes that the only good gentile is a "God-fearing" one — one who is attached to the synagogue and knows Moses. And the Paul of Acts finds most of his gentile converts in the synagogue; the only reported failure from his first mission is in Lystra among Zeus worshipers (14:8-18). Even within the narrative world of Acts, Luke makes clear distinctions among gentiles that indicates a preference for "God fearers" and proselytes who seem more ready to embrace the gospel and to live in appropriate ways with their Jewish sisters and brothers.

On an initial reading, the reader may wonder how James's interest in table fellowship within the Christian synagogues of the Diaspora relates to the biblical prophecy just cited. Is it part of his *halakhic* midrash on Amos or a pastoral exhortation detached from the prophecy? If the gentile believers in the church are the gentiles of the prophecy, whose salvation is then confirmed by Scripture (the Amos prophecy), then his exhortation for them to remain pure according to biblical teaching (Lev. 17–18) should not be viewed as odd. The same Scripture that includes "all the Gentiles who are called by God's name" in Israel's blessings now makes their civility toward Israel's God obligatory.

The consensus now reached by "the apostles and the elders, with the whole church" concerns the dissemination of James's *halakhic* reading of the Amos prophecy: they "choose" to send a delegation to Antioch "with the following letter" to read aloud to believers there. The literary convention of communicating a prior decision by letter is similar to the "double vision" (see 9:10-18; 10:1-16) in that the letter reads back into the previous narrative and fills in gaps with added detail. The result in Acts is a more fully nuanced account of important moments that clarify God's purposes and the motives of those with whom God participates in the church's prophetic mission.

The members of the delegation are introduced and given credentials appropriate to an important task: they are of one mind, beloved, "who have risked their lives" for the Lord's sake, with the personal integrity to confirm orally the validity of what is written (vv. 25-27). More important than these character qualifications, however, is that what is written and carried to Antioch "has seemed good to the Holy Spirit" (v. 28). The content of James's reading of Scripture agrees with the intentions of its author, the Holy Spirit (see 1:16). Any interpretation of Scripture that is a word on target must enjoy a consensus that includes God's Spirit. The implied response to such an interpretation is obedience. The repetition of James's purity code changes the order of prohibited practices, placing "fornication" last, and replaces "polluted by idols" with "sacrificed to idols" to make more explicit the specific religious practices considered subversive of the Christian worship of Israel's God in a mixed congregation.

The epistolary benediction concludes with an exhortation and a closing greeting, similar to what we find at the end of a Pauline letter. The exhortation — "if you keep yourselves from these, you do well" — underscores the importance of reciprocity in any covenant relationship. Its conditionality commends the importance of human accountability to God's purposes, discerned by James from Scripture. This is not a pointless formality, a polite way of saying goodbye to friends. There will be other disputes within emerging Christianity that will require turning back to James's reading of Amos for support and clarity in moving the word of God forward. In opening "the door of faith to the Gentiles" (14:27), the early leaders of the church have allowed for a set of other concerns that will require constant cooperation between the faith community and the Holy Spirit.

PART II: ENGAGING ACTS 15 FOR TODAY'S CHURCH

We have already seen several instances in Acts of the church dealing with change, making decisions, and experiencing and resolving conflict. In Acts 1 the church faced a crucial decision: they had to determine a successor for Judas, a new apostle. Conflict broke out in Acts 6 when, as the church grew, the system for distributing food to those in need within the community of shared goods proved inadequate. But no instance of change and conflict in the book of Acts proved more challenging than that created by the gentile mission. The challenge of this change and the experience of conflict come to focus and resolution in Acts 15 at the Jerusalem Council. What can this experience teach us in the contemporary church about dealing with change, facing conflict, and resolving it? Acts 15 is instructive about the processes for dealing with both change and conflict — and in the substance of the issue at hand. We shall look at both issues: (1) the process of facing and resolving conflict and (2) the continuing significance of this particular change for substantive issues facing the church today.

But before we turn to Acts 15, we offer several observations about conflict in contemporary congregations. On one hand, there is a good deal of conflict in the church, in both denominations and in local congregations. Too many congregations are like dysfunctional families, stuck in conflicts that are never resolved and that continue to debilitate the mission and life of those congregations, inflicting fresh wounds on anyone who gets too close. Partly in response to the negative witness of just such conflicted congregations, we sometimes come to the misleading conclusion that the healthy congregation does not experience conflict, or that a good congregation is one where all are constantly in harmony and agreement. But that picture too often turns out to be yet another kind of dysfunctional family, the one where differences are swept under the rug and people merely pretend that there are no disagreements or arguments, issues or conflicts. That is neither healthy nor faithful. By way of an alternative, one recalls the line of the great Jesuit theologian John Courtney Murray: "A good argument is a great achievement." Because we so seldom see "good arguments," conflicts that are engaged thoughtfully and respectfully, and where there is resolution for the good of the church, many congregations and pastors become conflict avoiders. Acts suggests another way. Conflict can be productive, a sign of life rather than death. While it is seldom easy, successfully dealing with change and the conflict change often brings may strengthen a congregation and make possible new chapters of life and ministry.

Acts 15 gives us a crucial illustration of the church dealing with change and conflict. We can be grateful that our scriptural narrative does not pretend that the early church experienced uninterrupted harmony and agreement. Rather, the church had to deal with change, and it had to deal with conflict; and the conflict had to be resolved. Clergy and other congregational leaders can turn to Acts 15 for guidance in teaching and preaching before conflict comes, and in so doing they may provide the church with resources for dealing with change and conflict.

Conflicts Have a Prehistory

Seldom, if ever, do conflicts in the church spring into full-blown existence at a given moment without a prehistory, that is, without roots or antecedents. This is true in Acts 15 as well. Well before the issue of gentile inclusion, the salvation of the gentiles, and fellowship in mixed communities of Jews and gentiles came to the fore in Acts 15, the vexed issue was brewing. One could trace it all the way back to the Gospel accounts of the ministries of Jesus, and even to the narratives of strangers and foreigners playing crucial roles in the Old Testament. For our purposes, though, we will note the shorter history that begins with Paul's conversion and call in Acts 9, Peter's ministry among the gentiles in Acts 10, and Barnabas and Paul's leadership of a gentile congregation in Antioch. Reports of these developments had already created concern within the Jerusalem church.

Pastors and church leaders who deal with change and conflict in their own congregations are well advised to probe beneath the surface, to go beyond the "presenting issue," to look at the dynamics of the community — the roles and the behaviors of those in authority — and to tease out the story of the matter at hand. If the first step in congregational leadership is to establish trust, the second step is to gain an accurate picture of reality, of what is really going on. Clergy and lay leaders cannot do this with a surface-only analysis, a scrutiny of the "presenting issue" alone. Ron Heifetz counsels leaders to "get to the balcony" to observe the patterns on the congregational dance floor below. Lovett Weems claims that the key question for church leaders is: "'What is the nature of the situation in which we find ourselves?' Anything less is inadequate as a basis for next steps. Once there is a correct definition of reality, then, and only then, can planning begin regarding appropriate actions."[1]

For example, on arriving at my own first pastoral call, I found a congregation in serious and painful conflict. The identified issue was the action, only a few weeks earlier, of our denomination's general synod to "affirm the civil rights of gays and lesbians." "This is an outrage," said some. "We demand that this congregation cut off all financial support to the denomination immediately." "This is a good thing," said others. "We support protecting the civil rights of all people, including gays and lesbians." Some others said: "We don't really know whether it's a good thing or a bad thing, but we do know that the synod speaks for the synod, not us. We're not sure this is the most important matter for our congregation right now." The surface issue was homosexuality, civil rights, and our denomination.

Probing beneath the surface, however, I noted those who were most vocal as well as those who stood on the sidelines and said little. I inquired about the departure of my predecessor, the former pastor, and about the interim experience of the congregation. Trading on my newness, I bought some time. I discovered that the civil rights issue was part of it, but only part. The larger conflict and question really concerned the theological identity of the congregation and its relationship to our denomination. During the period between my predecessor's departure and my arrival, a number of people who were theological fundamentalists had come into the congregation — some of whom became members, some not. It appeared that they wanted to detach the congregation from the denomina-

---

1. Lorett H. Weems Jr., *Take the Next Step* (Nashville: Abingdon, 2003), p. 41.

tion and move it in a much more conservative direction. The synod's action had provided the catalyst they needed. To be sure, there were real issues and there was a real conflict resulting from the synod's pronouncement. But in this congregation it was not limited to the civil rights of homosexual persons. It was a question of theological identity and denominational affiliation. That was the prehistory of this particular conflict: Would the church be theological centrist in orientation, or would it become more theological conservative, even right-wing?

Framing the Issue

It is the responsibility of leaders, after they have established the prehistory and context of an issue, to frame the issue or question accurately. Among scholars there is some division of opinion regarding the conflict before the Jerusalem Council. Was the question, Can gentiles be saved and participate in God's salvation without also being circumcised? Or was it, more broadly, a question of adopting Jewish practices and a Jewish way of life? Others suggest that the question was not about whether gentiles could participate in God's salvation. That was accepted. Rather, the question was: What is necessary for there to be fellowship — table fellowship — in this new and mixed community of gentiles and Jews? Whether the question was about salvation or fellowship, the matter was still one of Jewish life and practice and its place among followers of Jesus Christ. What, if anything, should be required of gentiles who were entering the life, faith, and fellowship of the church? In facing change, the church was confronted with the critical question raised by change: What is precious and what is expendable? What is core to our faith and identity, and what is not? These are certainly challenging questions, but they are also good questions — and important ones. They are crucial questions for healthy communities and congregations. Moreover, they are contemporary questions: What is precious and what is expendable for our congregations today?

Framing the question for discernment is a crucial step and skill. As we have noted earlier, some conflicts, because they are not accurately framed, are not productive or even capable of resolution. If the underlying question is, "How do we keep everyone happy?" then useful conflict — as well as resolution — is unlikely. Gil Rendle of the Alban Institute notes: "Systems are notoriously adept at colluding around answers that will not make a difference."[2] We might also observe that congregations are adept at colluding around questions that are poorly framed.

In the story of my first pastorate, the framing question, partly because my pastorate was so new, became: How can we be in fellowship with one another when we hold different views? And what is the basis of our fellowship? The next step for that congregation was to commit to participation in ten weeks of Bible study and prayer in small groups, with the groups made up of church members with diverse points of view. Seventy percent of the congregation took part in these groups over the next three months, building community, clarifying questions, exploring the core convictions of our faith. We worked carefully through 1 Corinthians, where congregational division and factionalism is a central focus. If we had simply taken a vote on denominational affiliation or on the civil rights of gays and lesbians, I believe that we would have been missing the real issues of the identity and direction of that congregation.

Hearing Testimony

In dealing with change and conflict, we should follow Acts in paying attention to the prehistory of the conflict and carefully defining the issues or questions for debate and discernment. In Acts the next move was for the body of apostles and elders to listen to the testimony of those involved. What had Peter, Paul, and Barnabas experienced? What did they perceive God to be doing? What was going on? Thus we have a deliberative body listening to the testimony of what people have seen, heard, and experienced. By definition, testimony is not primarily argumentation for a position. Rather, it is telling what we have witnessed — telling our story.

In the midst of congregational struggles with change and conflict, it is often both useful and necessary to invite testimony. People should be allowed to tell their story and their truth; they should be encouraged to speak in their own voice. "You're wrong, I'm right" is not testimony. Testimony is: "This is what I have seen. This is what I have experienced. This is my experience of God and of the Spirit." It is a truism of conflict resolution, but one that is nonetheless worthy of repetition, that often what people wish for and need the most is simply to be heard. In congregations we

---

2. Rendle, quoted in Weems, p. 40.

have to say, "Tell us your story. What is your testimony about this?" The council of apostles and elders listened carefully to the testimony and experience of Peter, Paul, and Barnabas.

Sources of Authority and Developing Paths for Resolution

The fourth move, depending on how we read and interpret Acts 15, is either the rendering of a judgment or a decision by James, or it is a proposal from James that is then accepted by the body. This procedural step raises several important questions for congregations today as they face conflict and change. Is there a recognized "teaching office" (or "magisterium") that has been designated and empowered to render judgments and plot decisions? Or, to put it another way, is there some source, position, office, or group of members who hold authority within the community, and if so, on what basis? Community, we would suggest, does require authority: that is, some office, body, position, or group of people who are able to render judgments and to establish norms for group life. Perhaps part of the reason that many congregations are averse to conflict today is that there is no recognized, accepted, or legitimate authority. Such authority could be vested in an elder such as James, or it could be a process of discernment to which the community agrees, or it could be existing norms that can be interpreted and applied to situations as they arise. In the absence of such an agreed-upon authority or shared norms and values, conflict resolution is nearly impossible, and conflict itself often degenerates into personal attacks. Before getting into an issue, a congregation should agree on what will function as legitimate authority for reaching a decision. Will it be the office of the pastor, or the congregation itself, or some combination of the two? What will function as an authoritative source of norms for our community of faith? Will it be Scripture, a creed or covenant, or the constitution or by-laws of the congregation?

Social analyst and critic Alan Ehrenhalt says: "There is no easy way to have an orderly world without somebody making the rules by which order is preserved. Every dream we have about re-creating community in the absence of authority will turn out to be a pipe dream in the end."[3] Here in the Jerusalem Council, the elder James plays such a role. After testimony has

3. Alan Ehrenhalt, *The Lost City* (New York: Basic Books, 1995), p. 21.

been heard and there has been "much debate" (v. 7), James takes the floor and says, "Brethren, listen to me" (v. 13). James bases his position and judgment in Scripture and renders a verdict and a proposal. The proposal is considered and supported by the entire body of the council as they seek the guidance of the Holy Spirit: "For it seemed good to the Holy Spirit and to us to lay upon you no greater burden than these necessary things" (v. 28).

From Democracy to Discernment

While different congregations and denominations have different histories and practices, congregations that attempt to deal with change and resolve conflict are not primarily engaged in an exercise in democracy, but an exercise in discernment. The distinction is a crucial one. Democracy, which honors important values, seeks the will of the majority; discernment seeks the will of God and the mind of Christ. In a gathering informed by the norms of democracy, everyone has a right to speak because everyone is entitled to his or her opinion. When engaged in discernment, we listen to others not because they have a right to their opinion but because we never know through whom the Holy Spirit may speak. Too often church meetings are conceived as exercises in democracy, attempts to discern the will of the majority and to line up the votes that will help the position of our choice prevail. Discernment is different: the focus is on being open to and discovering God's will for us. While discernment practice can also be abused, as a perspective and approach it is more congruent with the identity and nature of the church. Today many good guides to the traditional and ancient practices of congregational discernment are available.

The Jerusalem Council was an exercise in discernment. The council was composed of "apostles and elders," those with experience in seeking God's will. They heard testimony regarding believers' experiences of God; and they used Scripture to sanction and interpret a proposal that seems "good to the Holy Spirit and to us." Though few would claim that discernment can claim to know God's will fully or without question, the framing of such inquiry as discernment does make a difference — a positive and faithful difference.

Conflicts Have a Posthistory

In the case of Acts 15 and the Jerusalem Council, the matter at hand is not over and done when the council adjourns. Paul's mission to the gentiles continues to find a mixed reception among the believers in Jerusalem, which was one reason for Paul's return to Jerusalem later in Acts. Moreover, the terms of the James resolution and judgment need review and updating (Acts 21).

In the story from my own pastoral ministry that I have cited above, resolution came, in time, regarding the congregation's relationship with our denomination, and there was an interpretation of the denominational action and its significance for our congregation. Perhaps more importantly, there was a deepened and renewed understanding of what it meant to be the body of Christ, a body of "many parts, but one body." The resolution and affirmations we made at the time continued to be deepened and tested in future decisions in the life of the congregation. There was a need for ongoing pastoral work, both in teaching and in pastoral care, as the decision and resolution to our particular questions played themselves out. But as in Acts, the final test of the way the church dealt with the challenge of change and conflict really was the future health, faithfulness, and vitality of the congregation. Did we, as a community of Christ, grow stronger or weaker from the process we experienced and the decisions we reached?

To sum up the process we have derived from Acts 15, we see the following steps and convictions as central: (1) conflicts have a prehistory to which attention must be paid; (2) accurate framing of the issue and question at hand is crucial; (3) eliciting and hearing testimony is an important part of the discernment process; (4) prior agreement concerning what or who has an authoritative or normative role for a congregation is critical; (5) the church practices discernment, not democracy; (6) conflicts, once resolved, have a posthistory and require continuing interpretation and pastoral attention. In these six points or movements, Acts 15 shows the early church dealing with change and conflict, and it provides clues for congregations that wish to do the same today.

In the second part of this chapter, we shift our focus once again — from the process evident here to the substantive matters under consideration and to their significance — analogically — in the church today. We will consider two substantive matters here: (1) homosexuality and the church, and (2) Christian faith as a way of life.

Homosexuality and the Church

Many denominations and congregations are struggling today with the challenges of sexuality, and particularly homosexuality. May gay or lesbian persons — those who are openly so — be members of congregations? May gay or lesbian persons be united in something analogous to marriage in the church? May gay and lesbian persons serve in leadership roles in congregations, and may they be ordained to Christian ministry? The issues are complex and tangled. These conflicts have complicated prehistories and winding roots, both in the often harsh treatment of homosexual persons by their churches and in the larger matters of a sexually permissive and harmful society. We cannot pretend to address this issue in anything like an exhaustive way here, nor do we wish to do so. What we can do is suggest how Acts 15 and the matter of gentile inclusion may or may not be a pertinent analogy to the issue of homosexual participation in congregations.

We note two aspects of the church's debate over gentile inclusion — and in the Jerusalem Council particularly. First, there is the experience of God, of the activity of the Holy Spirit, showing Paul, Peter, and others that what they had held to be unclean is not unclean in God's eyes. In Peter's words, "God shows no partiality" (Acts 10:34). Moreover, in the Jerusalem Council the experience-based testimony of believers interprets Scripture, not the other way around. It could be argued that here "experience trumps Scripture." The experience of visions, of the baptism of the Holy Spirit, of the fellowship of Jews with gentiles, opens new insights into Scripture and its interpretation. Is it possible for the testimony of those who have the experience of Christian faith, the baptism of the Holy Spirit, and the fellowship of straight and gay to provide new insight into Scripture?

The second aspect of the Jerusalem Council decision moves in a different, though perhaps complementary, way. The resolution proposed by James includes purity practices that ancient Israel enjoined on resident aliens and sojourners in its midst. These include not worshipping idols, abstaining from sexual immorality, and observing Jewish practice with regard to food preparation and foods to be eaten. This shows an expectation of holy living and observing of purity practices as part of Christian life and fellowship. A crucial part of this injunction is abstaining from *porneia*, or sexual immorality. What, by analogy, might this suggest for the matter of homosexuality and the church? Does it mean that all homosexual acts fall under the proscription against *porneia?* Or might it mean that sexual promiscuity is proscribed but that covenanted and lifelong fidelity between homosexual individuals is not? Should the church ask persons who have a same-sex orientation to practice a celibate life, or is sexual practice within a covenanted relationship of fidelity to be accepted and supported? These are not easy matters or questions, and different Christians and communities of faith have come to different conclusions and resolutions about them. In some respects, we as the church in North America are engaged in a protracted season of discernment over this challenge.

We do believe that Acts 15 speaks to these challenging questions. We also believe that congregations and denominations that pay attention to the demands of a holy life for gay and lesbian persons do well to pay proportionate attention to what is required of heterosexual people.

Christian Faith as a Way of Life

We have previously noted the provocative observation of the biblical scholar James Sanders that Christianity took the *mythos,* or belief aspect of faith, while Judaism took the *ethos,* or the way-of-life emphasis. This is, of course, an extremely broad generalization for which there are many exceptions; yet it is useful if for no other reason than to call attention to Christian ambivalence about particular practices that embody and express a way of life that is pleasing to the Lord and holy. This ethos, or "way of life," aspect of faith has been undervalued and even considered suspect because of a disproportionate emphasis in North American Christianity on justification at the expense of sanctification and vocation. Or, to put it another way, the Protestant churches in North America have been heavily influenced by the Reformation themes of "salvation by grace alone." An emphasis on a way of life that is holy and pleasing to God has, with some notable exceptions, been subject to charges of "salvation by works," "works righteousness," or the heresy of Pelagianism. This is one of the central matters at stake in the book of Acts; it is the challenge we have identified as "gentilizing."

North American Protestant Christians have often been so aware of the threat of "Judaizing," particularly as discussed in the books of Galatians and Romans, that they have become overvigilant about undermining God's free grace with an emphasis on works. But the issue is not that simple, and North American Protestants have often been so zealous to avoid the Scylla of "Judaizing" that we have been less cognizant of — sometimes even blind to — the Charybdis of "gentilizing," or losing the Jewish context and inheritance of Christian faith. One particular form of the gentilizing threat to which the book of Acts is a response is the matter of faith finding expression in a concrete, specific, visible, and public way of life. Or to put it another way, does grace require a response that is a coherent way of life pleasing to God? We believe it does, and that the book of Acts points a way toward balancing the long-standing emphasis on *mythos* with a complementary *ethos*.

Acts envisions a way of life that is holy and that is constituted by both purity practices, those things from which Christians abstain, and resurrection practices, those things Christians do. In the next chapter we will pay particular attention to these resurrection practices under the heading of "marks of discipleship." Here we note the purity practices that were part of the resolution regarding the question of gentile inclusion.

Under the influence of Reformed themes and "by grace alone," many have looked askance at Acts 15 as a kind of hedging against the radical grace of Pauline theology. Acts 15 and its purity practices have been seen, at least by some, as a compromise of the true faith. We view it differently, and we view it in two ways. First, these purity practices remind contemporary Christians and their leaders that purity practices have a place, not as a way of winning salvation, but as part of the life of the redeemed. The three particular practices noted in Acts 15 are not without contemporary significance, though they may also be treated more analogically as well. Christians are, said James, to abstain from worship of idols. We may not have idols today in the same sense that the ancient world did, but we do have idols — that is, created things to which we ascribe ultimate value (we shall return to idols and idolatry in Chapter 12). Second, James speaks of sexual morality and abstaining from *porneia*. In a society that is sex-saturated, where sex is often separated from bonds of fidelity, and where pornography flourishes, this matter is very much with us. Finally, the purity practices James enjoins on gentiles extend to what foods are eaten and how foods are prepared. Again, though the specifics may be different, there is considerable reason today for serious consideration of such dietary concern. "We are," at least in some measure, "what we eat." In a world of fast food and prepackaged foods, what and how we eat does have religious significance — that is, these are not moot or anachronistic points or matters.

What constitutes a way of life pleasing to God today, and what purity practices are appropriate to such a life in North America in the twenty-first century?

Finally — and apart from these specific practices — the emphasis on a way of life, on things believers do and don't do, has another and contemporary implication. James draws from the Levitical holiness code those injunctions that are applied to resident aliens living in Israel for the particulars of Acts 15:21. These will be necessary for Jews and gentiles in the new church and body of believers to have fellowship together. In our own time, what are the practices to be avoided and observed in order that we not offend our sisters and brothers? We may speak of this as being "culturally sensitive," which is a contemporary term for it; or we may describe this as Paul might: abridging our freedoms out of respect for the conscience and scruples of others. In any case, we avoid certain practices and enact others for a higher purpose — participating in community together. Part of a contemporary Christian ethos in a multicultural world and church will be sensitivity to the ways and conscience of those whose culture is different from our own. We do well, at least in some matters, to limit our freedom and not insist on our own ways, so that fellowship may exist and deepen in diverse communities and congregations of faith.

STUDY QUESTIONS

1. What connection does James make between the believer's real-life experiences of God at work and the teaching of Scripture? Which is most important for discerning God's purposes in saving the world from evil?
2. Acts makes it clear that disagreement between earnest believers should never be left unattended; disunity subverts the church's sacred vocation. From your study of this passage, write out the "rules of engagement" that guide the settling of conflicts within the church?
3. There is much talk today among young adults about "purity," often leading to their commitment to "abstain" from behaviors contrary to health and healthy relationships. Translate the three "purity practices" listed in 15:20 (also in 15:29 and 21:25) — abstaining from worship of idols, avoiding sexual immorality, and a concern for diet and food preparation — for a contemporary campus or faith community. How might such a code of purity practices function today in marking out a people as belonging to God?
4. Review the section entitled "From Democracy to Discernment." Does what

you read there provoke any new ideas or plans for action? List them. Does this section rather trouble you? What objections do you register and why?

5. Wall and Robinson claim that many churches are so concerned about the "Judaizing" threat — "Jewish" works trump "Christian" faith — that they have more often ignored the "gentilizing" threat — "Christian" faith trumps "Jewish" works. Try to put these concerns in your own words. Are they, in your view, significant? Why or why not?

11 *Resurrection Practices: The Marks of Discipleship*

PART I: INTERPRETING ACTS 16:11-40 AS SCRIPTURE

Even though Paul's urban mission remains centered in the synagogues of the Diaspora, his divinely sanctioned turn toward Europe and its great Roman cities reflects changes in cultural scenery and thus of mission strategy. Yet even this story in Acts 16 finds Paul following a pattern he established in his earlier city crusades: on the Sabbath he goes to a place of prayer to worship Israel's God with attentive God-fearing gentiles (vv. 11-15). But this place is not an urban synagogue, nor is Paul invited to interpret Scripture for a congregation of devout Jews who are also gathered for worship. This is an informal setting at a traveler's riverside rest stop outside the city limits, and the most responsive person in a group of religious women is a God-fearing gentile merchant named Lydia. She is Paul's first convert in Macedonia, and her house becomes the site of Europe's first Christian congregation.

Paul encounters much harsher treatment within Philippi's city limits, where he encounters the possessed slave girl (vv. 16-18; cf. 13:6-12), whose exorcism provokes a sharp legal challenge from her greedy owners, laced with anti-Semitic propaganda, resulting in the arrest of Silas and Paul, severe flogging, and harsh imprisonment. As with the twelve before them (cf. 5:17-18; 12:4-11), however, they are miraculously liberated from their shackles — in this case by a timely earthquake rather than a heavenly angel (cf. 5:19; 4:31). Unlike the apostles, however, Silas and Paul stay put and sing the praises of God while other prisoners listen, much to the surprise of the warden, who awakens to opened prison gates and the expectation of a nighttime jailbreak (cf. 5:20-26). His astonishment at finding his prisoners still imprisoned occasions the famous missionary exchange between the terrified warden, who asks, "What must I do to be saved?" and Paul, who responds, "Believe on the Lord Jesus and you will be saved." The result is the warden's conversion (vv. 28-34).

Paul and Silas are released from prison the next day without a public trial. But rather than depart with grateful acquiescence, citizen Paul excoriates the city's magistrates for their abuse of Roman justice (vv. 37-38). They personally come, hat in hand, and escort Paul and Silas from jail, thus restoring the missionaries' credibility. But the two do not leave the city before making a quick house call on Lydia and the congregation of new believers who are now meeting in her home.

Two Women of Philippi

Acts provides a traveling itinerary to move the reader with Paul to Macedonia (vv. 8-12). The team's base of operations is Philippi, "a leading city of the district of Macedonia" and a Roman colony thoroughly influenced by Greek culture and literature. The plot line of Paul's Philippian mission is shaped by two different encounters with two very different women. The first is "a certain woman named Lydia" whom Paul meets on a sabbath in a makeshift synagogue — in this case located outside of town as a "place of prayer" — that he frequents while in Philippi. Evidently, there is no synagogue in the city, which may indicate the lack of a quorum of ten Jewish males to convene an assembly of Jews for worship. This lack of an urban Jewish presence may explain the spiritual climate Paul finds once he enters the city. The term "place of prayer" *(proseuche)* is virtually synonymous with a synagogue, even though its use here emphasizes its insignificant location: outside the city gates and by a small river on the southern edge of town. All of this suggests that Philippi is a city untempered by a prophetic word about Israel's God.

Paul's sitting posture with women who "had gathered there" may indicate the beginning of a worship service during which Paul acts as guest liturgist and preacher. Lydia is among the women with whom he speaks, and several features of her profile in Acts indicate her importance for the wider

Philippiain mission (see v. 40) and good reason for her conversion. One of the implied conclusions of James's programmatic commentary on Amos was that God-fearing gentiles attached to synagogues where Moses is preached are the best candidates for conversion to the Messiah (15:21). For this reason the reader recognizes that the details of Lydia's spiritual biography are similar to those of Cornelius (cf. 10:1-4): she is a "worshiper of God, who was listening to us" (v. 14). The repetition of her "eager listening" to Paul's preaching because "the Lord opened her heart" may well be the result of good character, which is seen in her hospitality toward Paul. This connection between hospitality — sharing goods with others — and responsiveness to the word of God is an important literary theme in both Luke and Acts (cf. Luke 24:29-31), and an indication of Lydia's spiritual authority as first convert and leader of the church in Philippi.

Lydia is a "dealer in purple cloth" from Thyatira, a city well known for its textile industry (cf. Rev. 2:18-29). Several details of her professional résumé indicate her success: she owns her own business and her own home. The text does not mention a husband, which may indicate either that she is single or that her husband is not a believer. Purple clothing marked out the rich and the royal in the Roman world, and it symbolized power and influence in Luke's world. A merchant dealing in purple cloth would be someone who rubbed shoulders daily with the rich and famous. The fact that Lydia is referred to by a personal name may also indicate her social prominence. In the narrative world of Acts, however, the materially wealthy are nonetheless spiritually impoverished. Lydia's response to Paul's preaching would seem to illustrate this theological trend.

Both elements of Lydia's profile in Acts, then, make sense of the story's conclusion, when an exonerated Paul and his missionary team visit the congregation meeting in Lydia's house on their way out of Philippi and on to Thessalonica. Her baptism, with her household, marks the beginning of a witness to Paul's God within a city where God has been made known mainly through the utterances of the demon-possessed.

Paul's exorcism of the divining slave girl recalls a similar encounter that Jesus had, which is found in the Gospels (Mark 1:21-26; Luke 4:41). Mark's version of the story is especially instructive. Jesus is at the beginning of his messianic mission and enters the synagogue at Capernaum to worship with other pious Jews. Among those whom Jesus' ministry provokes is a demon-possessed member of the congregation, who alone knows Jesus' true identity. The encounter is strange for many reasons;

however, its message is plain: Jesus' spiritual authority is aptly demonstrated when he expels the demon from the person. The same point is made in a similar setting here in Acts 16: Paul's spiritual authority as a prophet-like-Jesus — indeed, the public truth of the spirit's claim about his mission of salvation — is confirmed by this exorcism. Paul's Holy Spirit is greater than the evil spirit who speaks through the girl.

The species of evil spirit speaking through the girl is literally "a pythian spirit," recalling the Greek *pythōn* myth of the dragon that guarded the Delphi oracle at Mt. Parnassus and was killed by Apollo. In Luke's day its name and legend were attached to someone with clairvoyant powers or perhaps the trickery of a "ventriloquist." The powers or trickery of this slave girl are apparently extraordinary, or the Philippian public is extremely gullible, because "she brought her owners a great deal of money by fortune-telling" (v. 16). In Acts, where "property" serves as a barometer of spiritual life, such evident exploitation of another for profit is especially blameworthy, not only on the part of the girl's owners but of the religious climate of Philippi that would support their religious profit-taking.

The slave girl publicly proclaims her supernatural knowledge of Paul's mission, and she continues to do so "for several days." In fact, her divination that Paul and Silas are "slaves of the Most High God, who proclaim to you a way of salvation" (v. 17) ironically introduces the kerygmatic claim that Paul's conversion of the Philippian warden will later illustrate (vv. 30-31). There is also the sense that she unwittingly has thrown down a gauntlet of sorts to Paul. The term "Most High God" is also used in the worship of Zeus, to whom her own handlers may be attached. Paul, of course, is "slave" to the Most High God of Israel (cf. 7:48), and his exorcism of the girl's pythian spirit is a clear demonstration of his God's authority over Zeus and all other pagan gods of the Philippian pantheon. Paul's demonstration of God's power then clears the way for a fuller expression of his own spiritual authority when he leads the warden's household into the "way of salvation" (cf. 4:12; also 2:28; 9:2).

The formula Paul uses to expel the evil spirit from the slave girl harks back to Peter's command for healing "in the name of Jesus Christ" (3:6, 16; 4:10). The prophet's use of "the name" to heal and make people whole again is not magical but confessional: Paul's rebuke of the spirit expresses his certainty of God's triumph over evil. While the exorcism is an exercise of his spiritual authority, it is also symbolic of his kerygmatic claim that the risen Jesus is Messiah and Lord (cf. 2:36). This exorcism itself, then, aptly illustrates what Paul will later proclaim to the warden, fulfilling the slave girl's own prophecy: the Most High God saves the lost and makes them whole again.

Luke routinely uses property as a theological symbol in Acts. How people dispose of their possessions embodies their religious affections (see 1:16-20; 2:42-47; 4:32–5:11; 6:1-7; 10:44-48; 11:27-30, etc.). Here is another case in point, scored with sarcasm by Luke. The animus toward religious charlatans, especially those who are exploiting human "property" to satisfy their greed, is often expressed in Greco-Roman literature. Luke shares this distrust (cf. 13:6-11) and adds a deeply felt religious dimension here.

The owners' immediate response to the healing of their slave girl is hardly happy, which is to be expected: "They seized Paul and Silas and dragged them before the authorities" (v. 19). Their motive for doing so is seen as baldly financial: they perceive that their profits have gone the way of the demon! The judicial terms used by Luke in this passage indicate that they are bringing a lawsuit against Paul for loss of income. The "market-place" *(agora)* is the city's secular synagogue, where people assemble to conduct various transactions, including legal ones. The greedy owners follow a precise protocol in bringing their claims to the courthouse: they go first to the "authorities" who are responsible for public order, and they turn Paul and Silas over to the local "magistrates," who are responsible for settling civil claims.

Perhaps realizing that loss of income due to the loss of a pythian spirit would not work well in a public court disposed against religious quackery, the owners bring a more mean-spirited — yet appealing — accusation before the magistrates in two parts: "These men are Jews and are [therefore] disturbing our city." Their first charge appeals to Roman anti-Semitism; it is propagandistic without having any legal merit. The clear intent is to incite prejudice against Jews in a pagan marketplace, and it is this appeal that sparks the crowd's hostilities against Paul and Silas. The second charge appeals to the legal "principle of incompatibility," according to which it is considered unlawful within the premises of a Roman colony to proselytize converts to a non-Roman cult (v. 21). This charge is also without merit because by Paul's day the principle was no longer followed in legal practice, and there is every indication that Paul recruited converts outside the city limits at the place of prayer; thus he was not in violation of this law in any case — unless exorcising the slave girl's demon in Jesus' name constituted an act of proselytizing her.

It is significant that Paul's religious practices, which are linked to the place of prayer, are recognized to be Jewish and in sharp contrast to the Roman "customs" of Philippi. In fact, the mob reaction against Paul and Silas, obviously incited by the crowd's anti-Semitic sentiment, makes this point all the more clear. Luke portrays Paul once again as an exemplar of James's primary concern for Jewish purity on pagan turf. Paul has not contaminated himself by accommodating pagan forms of religious observance: he has not become a "gentilized" Jew.

There is no indication of a court verdict, unless the violent crowd is considered a jury of sorts and their attack on Paul and Silas an indictment of "guilt." Without being granted any opportunity to defend their actions, they are stripped and beaten with rods by order of the magistrates and are then thrown into prison, where they are "securely" guarded (vv. 22-23). The magistrates' injudicious actions will come back to haunt them by story's end.

The warden will play a role complementary to Lydia's in this story. His transformation as the story unfolds exemplifies the very stuff of the transforming power of God's grace that Paul proclaims. He is introduced to us as the lackey of civil authority who "follows their instructions" by putting Paul and Silas in maximum security, with their feet "fastened in the stocks" (v. 24). These images of harsh treatment and loneliness serve two purposes: (1) They recall the Lord's prophecy that Paul would "suffer for the sake of my name" (9:16). Paul is now in prison because he has exorcized the girl's divining spirit "in the name of Jesus Christ," thus fulfilling his commissioning prophecy. He's right where he should be! (2) The warden's actions also stage the miracle that follows: surely there is no escape from "the inner prison" when one's feet are "in the stocks."

In Acts prisons symbolize the location where a cosmic battle between God and evil (or Zeus) is waged. What Paul and Silas are doing there, as God's agents, exemplifies God's triumphant response to evil: they are "praying and singing hymns to God" (v. 25). Their acts of devotion are resurrection practices. The other prisoners listen to their witness, and what those prisoners hear interprets the earthquake as God's answer.

The earthquake strikes "suddenly" and opens doors and unfastens chains. But no one leaves. Why? Biblical narratives rarely supply motives for actions; readers must fill in the gaps. Perhaps if they had left, no one would have prevented the warden from taking his life — or the Lord from saving it. The text only tells the reader that the earthquake has awakened him. Why he would fail to check the cells before taking his own life is the stuff of legend. Nor does the story make clear why he would resort to such a drastic solution to his problem in any case. The reader does know — from their unconscionable treatment of Paul and Silas — the capacity for brutality of the warden's employers. But punishment by death would seem an unlikely result, since the cause is an act of God rather than professional incompetence. Perhaps the public shame that would come to him and his family when the story of a jailbreak got out to the local media was enough to make him consider suicide. He was given responsibility for these prisoners, after all, and his special instructions in the case of Paul and Silas may well have indicated their special importance. But that is also unlikely for the same reason: who could blame the warden for an act of God?

This logical conclusion is exactly the narrator's point: the warden's decision to take his life is due to a religious conviction, especially since the earthquake is known to be an act of divine intervention. It is likely he thought that it was an act of retribution from which his salvation is unlikely. If the reader reads this motive into the story, the warden's responses to Paul's saving call make perfect sense. Initially, he "fell down trembling before Paul and Silas" (v. 29; cf. 10:25), which recalls Moses' response to the burning-bush theophany, when he "trembled" before God (cf. 7:32; Heb. 12:21). The warden is terrified because he has "seen" his Maker.

After removing his prisoners from the prison, he asks them the famous question: "What must I do to be saved?" Although his desire for salvation may be nonreligious, the setting makes this interpretation unlikely: he would be asking Paul what must be done to save him from himself! More likely, the implied meaning of his question is religious and is a request to hear the gospel that Paul and Silas have been proclaiming to their fellow prisoners: in other words, What must I do to be saved by your God?

The reader should note the parallelism between Paul's own conversion story in Acts 9 and the warden's. Paul's transformation from persecutor of Jesus to a prophet-like-Jesus was also facilitated by divine intervention, and that supplies the subtext of the gospel he now presents to the warden (cf. 1 Tim. 1:13-16): "Believe on the Lord Jesus, and you will be saved — you and your household." The connection of belief and salvation is central to the theological shape of Paul's message in Acts (cf. 14:9; 15:11; Rom. 10:9) and provides a succinct formulation of "the way of salvation" called for by the slave girl's oracle (v. 17).

The repetition of "household" both in Paul's gospel presentation and again in the subsequent summary (vv. 31-32) recalls the imagery of a restored "house" of Israel from Amos's prophecy (cf. 15:16-18), again reminding the reader of Acts that the warden, along with Lydia, are those "households" of gentiles that God is calling out of the nations to share in Israel's blessings. What is striking about the warden's conversion story, and different from — though complementary to — Lydia's story, is that the warden is not a God-fearer who knows Moses, but a pagan. His conversion, then, suggests that beyond Palestine and Roman Asia (with its substantial Jewish Diaspora), in Roman cities such as Philippi, full of evil spirits, moral rogues, and anti-Semitic sentiment, Israel's God will still find a people from among the gentiles who "are called by his name" (15:17).

Just as in Lydia's case (v. 15), the warden's salvation is confirmed by his hospitality toward Paul and Silas. First a female God-fearer and now a male pagan, both with their families, evince the transforming work of God in their lives by acts of friendship toward Paul. In the warden's case, "he took them and washed their wounds . . . and brought them up into his house and set food before them." With this festive meal Luke adds that the "entire household rejoiced that he had become a believer in God." The combination of meal and joy strongly implies that their celebration gathered around the Eucharist, when Jesus' suffering is remembered as an act of redemption. The faithful reader is likewise compelled to read back into Paul's suffering for the sake of Jesus' name as a means of grace that brings the warden and his family onto the way of salvation.

Jailhouse Rock

The account of the warden's salvation is sandwiched between two successive chapters that tell of Paul and Silas's legal problems. The present passage continues this story from verse 23 ("the morning after" the great earthquake): Paul and Silas are back in jail. We are introduced to "the police," who play another role in the Philippian court system: apparently in this situation they are the official go-betweens who carry messages from the magistrates to the warden on prison-related matters, something like today's police. The passage is severely gapped. Luke is not interested in telling his readers what prompts the magistrates' decision to "let those men go," though we can imagine why.

Paul's response to this fairly casual liberation reflects the honor-shame culture of his world: he does not want the magistrates to brush the crumbs of their shameful behavior under the carpet of public attention. He wants them to receive their just deserts. He lists the grievances that resulted in his humiliation: public flogging, condemnation and incarceration of innocent Roman citizens, without benefit of trial or defense attorneys (v. 37). "Did you say 'Roman citizens,' Paul?" Gulp! Imprisoning and flogging a Roman citizen without trial was illegal; doing so publicly was a criminal act worthy of execution. No wonder "they were afraid when they heard that they were Roman citizens."

The stunning revelation that Paul and Silas are both Roman citizens requires a rereading of the evidence in a couple of ways. It more clearly reveals the slave-owners' original accusation as anti-Semitic and motivated by greed, which accusation the court had nonetheless embraced without question or due process. Succinctly put, Paul and Silas suffer because they are Jews, which perhaps more keenly underscores Jewish identity as a critical feature of Paul's biography and his mission according to Acts. Here also the Paul of Acts introduces what his letters do not: Paul is a Roman citizen — with all the rights and privileges due him. While the interpreter must set aside the historicity of Paul's claim, given that he never mentions it in his epistolary autobiography, it is an important feature of Luke's apologia in Acts. Although Paul rarely appeals to his citizenship in Acts, he does so strategically, and it remains in the reader's mind in any case.

In this regard, Paul's gracious response in accepting the magistrates' apology (v. 39) may be highly suggestive of Luke's literary shaping of the church's relationship with Rome. If so, his point is not to exonerate Rome of evils done against the church. Luke's depiction of Rome in Acts is at best realistic and hardly painted in a positive light. His point is rather to show Rome's inability — even its political weakness — to subvert the work of God's salvation in the world. Even Rome must come with hat in hand to the prophets of the "Most High God" to appease them.

The final snapshot in Luke's photo album of Paul's Philippian mission is of the departure of Paul and Silas from both prison and city, but only after "they went to Lydia's home to see and encourage the sisters and brothers there." Luke's nice literary touch effectively brackets the events of Paul's jailhouse experience with the story of Lydia's conversion. It is important to note the order of Luke's text in order to understand the significance of Lydia's conversion, since Paul does not depart the city until after he makes his house call to the congregation gathered in her home. Her home lies within city limits, so there is at last a place of prayer and witness to the "Most High God" and God's risen Christ in Philippi.

Luke includes this story of Paul's Philippian mission partly to add several qualifications to the verdict James has rendered at the Jerusalem Council (see 15:13-21, 22-29). Paul's Philippian mission is precisely the kind that worries James: Philippi is an overtly pagan city that is far from Jerusalem and has no meaningful Jewish presence. In an implicit response to James, then, Luke portrays Paul as the very personification of a faithful Jew within an anti-Jewish culture; and his personal story is one of suffering as a Jew (cf. 9:16). Paul's mission results in a quorum of believers gathered in Lydia's house, which is a substitute for a city synagogue, to worship Israel's God, whose intervention on Paul's behalf has helped preserve the church's Jewish legacy on pagan soil.

PART II: ENGAGING ACTS 16 FOR TODAY'S CHURCH

Lutheran pastor Michael Foss, in his book *Power Surge* and in other writings, claims that the great challenge facing numerous congregations in North America today is to make the shift from "a culture of membership" to "a culture of discipleship." Though we cannot fully explore Foss's thought here, we can join Foss in noting that churches too often turn into clubs where the real purpose is to satisfy the members. And when that happens, churches have lost their central purpose — which is to "make disciples," to help people become, live, and grow as disciples of Jesus Christ. As we have noted above, conversion and call are linked. A change of heart (conversion) needs to find expression and embodiment in a change of life (discipleship). We are called to a new and particular way of life, which finds expression in particular practices, or marks of discipleship.

In my experience, the distinction between the congregation that is a "culture of membership" and the congregation that is a "culture of discipleship" may also be suggested in the following way: when members of a congregation gather and discover that they do not all already know each other, they will introduce themselves by saying how long they have been a member of that particular congregation. That is, of course, useful information, but it may not be essential information. Moreover, stating how long we have "been a member" often seems to have the effect of establishing a pecking order: the longer one has been a member, the higher one is in the pecking order.

Imagine a different pattern of introductions in a congregation, one that seeks to be a culture of discipleship, a congregation where the emphasis is on conversion and call and on making disciples. A person in such a congregation might introduce herself, not by saying how long she has been a member, but by saying a few words about how it has been going for her lately in her life as a follower of Christ — as a disciple. What is she working on in her life of discipleship? What is most challenging in that life, and what is most rewarding? It is true, of course, that anything can be misused, and a new or different pattern of introductions as just described could itself become a way of establishing a pecking order. Yet, with appropriate pastoral teaching and guidance, this seemingly innocuous shift could prove significant. People would be narrating their stories of discipleship, their struggles as well as their successes. Without ever needing to say so explicitly, they would shift the focus of the church from membership and member satisfaction to discipleship and following Christ in our daily lives.

Conversion or transformation may begin one's life of faith (Paul) or may initiate a new chapter or movement (Peter). In making disciples, the church builds on such experiences, helping them find meaning and expression in everyday life as well as deepening and expressing them through particular ways of living. Earlier we have discussed both "purity practices" (i.e., those things from which believers abstain) and "resurrection practices" (i.e., those things that believers do). Those who are in Christ have become, by the act and grace of God, new. Such is the indicative of the gospel, and the indicative leads to the imperative: "In Christ you are reconciled with God, therefore, be reconciled." You are — therefore be. Both the purity practices and the resurrection practices of the church are ways of living out the new life, the reconciled life, which is ours by God's grace and gift. They are not ways of earning grace or of succeeding at being a Christian. They are ways of responding to God's love and growing in our life as those who have been loved and who know it.

This episode in Acts 16 is one of several passages in which readers of Acts may find the "resurrection practices," or marks of discipleship, highlighted. Acts 16 does not provide a definitive or systematic treatment of resurrection practices, but it does illustrate them. We find in Acts 16 helpful guidance for congregations that wish to speak of specific, concrete, and public marks of discipleship. Here we pay particular attention to the following "marks": hospitality, justice, suffering, worship and prayer, and teaching and learning. Congregations that wish to give attention to specific marks of discipleship may find this listing helpful, even as they adapt it to specific situations and express it in different terms or language.

Hospitality

As a starting point, it may be useful to distinguish hospitality from fellowship, though fellowship — *koinonia* — in the Christian community may be another mark of discipleship. Hospitality and fellowship are related, but also distinct from each other. Fellowship is the experience of community, of care, and of life together among believers within the Christian community; hospitality is the welcoming of the stranger, providing care and support and welcome to those who are not already part of the community or congregation. And it may well mean providing welcome to those who are "not like us."

Often fellowship, in practice, has come to mean loving those and caring for those who are pretty much like us, or who we anticipate will turn out to be pretty much like us, if only we get to know them better. "The more we are together," as the children's song puts it, "the happier we'll be." Well, maybe. But hospitality does not make such promises. Sometimes hospitality is easy and brings many evident blessings; sometimes it is not so easy, and those we welcome as guests may prove more angular or difficult than we might wish or expect. Strangers can sometimes become friends, but sometimes they remain strange — and strangely "other." Moreover, hospitality is a concept very different from "friendliness." Of course, true friendship is both a great gift and a demanding task, but sometimes the contemporary church aims for a "friendliness" that is superficial, that is, the friendliness of "our gang" or our club. We think of ourselves as friendly and describe our church as "a friendly church." That may be a genuine strength, or it may mean that here we keep things pretty superficial because going deeper might disrupt the appearance of friendliness.

Hospitality is the welcoming of and caring for the stranger and sojourner among us, the resident alien, the immigrant, the refugee, or simply the newcomer to town or church. Hospitality was a crucial practice of life in the arid Middle East of the early church; but it is a practice very much at risk in contemporary North America, where we are taught to be watchful of strangers and suspicious of them. In such a context, the counsel of the letter to the Hebrews, "Do not neglect to show hospitality to strangers, for by doing so some have entertained angels unawares," may sound not only unwise but downright subversive.

This passage in Acts 16 both begins and concludes with the acts of hospitality of a Philippian woman, Lydia, as she welcomes Paul and Silas to her home. Opening her home to these preachers and prophets-like-Jesus follows on Lydia's baptism: grace elicits response. God's grace makes us gracious. "If you have judged me to be faithful to the Lord, come and stay at my home," says Lydia to Paul and Silas (v. 15). Again, as the mission to Philippi concludes, Paul and Silas go "to Lydia's home," where they meet with and encourage the congregation (v. 40). In welcoming Paul and Silas to her home, Lydia not only welcomes those who are strangers and outsiders to Philippi, but more: these are Jews, and Lydia is a gentile; they are men, and she is a woman (and nothing in the report suggests that Lydia is married or that there's a man at home); Lydia is the head of a household and is a businesswoman, while Paul and Silas have no visible means of support. Thus all the divisions that Paul cites in Galatians 3:28 are met and transcended here in this Acts story: "slave and free" (social class), "Jew and gentile" (cultural and ethnic), and "male and female" (gender). Hospitality does indeed mean welcoming the other.

But these bookends of hospitality are not the only such instances in this narrative. The Philippian jailer also practices hospitality: after receiving the teaching of Paul and Silas about Jesus and coming to faith, the jailer opens his home to these traveling teachers — who just happened to be his prisoners! That represents a big step beyond the ethnic, gender, and social-class distinctions: welcoming the prisoner! Hospitality, welcoming the stranger as God has welcomed us, is a resurrection practice and mark of discipleship.

But we do not need to construe this as merely a personal practice. Hospitality can be a resurrection practice and mark of discipleship for the church as a community. One of the ironies of the Christian church today is that some of the very congregations where members pride themselves on their friendliness and wonderful fellowship may seem anything but friendly to the outsider, the newcomer, or the stranger who may be a little or a lot different. This is not to say that the experience of friendliness and fellowship of members of the congregation is not real. Certainly, it is; but it is also limited. The congregation that someone on the inside may describe as "just the warmest group I know" may seem to a stranger to be "a very cold church."

This suggests that fellowship, the tie that binds the members and believers of a faith community together, must always live in a certain creative tension with hospitality — welcoming the stranger. If the latter does not exist, while the former does, there's a good chance that what we have is not so much "church" as "club." True church does have *koinonia*, a genuine sense of Christian community and fellowship; but it also has a hospitable spirit, a capacity to welcome the stranger and sojourner. This sense of the church has both a clear center and open boundaries. In fact, that combination may be one of the best marks of a truly healthy congregation. On one hand, there is a clear center and a sense of itself; on the other, the strength of that center allows openness at the edges. Sometimes a very warm and tight community lacks a truly strong center in faith and in the living God, which is exposed in an attitude of suspicion or simply failure to notice the visitor, the stranger, the outsider. Healthy congregations, like healthy individuals, have sufficient strength in themselves and their core that they are able to welcome others, take an interest in them, receive the gifts the stranger brings — which she will share if made to feel "at home."

Justice and Liberation

While staying with Lydia and in Philippi, Paul and Silas attract the attention of a demon-possessed slave girl, whose disorder her owners have exploited for profit. She has made a good deal of money for them by telling fortunes in this pagan and superstitious city. She begins to follow Paul and Silas around Philippi in a way we have come to expect of those who harbor a demonic spirit: she knows and understands that Paul and Silas represent both threat and hope. They are a threat to the power of the demon that has the girl in its grip. But they represent hope to the girl herself, hope of liberation both from the demon and from her owners and their exploitation of her vulnerability and disorder. Paul confronts the demon and exorcises it, leaving the girl in her right mind and free.

We don't know what happens to her next, but we do know what happens to Paul and Silas next. The owners of the slave girl trump up charges against Paul and Silas: disturbing the order and introducing alien customs.

They don't come right out and declare that their vested economic interests have been jeopardized, preferring to advance more general and high-sounding accusations that might appeal to the Philippi magistrates. They drag Paul and Silas to the marketplace, where the local magistrate is only too happy to serve commercial interests. The magistrate has Paul and Silas flogged and jailed for their public ministries of justice and liberation. They have intervened so that the weak can no longer be exploited by the strong, a steady theme of biblical faith — as well as a resurrection practice and mark of discipleship.

Whenever contemporary Christians challenge those who exploit the weakness of others for personal and private gain, such ministries of justice and liberation are at stake. Moreover, they may incur a similar displeasure from vested interests. Seldom will such vested interests announce their self-interest directly, but they may accuse advocates and enactors of justice and liberation of undermining private ownership or disturbing community values. But make no mistake: Christian faith and discipleship do have implications for business, whatever our business may be, whenever the weak and vulnerable are being exploited by the strong and powerful.

Paul's justice ministry is not, however, limited in Acts 16 to the liberation of the slave girl and the challenge to her exploitative owners. In the final scene of this ministry in Philippi, Paul and Silas are back in jail, where they have apparently returned after baptizing the jailer and his household. In the wake of the earthquake, the magistrates seem content to merely release Paul and Silas and tell them to get out of town. But Paul will have none of it: he reveals that they are Roman citizens, which means that the magistrates have violated their rights as citizens. Paul insists that this abuse of power and law come to light and be addressed.

This suggests another way in which Christian ministries of justice take shape, particularly in relation to civil authorities. The church may serve God and the whole community by insisting on holding civil authorities accountable to their own laws and responsibilities. Of course, we in the church have at times found the tables turned, when civil authorities call us to account. We recall that it was an Egyptian pharaoh who lectured Abraham on ethics early in the story of Abraham and Sarah. The church is hardly above judgment itself. Today civil authorities may need to hold the church to account in matters of tax fraud, clergy sexual abuse, and other moral and ethical failures. But Paul and Silas's ministry does illustrate an appropriate and necessary public-square role for the church in addition to the work of liberation. Civil authorities, according to Scripture, have an appropriate and necessary place and role. Christians are called to respect this place and role, and when it becomes necessary, they must insist that such authorities do what they are supposed to do, whether it be to distribute benefits to Medicare recipients who are entitled to them or to enforce environmental regulations against corporate offenders.

Suffering

We have already noted that Paul and Silas experience the truth of an old quip: "No good deed goes unpunished." Just as Jesus is seldom thanked for giving sight to the blind or healing the lame, so Paul and Silas are not thanked for their healing. Instead, they are flogged and jailed. They suffer for their faith and discipleship, but their suffering has a different tone and character from some other experiences of suffering. Consistent with the overall story of Acts, they may be victims of suffering, but they show no victim mentality. Quite the contrary, while in jail Paul and Silas pray and sing hymns. Theirs is not meaningless suffering: it is meaningful because it is suffering in the cause and service of Christ.

Even if, as is most often the case, our own situations are not quite as clear and unambiguous as the story of Paul and Silas appears to be, we can take from this story — as well as from the whole gospel — a different perspective on suffering. As a pastor, I often note that when people experience suffering, when their good deeds arouse resistance or resentment or jealousy, contemporary disciples conclude that they must be doing something wrong, that they are at fault. Among both clergy and laity the assumption seems to be, "If I were truly and faithfully following Christ, everyone would love me, appreciate me, and reward me." Again, maybe not. While contemporary disciples should not indulge in masochism and should always be prepared to learn from resistance and opposition — and should not assume that they are in the right — neither should they assume that they are in the wrong, nor that opposition or suffering means something is wrong with them. At least on some occasions we can and should expect opposition and suffering in the cause of what is right.

Worship and Prayer

In this Acts 16 story we see a vigorous life of worship and prayer shared in community. As the Philippi venture begins, Paul and Silas make their way to a place of worship outside the city gates and share in worship and prayer there. Later they will worship in one of the strangest places — in jail — and with the jailer's entire household in his home. What do Christians do in jail? They pray, sing hymns, and worship God, of course. And this worship is also witness. As the story unfolds, we see that the jailed prisoners, Paul and Silas, are actually free, while the jailer and magistrate, not to mention the owners of the slave girl, are in chains, though they are spiritual chains. Worship and praise to God while they are in chains and in jail is the disciples' way of affirming that they are free even though in jail. They are free because they worship the true God, and no civil power or authority is capable of making them captives.

The variety of settings in which disciples are caught up in worship and prayer in Acts suggests that the church today needs to equip and prepare us to worship wherever and whenever we find ourselves, and not to be completely hamstrung if we find ourselves without a sanctuary, hymnals, instruments, candles, choirs, or worship leaders. Years ago a group from our congregation traveled to Nicaragua, where we were welcomed into the homes of Nicaraguan Christians. After a generous and delicious dinner, our hosts rose and said, "We would like to sing for you." They broke into beautiful renditions of hymns, which they sang in harmony and without instrumental accompaniment or hymnals or music. I was thoroughly enjoying this until I realized that the inevitable was coming, namely, that they would say, "Now, you sing for us." When they did, we had to admit that without hymnals we were lost — we weren't able to sing, which was a sad state of affairs. On the remainder of that journey we spent our free time committing our favorite hymns to memory.

Acts suggests that the church today should prepare people to sing the Lord's songs wherever we find ourselves. At another congregation in Nicaragua, we were about to have dinner in the church hall when, suddenly, the lights went off all over Managua. We North Americans wondered what to do and what would happen next? The Nicaraguans knew what to do. They began to praise the Lord by singing hymns with great gusto and joy, as some among them fetched and lit candles.

Teaching and Learning

Not only do Paul and Silas worship robustly while in jail; throughout this story they are engaged in a ministry of teaching, while others participate in learning. Paul and Silas teach and interpret Scripture at the riverside with Lydia and others. Later they proclaim and teach in jail, and then subsequently in the jailer's home and to his entire household. Such teaching imparts a new story, the story of the lordship of Jesus Christ. This story reinterprets experience, giving new meaning and new possibilities. Such teaching and learning of the gospel, of God and of Jesus, is also a resurrection practice and a mark of discipleship.

Often the church has put most of its educational eggs in the children-and-youth basket. There is, of course, nothing whatsoever wrong with a great teaching and learning ministry for children and youth. But there is something wrong when it stops there. When, as is too often the case, our teaching ministry for adults is either limited to a very small slice of the congregation or is nonexistent, we are not doing a good job of making disciples or equipping the saints for ministry. There are a growing number of excellent resources congregations can use to strengthen their adult teaching and formation ministries. Moreover, pastoral leaders must themselves be teachers of the faith, and they must train and equip others to teach.

One might draw attention to other resurrection practices in Acts 16 — and certainly in the larger text of Acts; but perhaps we have made the point for our purposes. Christian faith is not only a matter of beliefs (*mythos*) but of practices (*ethos*), and of a way of living. Such practices and ways of living both deepen and sustain our faith. But they do more: they express and embody it in public ways. Some years ago, President Jimmy Carter's pastor made headlines with his sermon title, "If being a Christian were a crime, would there be enough evidence to get you convicted?" Resurrection practices or marks of discipleship give evidence to a broken world of our faith and of God's grace and presence.

We would encourage congregations, perhaps in dialogue with the book of Acts, to develop their own "marks of discipleship" and to place those at the center of their congregational life. The five we have noted here provide a starting point, though they may, of course, be given different expressions. For example, a congregation, working from these five, might speak of the following marks of discipleship: sharing of goods in community, participation in ministries of service and justice to the world, tribulation in faith, sharing in life of worship and praise, and finally, study of Scripture. It seems both helpful and honest for congregations and pastoral leaders to speak openly of what they expect: that being a Christian is not a matter of tacit agreement but of a way of life. Perhaps the language of discipleship is not for everyone. It doesn't have to be. Some congregations may find that it works better in their setting to speak of "faith practices" and "growing in faith." Others will find other language more fitting for their contexts. The point is not so much the language as it is a specific and public way of life through which we grow in, are sustained by, and express and embody our faith for the good and blessing of the world.

STUDY QUESTIONS

1. Christian discipleship is countercultural. What characteristics of Lydia's persona are countercultural within the narrative world of Acts? How do her actions contrast with those of others portrayed in this story?

2. What accusations are leveled against Paul and Silas that lead to their arrest? Under what circumstances does Paul appeal to his Roman citizenship? How does this narrative detail help to define the church's relationship with the state according to Acts?

3. The story of Paul's Philippian mission is strategic in the contribution Acts makes to a biblical theology of salvation. Describe the various patterns of conversion found in this chapter. How does this chapter define salvation — from what threats and for what purposes are a people saved?

4. Discuss the difference between "a culture of membership" and a "culture of discipleship." What implications do you see for your congregation?

5. Note the differences between Lydia and Paul and Silas: culture, gender, economic means. Have you experienced hospitality extended from someone quite different from you? How did it affect you?

6. Which of the "resurrection practices" or "marks of discipleship" discussed in this chapter speaks most powerfully to you and why? They include hospitality, justice and liberation, suffering, worship and prayer, and teaching and learning.

12 *Spirituality: Its Lure and Danger*

PART I: INTERPRETING ACTS 17:16-34 AS SCRIPTURE

Although a bit tattered by comparison to its golden age of Pericles and Socrates, Athens is still a great university town where important ideas hold value for the intellectually curious when the Paul of Acts delivers one of his three major missionary speeches — and the only one to pagans. Its religious subtext is a response to the city's pervasive idolatry, which not only "deeply distresses" him (v. 16) but which he also considers nonrational. Great learning has not eliminated false religion from Athens.

Upon his arrival in Athens, Paul visits the city's synagogue and then the town square, where he "argues" with all those he encounters (v. 17). Philosophers are among Paul's conversation partners even though they fail to grasp what he proclaims to them and so make two errors of judgment: they question his spiritual authority, calling him a "babbler," and confuse his teaching about Jesus' resurrection with propaganda about "foreign deities." Because they fail to recognize Paul as a teacher of Israel, whose religion is approved for Athenians, they lead him to the Areopagus, where he explains his "new teaching" (vv. 19-21). Paul does so in a speech of uncommon power that both legitimates his spiritual authority and examines the claim that he teaches "foreign deities" (vv. 22-29), before turning to his "new teaching" about Jesus and the resurrection (vv. 30-31). Characteristically, his call to conversion results in a divided house (vv. 32-34).

A Marketplace of Ideas and Idols

Paul is "deeply distressed" to find a great city "full of idols." Although there is evidence that these "idols" were valued as great works of art, Paul's response to them is not one of aesthetic evaluation but of spiritual outrage. "Deeply" translates the Greek phrase that literally means "his spirit within him," and it refers to his spiritual life — his mind and soul — which is shaped by Israel's theological beliefs. The Old Testament teaches against the use of manufactured images in religious observance, since they domesticate God and subvert the worship of Israel's God, the only God (cf. Exod. 20:4; Deut. 5:6-10). What is evidently shocking to the Jewish Paul here in Acts is the sheer number of idols he finds in Athens, which compounds the religious offense. The word translated "full of idols" is found only in this text in the New Testament and conjures up the image of a "forest" or "feast" of idols.

If the pervasive idolatry of Athens is distressing for the Jewish Paul, it is even more so because Athens, unlike Philippi, has a Jewish synagogue that clearly has had little positive influence on the city's religious life. Israel has had no mission to the pagans in the Diaspora; so Paul's mission is a novelty act. Indeed, the philosophers' misunderstanding of Paul's proclamation of Jesus in the marketplace is due in part to their general ignorance of Jewish history and religion. So Paul's message fails to impress them.

Acts reports that Paul "argues with the Jews and devout gentiles" of the Athenian synagogue (v. 17; see vv. 2, 10). In this setting, Luke's choice of words, "to argue," is strategic because it recalls the legendary figure of Socrates, whose public persona was to make himself available to citizens in the "marketplace" *(agora)* for philosophical debate. Earlier stories of Paul's urban mission provide details of what he argues: the resurrection of Jesus discloses that what God has promised according to Israel's Scripture is now being realized.

Among those in the *agora* are "Epicurean and Stoic philosophers who debated *(symballō)* with Paul." The style of discourse is indicated by the choice of *symballō* — a favorite word of the narrator — which denotes a collegial exchange toward a constructive end (cf. 4:15; 18:27; 20:14; see also Luke 2:19; 14:31). The impression is of an honest exchange between "scholarly peers," and not a contentious retort that some translations connote.

Paul's conversation partners include members from divergent schools of philosophical thought in Athens, though all are interested in practical rather than theoretical discussions. In Paul's case, the gospel demands a practical discourse because the reality of Jesus' resurrection influences all of life. Epicureans were materialists and believed that human life exists by natural chance. Personal pleasure was the aim of human existence, not religious devotion, since a personal god who could make a practical difference in the outcome of a happy life does not exist. Significantly, they were harsh critics of idolatry as well. Their criticism of Athenian folk religion was that any offering to gods who are impersonal and cannot respond is nonrational, because molten gods are incapable of producing personal happiness. Little did they realize that Israel's Scripture offered the same criticism regarding the foolishness of idol worship (e.g., Isa. 44:9-20).

Stoics, on the other hand, were hard rationalists who were guided by their analytical observations and careful reasoning. They sought to live in harmony with all the institutions of daily life, and they were duty-bound to do so. Stoics believed in the solidarity of the human race and in a "personal" deity in whom "we live and move and have our being" (Acts 17:28). However, theirs was a civil religion whose god accommodated diverse human culture rather than a transcendent One who stands in judgment over citizens and cities according to God's purpose rather than Athens' prerequisites.

The initial impression made on the audience overhearing their discussion concerning "practical reason" is that Paul's claims for the risen Jesus are ill-conceived and intellectually impoverished: he is a "babbler" (*spermologos:* literally, a "seed picker") of old ideas that are irrelevant or unimportant for Athenians. This mocking term challenges Paul's intellectual authority to contend for a superior account of practical divinity. He is a teacher who picks up the "seeds" of another's intellectual property and has nothing important to contribute to a public discourse on true religion. While the authority of God's prophet must be measured by different criteria than in Athens, he is being tested here; and whether or not he passes his test determines whether he will have an audience to hear the gospel at the end of the day.

The second and quite different challenge from his opponents is that Paul lobbies for "foreign deities" (see 16:21). The earlier reference to Socrates as a public philosopher is now relevant: Paul joins the company of Socrates, who was also charged with propagating strange gods in Athens, which was a capital offense in the birthplace of democracy. Athens' definition of political correctness valued "common ground" more than any other civic virtue. Not only is the tragic fate of Socrates a subtext of Paul's response to his Athenian opponents; his very status in the marketplace of ideas has been challenged. He is judged an incompetent "seed-picker" who traffics in irrelevant religiosity. The Areopagus of Athens is the tribunal where a final verdict on Paul's intellectual chops will be rendered, and this is where he is now taken.

The meaning of "took" *(epilabomenoi)* is ambiguous: it can be translated either "to arrest" (to take into police custody) or "to accompany" (to take along with). Since the decision one makes about the meaning of Greek words is largely determined by their use in narrative context, *epilabomenoi* here would seem to denote an action appropriate to the Areopagus (literally, Mars Hill), for this is where Paul is taken. Whatever decision the translator makes also determines whether he will read Paul's Areopagus speech as a legal defense, a scholarly discussion, or both. In my view, Paul is not arrested. The original judgment of his intellectual authority and the viability of his practical theology have now given way to a benign interest in his "new teaching." In this sense, then, Paul "accompanies" (rather than is arrested by) his detractors to the Areopagus, where the content of his teaching will be more rigorously examined by the high standards of the Athenian philosophical tradition.

The Areopagus was the name given to an elevated, open-air site just to the west of the Acropolis in Athens, where there was sufficient room to hold senate meetings or public debates. The impression of this story's plot line is that the *agora* is too small a site to accommodate the large crowds attracted to Paul's message; here is the proper stage to defend his intellectual prowess and strange "new teaching." The Areopagus also refers to the council of philosophers (v. 33) who refereed these public spectacles in ancient Athens, and rendered verdicts on which side prevailed. Paul's rivals, then, are scholarly foes, and this council is comprised of his peers: they are more intellectually curious than hostile.

If the Areopagus seeks only to review Paul's teaching, its leading question is appropriate to the task: "May we know what this new teaching is that you are presenting?" (v. 19). The potentially dangerous charge of teaching "foreign deities" has been dropped, replaced by their desire to learn something of Paul's "new teaching" that "sounds strange to us." Luke explains this apparent shift of motive as a keen and well-known Athenian curiosity in "something new" (v. 21). While a scholar's interest prompted by new ideas seems good at first reading, the council's disappointing response to Paul's speech (see vv. 32-34) may suggest the narrator's irony. If a scholar's curiosity leads only to investigating new insights but not toward a clear and certain resolution, the result will almost always be an unsatisfying relativism. The gospel's call for repentance here (vv. 30-31) represents a closure of sorts to wrong ideas and commences the repentant believer's journey in a new direction — toward a specific destination. Luke's parenthetical comment about Athenian curiosity both occasions Paul's speech and explains why his call to conversion is then rejected by the intellectually curious, who may see this prophet's definitive claim for ultimate truth and his implicit call for repentance as unsettling.

Paul's Mars Hill Speech

Although presented in different words, the broad structure and the content of Paul's Areopagus speech are similar to what we find in Acts whenever a prophet-like-Jesus faces opposition. In fact, Paul gave the précis of this speech earlier at Lystra, where he championed "the living God, who made the heaven, the earth and sea and all that is in them" and asserted its predicate "that you should turn from these worthless things to the living God" (14:15). But he is now in Athens and before the renowned Areopagus, where he is asked to defend the gospel of a "new religion" that he has introduced into public discourse. This is heady stuff indeed!

R. Garland recently has demonstrated that three claims were necessary to legitimate a "new religion" in ancient Athens: (1) the sponsor of a new religion must claim to represent the "new" deity in question; (2) he must prove that this deity is eager to establish residence in Athens; and (3) the deity's residence in Athens must provide some benefit to all Athenians as the civic mark of its good will.[1] Luke may well have known these criteria and thus reshaped Paul's Mars Hill speech into a defense of the Christian gospel for all pagans — a role it continues to perform to this day. Accordingly, Paul introduces himself as an authorized herald of a living deity whose transcendent residence above the earth requires no Athenian residence, priesthood, or religious practices (vv. 24-29). Paul's deity thus does not seek formal induction into the Athenian Pantheon — of this the

---

1. R. Garland, *Introducing New Gods: The Politics of Athenian Religion* (London: Duckworth, 1992), pp. 18-19.

Areopagus need not worry — but rather seeks to judge and save all repentant Athenians as disclosed in the resurrection of Jesus. And of this they should worry (vv. 30-31).

The speech has been cued up by a dramatic gesture: "Paul stood in front of the Areopagus" and addressed his listeners directly by name, "Athenians." Paul must win the right to be taken seriously, so he first responds to the criticism that he is a babbler of second-hand ideas and hence without scholarly credentials in the city where Dr. Socrates once taught. The scholar's most important talent is the capacity to make careful observations. Paul's first words intend to cultivate the impression that he is a skilled practitioner of the scholar's trade: he "went through the city" taking notes and "looked carefully" at all the available evidence in coming to the conclusion that the Athenians are "extremely religious [*deisidaimonisterous*] in every way." The superlative *deisidaimonisterous* could mean that they are either superstitious, a vice of the intellectually impoverished, or keenly pious, a virtue of the educated person, according to Greek philosophy. Whether to correct their superstition or inform their piety, Paul's opening words solicit a positive impression while also clarifying his motive: he intends to address his audience as religious people in a religious idiom about religious matters in anticipation of a religious response — that is, conversion. While doing so, he also challenges the perception that his lack of a scholar's talent disqualifies him from the marketplace of compelling religious ideas.

Paul's authority has also been challenged because he is "a proclaimer of foreign deities" (v. 18), or, as the council more politely rephrases the philosophers' earlier charge, for presenting "new teaching" that "sounds strange to us" (vv. 19-20). In response, Paul playfully notes one altar's inscription, "To an unknown God," providing evidence of superlative piety: You are so religious that you worship gods you don't even know! Indeed, they live in "times of ignorance" (v. 30), when what is unknown about god is the hallmark of a people's religious devotion.

With this stunning description of Athenian folk religion, Paul has positioned himself to declare boldly the purpose of his mission in Athens: this God you worship in ignorance "I proclaim [*katangellō*] to you." While his Athenian listeners could not have known the powerful resonance of Paul's assertion, readers do. The use of *katangellō* brings to mind its richly textured meaning in Acts, where the verb is repeatedly used of the church's prophetic witness (cf. 3:24; 4:2; 13:5, 38; 15:36; 16:17; 17:3). Thus, in the guise of a philosopher-like-Socrates, Paul discloses his true vocation as a prophet-like-Jesus; and as a prophet-like-Jesus, he defends his spiritual authority as the inspired medium of God's word to expose the theological ignorance of these learned people and to bid them to repent and turn to the one true God for salvation from certain judgment (vv. 30-31).

The main body of Paul's speech is a logical sequence of theologically dense statements. Most scholars detect a prophet's "theo-logic," something like a confession of Jewish faith in the idiom of Greek philosophy. Axiomatic and essential to the prophet's rationale is a profession of Israel's monotheism: God is "the God" (*ho theos*: v. 24; cf. Deut. 6:4). God is neither dependent on nor divided by another deity. Nor does God's existence depend on a philosopher's claim that God has a legal "right" to exist in Athens.

God "made the world [*kosmos*] and everything in it" (see 4:24; 14:15) without the aid of another deity, and God is therefore "Lord of heaven and earth" (cf. Luke 10:21). These first two assertions are logically related because the Creator justifiably takes responsibility for and has authority over what is created; this conclusion appeals to Stoics (v. 18), whose core belief in human solidarity is predicated on a belief that the Creator is the sole source for the living.

The reasonable deduction that Paul draws from this formulation of God's sovereignty is that no creature of the natural kosmos — this "world" that is designed, arranged, and brought to order by a single Creator — is capable of domesticating God: this one and only Creator is a living God who "does not live in shrines made by human hands" (v. 24c; see 7:48; cf. Isa. 57:15-16). Nor does God require religious artifacts "as though [God] needed anything" (v. 25a; cf. Amos 5:12-23), a conclusion that would have appealed to the Epicureans in Paul's audience, whose functional atheism was predicated on the belief that any deity worth worshiping should need nothing from anyone (see v. 18).

Rather, Israel's God is a gracious benefactor who "gives to all mortals life and breath and all things" (cf. Isa. 42:5; Gen. 2:7). This same assessment of God's goodness can be seen in Peter's stunning theological claim that a sovereign God freely dispenses the gifts of salvation to all who repent and believe without prejudice (cf. 10:34).

On the foundation of this series of more general claims in defense of Israel's God, Paul narrows his focus to God's relationship with people to make his most dramatic claims for God. Even as Paul claims that everything derives from one God, he goes on to declare that from one human stock (i.e., Adam and Eve) many races/nations descend "to inhabit the whole earth" (v. 26; cf. Gen. 1:24-25; Rom. 5:12-14). This pairing of one God with a single human family ensures that the "many" who physically descend from Adam and Eve also share a common religious ground, whether people recognize it or not.

Paul concludes that this God who has created the human family also "allots times . . . and boundaries" that circumscribe human existence. While his commentary is laden with the philosophical ideas of his day, the point he ends up making is practical and straightforward: if the Creator takes such care of the creation, then it is illogical to suppose that the Creator would abandon it to fend for itself (cf. 14:16-17). In this regard, Paul implies a second concept that is axiomatic of biblical faith: God's purpose for reordering human life is "so that humans would search . . . grope . . . and find God" (v. 27a). God creates an environment that aims at a personal relationship so that God "is not far from each one of us" (cf. Rom. 10:8; Ps. 145:18). In setting forth this theological claim, Paul prepares the audience for his move toward Christian proclamation, where he will contend that the Creator makes a world in which all people are in close proximity to God in order to deliver them from judgment (vv. 30-31).

The appeal to relevant evidence is a crucial feature of all the speeches in Acts. To an audience of learned nonbelievers, Paul draws support from a contemporary poet, probably a Stoic, to confirm his point: "In him [*en auto*] we live and move and have our being" (cf. Titus 1:12). Although the Stoics of his audience may well have taken Paul's appeal as confirmation of their pantheism — as though God's proximity to us is due to our participation in the divine — they almost certainly would have understood *en autō* as instrumental: that is, "by him" means humans exist "because of" God.

Paul's second citation from a philosopher-poet undermines the deep logic of the city's idolatry: "Since we are God's offspring, we should not think the deity is an image formed by humans" (v. 29). Idols can't reproduce "offspring." Paul exposes the faulty logic of a religious devotion whose chief symbols — shrines, idols, foods offered to gods, pagan rituals — are inconsistent with the inherent character of God's personal relations with humankind. The Creator must be worshiped in accordance with who God is and what God has made; religious observance must be of a kind that embodies humanity's kinship with God. The substitution of inanimate materials for the living God makes no sense.

Paul's "Altar Call"

In a few statements Paul has captured the essence of Israel's God, who is at once transcendent yet personal, sovereign yet fully engaged in human life. In doing so, he also exposes the logical flaw of pagan religion and suggests that the inward distress he experiences when observing its idols is not merely spiritual remorse but also intellectual outrage. Therefore, Paul recalls Peter's earlier ironic criticism of pious Jews whose continuing ignorance of Israel's Scriptures, the authority of which they firmly embraced, subverted their prospect of salvation (cf. 3:17-19). This benevolent God "overlooks" the ignorance of these learned philosophers and has graciously brought them a prophet-like-Jesus (Paul) to expose their intellectual darkness with the light of God's word (v. 30; cf. 3:17; 13:47). According to Acts, then, the spiritual crisis facing Israel is precisely the one facing the nations: ignorance of God's word.

Such a crisis is settled only by the prophet's proclamation of God's word in an idiom receptive by every audience it addresses. Paul's reference to two redemptive seasons — "times of human ignorance" and a "day of judgment" — recalls Peter's reference to similar seasons: "times of refreshing" (3:19) and "times of universal restoration" (3:21). The theological subtext of Peter's "times," however, is God's faithfulness to the promise of Israel's restoration, whereas the relevant subtext of Paul's speech is the universalism of God's salvation (cf. Rom. 1:18–3:26).

The warrant for turning to God and away from idolatry is that God "will have the world [*oikoumenē*] judged in righteousness" (v. 31; cf. Amos 5:18; LXX Pss. 9:8; 66:4; 95:13; 97:9). Paul's turn to the future is yet another feature of his gospel appeal that follows the deep logic of Peter's second missionary speech (3:17-26). Paul's emphasis, however, is on universal judgment rather than "the time of universal restoration." The universalism envisioned by both prophetic speeches is concentrated on the ultimate importance of the Lord's return both to judge (i.e., purify) and to restore the *oikoumenē* — another word for "world" that refers to its inhabitants (v. 6; 11:28; 17:6; cf. Luke 21:26). The use of "righteousness" in Paul's altar call probably alludes to the legal criterion of Athenian democracy: God will impartially use a common standard on the final "day of judgment" to render a fair verdict of every person's eternal destiny.

What's left for Paul to clarify is what standard of "righteousness" will be the basis for God's verdict to be rendered on that final day. The reader of Acts will draw the unstated inference from Paul's exhortation to repent that the criterion is whether people repent of the "pollutions of idols" and turn to the living God in faith. Paul is more interested in pressing for the urgency of the matter. This day of universal judgment (and restoration) is "proven" imminent by the resurrection of "a man whom God has appointed" (i.e., Jesus; cf. 2:22-24, 36). Of course, the faithful reader knows where to find this man's story (in the four Gospels) and thus how to continue where the Paul of Acts leaves it.

The response to Paul's exhortation to repent on the basis of the resurrection is mixed here in Athens, as the reader of Acts would expect. Clearly the resurrection remains a "strange teaching" to the Athenian scoffers (v. 32a), even if they are now wrapped up in a robust common ground of theological and philosophical ideas. That these ideas are generally accepted and found stimulating may well be indicated by the response of some others, who say, "We will hear you again about this." Significantly, Paul is neither mocked nor disabused of his authority to argue his case; even though the response is not great, he leaves them as a free man (v. 33). Indeed, Luke makes note of two Athenians, Dionysius and Damaris, who hear God's word in faith and turn to God's Messiah for their salvation.

PART II: ENGAGING ACTS 17 FOR TODAY'S CHURCH

Many of the scholars and students of religion who wrote during the 1960s and 1970s are surprised, even embarrassed, today. They predicted the demise of religion: secularism was on the march, and we modern, secular people would, before long, feel no need for religion, for God, or for churches and other religious institutions. A fair number of the "scholars of secularism" imagined that by the time the twenty-first century dawned, ours would be a completely secular society with only remnants of religion, spirituality, or Christianity.

Their prognostications were not completely off track. North America has become, in many ways, a much more secular and post-Christian society than it was fifty years ago. Nevertheless, interest in things religious and spiritual hardly seems to have disappeared. On the contrary, "spirituality" has become almost a buzzword. There are new forms and expressions of spirituality everywhere, from the workplace to the college campus, from the mosque to the yoga studio down the street. Certainly one of the most commonly repeated ways that people today describe themselves is: "I am not religious, but I am spiritual." In some ways, contemporary North America resembles first-century Athens, where Paul walked among a forest of gods and observed that the Athenians were very, very spiritual. Paul's experience in Athens, that great center of culture and learning, may have something to say to Christians, pastors, and congregations today as we try to negotiate our way in a culture with a smorgasbord of spiritualities. How are we to respond to the person who says, "I'm spiritual, but not religious"? How are we to respond to a culture with so much apparent spiritual interest?

Paul's own response is instructive in its nuanced manner. While he is troubled by what he sees in Athens, Paul does not respond in a simply or overtly negative way. He does not immediately dismiss or deplore all the spirituality of Athens; nor should the church simply dismiss or deplore the interest in and openness to spirituality in twenty-first-century North America. Nor does Paul unequivocally embrace it all. His response includes not only recognition of its reality and the potential of the Athenians' spiritualities but also a challenging and honest engagement with them. We Christians do well to learn from Paul and to respond with similar sensitivity and nuance to the widespread interest in spirituality in our time.

As the claims and values of modernity have waned among us and there is a loss of confidence in modernity's sources and values — reason, rationality, progress based on science and technology — there is a searching for new sources and different values. With reason and rationality no longer holding uncontested dominion, other ways of knowing have found new expression, including the mystical, the sacramental, and the spiritual. One way to understand "spirituality" as it is expressed today has been suggested by Eugene Peterson: "Its current usefulness is not in its precision but rather in the way it names something indefinable yet quite recognizable: transcendence vaguely intermingled with intimacy. Transcendence: sense that there is more, a sense that life extends far beyond me, beyond what I get paid, beyond what my spouse and my children think of me, beyond my cholesterol count. Intimacy: sense that deep within me there is a core being inaccessible to the probes of psychologists or the examinations of physicians, the questions of pollsters, the strategies of advertisers. Spirituality, though hardly precise, provides a popular term that recognizes an organic linkage between this beyond and within that are part of everyone's experience."[2]

Paul Engages the Public Square

The longing for transcendence, the search for intimacy, and the linkage of these two, Peterson suggests, are at the root of the current blossoming of spirituality. Christians can, and should, appreciate both longings and recognize them as part of their own faith experience. In this sense, the contemporary interest in spirituality provides, as did a similar interest in Athens for Paul, a point from which to begin a conversation, a place on which to build. And that is exactly what Paul does: "Athenians, I see how extremely religious you are in every way. For as I went through the city and looked carefully at the objects of your worship, I found among them an altar with an inscription, 'To an unknown god.'" Paul takes the opening that they provide. More than that, he affirms their own religious language when he quotes poetry from the Stoics: "For 'in him we live and move and have our being,' as even some of your own poets have said." Paul does not discount or dismiss the religious or spiritual interest of the Athenians, but he carefully observes it, engages it, and builds on it.

Yet, whereas Paul does observe and engage Athenian spirituality, he does not simply affirm their spirituality and leave it at that. He doesn't say, "You have gods, I have a God. Ain't it great? We're all just believing different forms of the same thing." Instead, Paul also challenges Athenian spirituality, as contemporary Christians should challenge and engage contemporary spirituality with both humility and conviction. Before saying more about just how Paul does both engage and challenge Athenian spirituality, we must note that, in Athens, Paul is out there on their turf — first in the marketplace and then in the place of public debate and judgment. There has been a Jewish synagogue in Athens for a long time, but its members have not been out there engaging the Athenians or their spirituality. While it's historically true that the Judaism of the time had no mission beyond its own community, Paul's venture into the marketplace and public square is instructive.

Too often Christians and pastoral leaders today shy away from the

---

2. Eugene H. Peterson, "Missing Ingredient," *Christian Century* (March 22, 2003), p. 30.

marketplaces and public squares of our own world. Like Athenian Jews, we huddle together. Though Paul did not enjoy spectacular success in Athens (two converts, at least that's how many Luke mentions), he did venture out on the edges, out to the margins, as Acts so often does. This is a story of innovation and adventure that challenges contemporary churches and their leaders for not taking the risk of such engagement, though we may make many pronouncements of our care and concern for the wider world.

Working with congregations, I sometimes note the huge proportion of time spent by a congregation's ordained leaders attending meetings of various boards and committees. All this training and talent is focused, so to speak, in the cranium of the body of Christ, and very little out at the nerve endings, where the body touches the world. Sometimes I make a suggestion: "Tell your pastors to give up half their meetings and spend that time in evangelism." Instead of the metaphor of running a battleship, we need more windsurfers, people out catching the wind of the Spirit. I understand that ministry to the congregation is critically important, but I also see that Paul ventured into the marketplace and the public square, that, rather than devoting all his time to the internal life of the church, he engaged the wider culture. So should the pastors of the church today. So should all believers in congregations today. We need fewer battleships and more windsurfers.

Paul Critiques Athenian Spirituality

In the *agora* and at the Aeropagus, Paul engages Athenian spirituality in ways that may be instructive to contemporary Christians who would risk engaging people and their spiritual longings today. In doing so, Paul does bring to light some of the dangers of spirituality, then and now. We read in verse 21: "Now all the Athenians and the foreigners living there would spend their time in nothing but telling or hearing something new." There was a fascination with the latest thing and newest trend that seems very much like aspects of our contemporary cultural and spiritual interests. Sometimes it is just "one thing after another": this guru, that text, this method of meditation, a book with a life-changing technique, an institute or workshop you can't miss, or an appliance that will revolutionize your life. Spirituality, too, can begin to sound like something from commercials offering "an amazing product that cuts, dices, slices, makes Julienne fries, and folds into an easy-to-use pocket knife that you can get immediately by calling the toll-free number at the bottom of your screen!"

Beneath this is a deeper issue that is at the heart of Paul's distress over the forest of idols in Athens. "Idols" meant those man-made objects and representations to whom people attributed divine or magical or spiritual powers. The danger in this — as Jews understood, and Christians should — is our perennial human attempt to gain control, to domesticate God or gods, to put them in service to us. Indeed, one danger of contemporary spirituality is that it becomes just another way of "meeting my needs," making my life a little better, or of making me feel better about myself. We should forgive others, not because Christ commanded it, but because we will feel better and live longer. We should pray, not because it acknowledges our daily dependence on God, but because it will soothe our nerves, lower our blood pressure, and generally make our lives a little better.

Another, somewhat different way to look at this is to return to the notion that ours is a therapeutic culture, a culture where almost everything is put in service of the self, where self-fulfillment and self-realization have become the self-evident *telos*. When this is applied to religion and spirituality, the result is the instrumentalizing of God. Rather than being an end in himself, God becomes an instrument toward the realization of our own predetermined ends. But God, as ultimate reality, is by definition not an instrument of our purposes. Thus Paul speaks of God as "the God who made the world and everything in it, he who is Lord of heaven and earth, [who] does not live in shrines made by human hands, nor is served by human hands, as though he needed anything, since he himself gives to mortals life and breath and all things" (vv. 24-25). God alone is God! The point is hardly to say, "My God is better than your god." It is, rather, to say that God — in order to be God at all — is the source and end of all things, not the instrument of other goals or ends, however noble, endearing, or persuasive those goals may be. "From one ancestor he made all nations to inhabit the whole earth, and he allotted the times of their existence and the bounds of their habitation" (v. 26). If God is not truly God — ultimate, holy, and sovereign — then don't bother. Hence Paul's deep distress over finding a forest of gods. It is not just that they worship the wrong God but that they have effectively destroyed the very notion of God.

In Athens the attempt to domesticate God, to control the mystery, went beyond the personal to the life of the city. Those deities that wanted

— or their handlers wanted — to have a place in Athens had to show that they would make a positive contribution, that they would add to civic health, happiness, and contentment. No disturbing deities allowed! Perhaps this sounds a bit far-fetched, but think about the way Christianity is often supposed to play a role in helping us all get along and be a better city. Think about the way Christianity and the Cross are sometimes called into service on behalf of the nation and flag. We would like to think that by now we have it figured out better than did those Athenians, who insisted that prospective gods must provide some benefit to all Athenians as the civic mark of good will. But at least sometimes we ourselves expect our God to be on the side of stability, order, and the powers that be, assisting in making our town a nice place to live and work. Again, the problem is that this inverts the biblical understanding of our relationship with God. It is not God who is to serve us; we are to serve God. It is not God who must prove his usefulness; it is we who must prove our justice and righteousness. It is not the God of Jesus Christ who must fit into our world and way of doing things; it is we who must be transformed by the renewal of our minds that we not conform to the present age (see Rom. 12:1-2)

This matter comes to a head when Paul uses the *R*-word so prominent throughout the book of Acts: "While God has overlooked the times of human ignorance, now he commands all people everywhere to repent" (v. 30). There is a basic difference between a religion or spirituality that offers to improve our lives on our terms and a religion or faith that calls us to repent, to change our hearts and minds. Theologian Reinhold Niebuhr understood the difference:

> Repentance is the basis for faith, because when I face the ultimate situation in the dialogue with God, I find that I am making too much of a claim for myself. This is the perpetual human situation. We are all creatures who have this peculiarity. We are in the flux of events, and yet we transcend them enough to know that we are in the flux, and to be worried about it. So we pretend that we are not in it, that we have a mind that transcends it, that we have a power or a virtue which can defy death. The basic sin which is discovered in the encounter with God in Christ is the sin of pretension and pride. I think I am a good man. I pretend that I am a virtuous man, and a wise man, until I confront God in Christ, and then I know that I am in the wrong before him because of all these pretenses. I have completed

my life falsely from the standpoint of myself, on the basis of my pride. So it is necessary that I die to my own self if I would truly live."[3]

Paul's call to repentance was nothing less than a call to die to the self that one might truly live. The Athenians did not, by and large, go for it. People in affluent, well-off, highly educated, and privileged populations often do not. "We will hear you again about this," they said to Paul as they folded their chairs and took their leave (v. 32). They were certainly polite, but not interested — not in repentance or new life. The price was too high. The Athenians, a wonderfully curious people very much interested in whatever new idea or insight might come down the pike for their intrigue and entertainment, were not much disposed to "lose themselves" that they might "find themselves." Interesting ideas are great, but don't ask us to really make any commitment.

Today some people who are fascinated by spirituality will respond in similar ways when their self-centeredness is challenged, when they are presented with a God who cannot be reduced to fit their world or domesticated to serve their agenda. Not every time that a prophet-like-Jesus preaches in Acts is there a great harvest of souls — several thousand joining up and following the Way. Here in Athens only two are reported. Not a large coming forward at the altar call. But maybe that's okay. Paul engaged the marketplace, entered the public square, and preached the gospel. He proclaimed God's Word. Some days the altar call is huge, but many days it is not. Neither success nor failure invalidates the proclamation. Furthermore, we cannot know whether the Athenian response was merely a polite evasion. Maybe some of those Athenians did hear Paul that day and then another Christian preacher on another day, and maybe more turned to repentance and belief after the evangelist and his reporter had left town.

In our day, spirituality holds within it a great lure and potential: people long for the beyond and hunger for the within — for both transcendence and intimacy. These hungers are real and powerful, and we should respect them and take them seriously. But there are dangers in the contemporary enthusiasm for spiritualities: if they remain but another form of self-aggrandizement, they will revel in the perpetual unknown and forever uncertain, and they will not take the risk of "naming the name." People

---

3. Niebuhr, *Justice and Mercy* (New York: Harper and Row, 1974), p. 130.

may fabricate gods to serve their needs, whether individual or social, rather than serving God and finding the self in losing themselves. They have no place for a God of judgment and grace, a God who is less concerned to make our lives a little better than to make us new. Contemporary spirituality's popularity represents both a great opportunity and a great challenge.

STUDY QUESTIONS

1. In this narrative, Paul assumes the role of a "Christian Socrates" who delineates the evidence by which the "unknown deity" of Athens is actually the God of Israel. Identify and discuss the most influential philosophies of today and match them with those against which Paul contends in Athens, in particular regarding beliefs about the existence of God, natural/material vs. supernatural/spiritual, and the future.

2. Do you think Paul's arguments in his famous Mars Hill speech, translated for today, would resonate among today's most thoughtful pundits and intellectuals? Why/why not?

3. The Paul of Acts is a skilled communicator across different cultural lines and to different audiences. How does he interpret the centrality of Jesus' resurrection in this Athenian setting? Compare his interpretation adapted for philosophers to claims made about the resurrection in other passages you have studied in Acts.

4. Do you see current interest in "spirituality" as positive or negative? Why?

5. Would you say that your congregation is more like a battleship (a lot of focus on "the bridge," centralized decision-making, and organizational maintenance) or like a windsurfer, dispersing energy into the world, making quick turns, and catching the wind?

6. The Paul of Acts not only challenges self-centered distortions of God's existence but also any attempt to make Athenian deities responsible for the city's welfare. Draw parallels to the church's response to the promotion of "civil religion" in today's society.

13 Leadership for the Church

PART I: INTERPRETING ACTS 20:17-38 AS SCRIPTURE

Paul's speech to the Ephesian elders at Miletus brings to a fitting conclusion his Asian and European missions. In contrast to Paul's missionary speeches and legal briefs, this speech addresses an audience of believers similar to those implied by his New Testament letters and is occasioned by similar concerns and interests. For this reason, an analysis of this passage may prove especially useful in orienting students to the Pauline letters: here is a portrait of the canonical Paul, the implied author of the collection of thirteen Epistles that follow the Acts of the Apostles.

The question of the speech's literary genre is also pertinent to any discussion of its wider role within the New Testament canon. There is virtual unanimity among commentators that this is Paul's "farewell" speech, which publishes his "last will and testament" to a gathering of close associates and friends shortly before his death. But there is one problem with this consensus of opinion: Paul does not die in Acts. For this reason, I am inclined to say that the purpose of this speech in Acts is to facilitate Paul's successors in Roman Asia, to discharge responsibility for the mission there to those appointed to succeed him. In his absence, these church elders will continue what he has already begun to do and teach.

In this sense, the role of this speech in narrating Paul's mission in Acts is similar to the opening narrative of the apostles' succession of the living Jesus (cf. 1:1-11; also 12:1-17; Luke 22:14-38; 24:36-53). In that earlier story in

Acts, Jesus prepares the apostles for their future ministry in light of his imminent departure in a number of ways: (1) by reviewing and interpreting his past suffering, proofs of his resurrection, and his message of God's kingdom (1:3); (2) against the horizon of his future ascension/departure from them (1:2), (3) and retrospective of John's promise of the Spirit (1:4-5), (4) the Lord charges his apostles to bring a Spirit-empowered witness of him to restore Israel as a light to the nations (1:6-8). (5) The succession is only completed after his physical departure (1:9-11). The purpose of Jesus' final speech to his apostles is not to bid them farewell but to commission them for a future mission that continues what he has begun to do and to say as the Messiah (see Acts 1:1).

If Paul's Miletus speech and departure from Asia is roughly analogous in form and function to Jesus' final speech and departure from earth, I propose the following outline of the present passage: (1) Paul rehearses his past ministry, relating his suffering and testimony (vv. 18b-20), (2) against the horizon of his future departure from them (vv. 21-25), (3) and in retrospect of his ministry among them (vv. 26-27). (4) Paul then charges the Ephesian elders to care for the church of God (vv. 28-35); (5) he completes his succession with his departure from them (vv. 36-38). Paul's purpose is pastoral preparation: his aim is to equip his successors to continue what he has begun to do and say in Ephesus, knowing that his departure from the city and its Christian congregation is now final (v. 25).

Paul's speech cultivates the faithful reader's confidence in his exemplary persona and trustworthy instruction, which has lasting importance for the church catholic in every generation. By extension, then, the Pauline letters provide their readers with an interpretation of God's Word, complete with Paul's personal testimony, which has lasting importance in their Christian formation. In this regard, the themes of his speech suggest touch-points with his letters that help fashion a coherent theological understanding of their collective witness to "the whole counsel of God": for example, faithful and humble leadership, costly suffering in consecrated service to God, congregational welfare over personal gain, and various threats against the church.

Paul's discourse also concerns those who are responsible for transmitting his legacy to still others in his absence. By extension, if the Pauline letters are the textual depository of Paul's legacy, then the future of this collection within the church is predicated on the ongoing use of them by faithful interpreters who firmly embrace the importance of Paul's testimony to God's grace and seek to imitate his faithful service to God's call-ing. The responsibility of interpreting Paul for the next generation of be-lievers is no longer a matter of casting lots or of holding ecclesial office but of good character and orthodox beliefs in faithful imitation of Paul (cf. 2 Tim. 2:2).

Paul's Importance for the Church's Future

A brief introduction to Paul's speech (vv. 17-18a) sets its stage and tone: he "sends a message" (*metakaleomai*) to Ephesus asking that the "elders of the church" meet with him in Miletus. The narrative assumes that a council of elders leads in the formation of Christian congregations from the very be-ginning of the mission to the nations (cf. 11:30; 14:23; 15:6; 16:4). The use of *metakaleomai* suggests that this is a meeting according to God's plans, which gives it an air of importance (cf. 10:32).

The first half of Paul's speech concentrates his listeners' attention on his legacy. It is enclosed by an apologia of his past ministry at Ephesus, which he characterizes as faithful both to his prophetic calling (vv. 18b-21) and to his congregants (vv. 26-27). Sandwiched between is a prophecy of his future suffering in Jerusalem (vv. 22-24) and an assertion on this basis that he will not return to Ephesus (v. 25).

In a single Greek sentence, the Paul of Acts defends his Asian mission, centered in Ephesus, in two integral movements. He first appeals to the en-tire body of evidence of "how I lived among you" (v. 18; cf. 1 Thess. 2:1-2; 5:10-11; Phil. 4:15), a life characterized by his humble service to the Lord and by his costly endurance of "the plots of the Jews" (v. 19; cf. 2 Cor. 1:3-11). The importance of "humility" in Paul's retrospective is intensified by its rarity. It is used only here in Acts, infrequently in the New Testament, and not at all in the Septuagint. Significantly, its use in the New Testament is mostly by Paul and found in the virtue catalogs of Ephesians (4:2) and Colossians (2:18, 23; 3:12) — writings whose Pauline traditions, largely shaped after his death, are closely associated with those of the Paul of Acts.

While testimony to his humility reflects Paul's commentary on the be-liever's inward affections (cf. 2 Cor. 10:1; 11:7; 1 Thess. 2:6), his appeal to consider personal suffering represents a more empirical line of evidence that invites his listeners to evaluate his devotion to Christ (cf. 9:16) and to them. The reader, too, can participate in this review of Paul's life by recalling his difficulties in Ephesus layered into the earlier narrative of his mission there (cf. 19:8-10; 20:3).

The second broad movement concerns the disposition of Paul's pastoral obligations to the Ephesian church. His description of prophetic tasks performed is exemplary of Christian leadership into the church's future, and he will later recall these same images as characteristic of ministry that continues his legacy in his absence. He declares that in general he "did not shrink [*hypostellō*] from doing anything helpful." Luke uses the root word for "apostasy" *(hypostellō)* in two related senses here and elsewhere in Acts. On the one hand, Paul does not "shrink" from his calling to teach the congregations founded by his mission ("house to house," v. 20), unlike Judas, for example, whose betrayal of Jesus was a repudiation of his divine appointment to care for the messianic community (1:16b-17). On the other hand, Paul does not "shrink" from the message he publicly proclaims "to Jews and Greeks about repentance toward God and faith toward our Lord Jesus" (v. 21; cf. Rom. 10:8-13). Not only is there a practical apostasy that Paul avoids in his regular ministry among believing households; there is also a theological apostasy that he avoids in defending the truth claims of the gospel, which he summarizes using the familiar catchwords of Acts — "repentance" and "faith." The Paul of Acts does not need to remind the reader of those places or of that biblical protocol that he follows, whether as a philosopher in Athens or a prophet in Jewish synagogues, to faithfully argue the gospel's case (v. 24).

Paul signals the shift from apologia (in retrospect) to prophecy (in prospect) with the transitional phrase "and now I. . . ." Even as he shows his faithfulness through his costly devotion to the tasks of the prophet-like-Jesus, he is also faithful to (or "captive/compelled" by) what the "Holy Spirit testifies to me in every city that imprisonment and persecutions are waiting for me" (vv. 22-23). He does not mention details of a particular revelation from the Spirit to him; in fact, he claims that he does not know what will happen to him in Jerusalem (cf. Rom. 15:30-32). Commentators have long noted the parallelism between Paul's prophecy and Jesus' prediction of his passion in Jerusalem. While this is certainly characteristic of Luke's typological shaping of his narrative, and perhaps is a subtext of this part of Paul's speech, the prophecy is still much too vague to assert that Paul's final Jerusalem visit is of a type with that of Jesus. Paul did not die there, nor does he know what will happen to him there.

That he should expect suffering to await him in Jerusalem is no different from what he expects in "every city," since Jesus prophesied that Paul's mission would result in his suffering for the sake of the gospel (see 9:15-16). Conflict is the inevitable result of preaching Jesus (cf. Luke 2:34). Furthermore, it seems more likely that the compelling motive of Paul's journey to Jerusalem as a religious pilgrim is in keeping with his observance of Jewish practices (v. 16) rather than as a Christian martyr. While he can claim, "I do not count my life of any value to myself" (v. 24a; cf. 2 Cor. 4:7–5:10; 6:4-10; Phil. 1:19-26), the revelation to which he refers must be of an earlier vision that disclosed Rome, not Jerusalem, as the place where he will "finish my course and the ministry that I received from the Lord Jesus" (v. 24b; cf. 1 Cor. 9:24; Phil. 3:8-13).

For these reasons, Paul's statement of departure does not predict a Jerusalem "passion." His emphatic assertion that these Ephesians "will never see my face again" must be understood in terms of his earlier vision of a new mission field in Rome, which requires his departure from them and a succession of his leadership in Asia. His repetition of the central task of his prophetic vocation in Ephesus — to "proclaim the kingdom" — indicates that his farewell concerns the Roman mission and not a Jerusalem passion, and it recalls Jesus' paradigmatic prophecy about the inspired witness of his successors that includes teaching about God's kingdom at the "end of the earth" (see 1:3, 6; 14:22; 28:23, 31; cf. 1 Cor. 6:9-11; 1 Thess. 2:12; Col. 1:13).

Paul concludes his personal reminiscence by again declaring that he "did not shrink" from his prophetic obligations in proclaiming the gospel in Ephesus (v. 20). The striking declaration that he "is not responsible for the blood of any of you" (v. 26) recalls his earlier indictment of unrepentant Jews in Corinth (cf. 18:6), which presumed that they no longer could excuse their rejection of God's gospel on grounds of their ignorance of its claims and Scripture's warrants. Paul's preaching ministry has clarified God's script of salvation's history, and thus to refuse his message is to refuse God's invitation. In this new setting in which Paul addresses believers, the issue is not the salvation of his listeners but their succession of Paul's mission in Ephesus. Whether or not the foundation he has laid in that city continues to be built on is no longer in his hands; his departure signals the official beginning of their own ministry in his absence.

The addition of a final summary of Paul's gospel, "the whole counsel [*boulē*] of God" (v. 27; cf. Eph 1:11), delineates the theological boundaries of that ecclesiastical foundation. Elsewhere in Acts, *boulē* denotes God's sovereign purpose that is worked out in the Messiah's mission (e.g., 2:22-

23) and now in the church's mission under the aegis of the Holy Spirit (cf. 4:28-31). There is no Pauline teaching that deviates from God's *boulē*, and thus Pauline teaching is "canonical" in congregations founded by it. The implication is that God views any deviation from his catechesis apostasy; and such apostasy would subvert God's scripted plans for salvation's progress into the future of Ephesus.

In the second half of the speech, Paul shifts from a description of his past and a prophecy about his future to the terms of his succession in Ephesus. He discharges the elders (here referred to as "overseers," without any change of meaning) to their ministry in ever-vigilant expectation of coming dangers (vv. 28-31). He goes on to exhort them to follow his and the Lord's example of leadership within a community of goods that cares for the poor (vv. 32-35). Paul's rehearsal of the dangers that will face the elders following his departure is enclosed by his charge for them to "keep watch over yourselves and all the flock" (v. 28; see 5:35b) and to "be alert" to his pastoral example (v. 31). The shepherd watching over his flock is a familiar biblical metaphor of the leader's provident care over Israel, of which the Paul of Acts is exemplary. He presumes that they will be competent to do so because "the Holy Spirit has made you overseers," which not only suggests the mediation of the Spirit's power for ministry but also the Spirit's authorizing "mark" in their lives that others have recognized (see 6:3-4).

While the role of elders to pastor "the church of God" seems clear enough, it is confused by the relative clause that follows — "which God bought with his own [*idios*] blood," a clause that is obscure in both its literal sense and its purpose within Paul's speech. That God acquires a people by saving them from destruction is a biblical idea (cf. Ps. 74:2), and it is probably Paul's meaning here. But that God did so by means of God's "own blood" is very difficult to understand theologically. A few commentators think that *idios* as used here is a term of endearment — implying God's "own" Messiah. Others suggest that Luke has combined fragments from two Pauline formulae about "the church of God" and "Christ purchases the church for God by his blood" and has made a grammatical mess of it, perhaps due to his lack of theological interest in the efficacy of Christ's blood in saving people from their sins. In any case, the lingering impression left by this phrase is that the church must place extraordinary value on God's sacrificial love, and in this light the church's leaders must take their own calling with utmost seriousness.

233

The ethos shaped by Paul's repeated exhortation to pastoral action is of a community whose beliefs and practices rub against the prevailing norm, which is certainly in line with the preceding narrative of his controversial Ephesian mission. And he must realize that his departure and the loss of his public charisma will occasion a serious challenge to the purity of this ethos. He notes, then, two potential dangers: false teachers will come as "savage wolves" from the outside, and even "from your own group" inside the flock of God (vv. 29-30). The catch phrase echoes Jesus' reference to "savage wolves" (see Matt. 7:15; 10:16; Luke 10:3; John 10:12), which is what he calls those teachers of Israel who reject his messianic word and in doing so lead the flock of Israel astray. The phrase has a similar ring in Paul's speech. In this case, the "savage wolf" is any teacher who "distorts the truth" of Paul's teaching within those congregations founded by his mission (cf. 13:10).

Paul's warning of false teaching within the church is unusual in the book of Acts. The repetition and variety of references to Paul's teaching in this speech underscore the importance of theological purity in maintaining and transmitting his legacy to the next generation of believers. Further, Paul calls upon the memory of the elders to "remember that for three years I did not cease night or day to warn everyone with tears" (v. 30; cf. 2 Cor. 2:4). Luke's characteristic use of hyperbole again underscores the value of Paul's personal example, which also carries canonical status within the ongoing community.

A Fond Farewell

A rhetorical shift from warning to encouragement is once again marked by the repetition of the transitional phrase "and now. . . ." The final lines of Paul's speech combine blessing (v. 32) and exhortation (vv. 33-35), similar to the benedictions in his letters. The main thread of the speech remains fixed on his "message" *(logos)* of God's grace (see v. 24; 14:3; 5:32). The edifying connection of Paul's gospel with the "building up" *(oikodomeō)* of his successors for their future "inheritance" reflects Pauline themes, even if here they are in the Lucan idiom.

In the context of Acts, however, the use of *oikodomeō* to encourage the spiritual formation ("building up") of elders glosses the use of *an-oikodomeō* in Amos's prophecy of a "rebuilt" Israel (cf. 15:16-17) to remind the reader that God continues to fulfill the promise of a restored Israel's mission to the nations even in Paul's absence through the ministry of the church's elders. In this regard, then, Paul's concluding admonitions reflect the concerns expressed by James regarding whether the mixing of uncircumcised gentiles with repentant Jews in the synagogues of the Diaspora will result in the attenuation of the Jewish legacy within the church (cf. 15:20-21, 29). Even as Acts has carefully depicted Paul — and thus his legacy — as Jewish, the reader should note the implied connection between his final exhortations and the cautionary notes sounded earlier by James regarding the social solidarity of the community.

Even if James's principal concerns are to maintain this sense of solidarity by abstaining from the pollutants of pagan religion, Paul's concerns are more ethical and echo the social practices of the community of goods (cf. 2:42-47), especially within the acquisitive culture of Ephesus (cf. 19:25b-27): the dispossession rather than "coveting" of property is the measure of one's spiritual maturity (v. 33; cf. 4:32-35); and working with one's hands to earn one's keep (v. 34; cf. 18:3) is motivated by the evident need "to support the weak" (v. 35). As with the content of what is taught, these moral norms are in imitation of Paul and obedient to Jesus' command that "it is more blessed to give than to receive." Although this saying is not found in the Gospel tradition, it agrees with the plain sense of Jesus' teaching (cf. Luke 6:35-38). In any case, the purpose of Paul's appeal is to underscore the practical truth that the community's solidarity is only as strong as its commitment to its own "weak" (cf. 4:32-35; 6:1-7). Finally, it is not his example but because of the command of Jesus that Paul can also say that "we must *(dei)*" help the poor and powerless — a practical necessity according to God's Word. This practice remains the social mark of the community of goods in whose life the kingdom of God has been restored by God's grace.

The concluding panel casts a poignant image of a fond farewell. The sheer weight of the emotional terms Luke layers into this scene ("much weeping," "embraced and kissed Paul," "grieving because they would not see his face again") highlights the theme of Paul's departure from Ephesus in the speech itself (vv. 25, 29) and all that is staked out because of it. A frequent interpretive mistake is to say that, since Luke is writing from a perspective after Paul's death, he must be writing *about* Paul's death: the sorrow and affection poured out on him foreshadow what might take place at his funeral. As I have argued in this commentary on the Acts 20 speech, the

Paul of Acts addresses the importance of an orderly succession of ministry in Ephesus, which is occasioned by his departure for a new mission elsewhere (i.e., Rome; cf. 19:21) and not by his so-called passion in Jerusalem. The finality of Paul's farewell, when "they accompany him to the ship," simply makes more urgent the elders' compliance with his instructions.

PART II: ENGAGING ACTS 20 FOR TODAY'S CHURCH

Though eight chapters remain in the Acts of the Apostles, chapters that tell the story of Paul's journey to Jerusalem and, after that, to Rome, the end is in sight, and another narrative of succession is at hand. Acts began with a narrative of succession — a leadership transfer in the first chapter. Now we come to another narrative of succession, this time a transfer of leadership by Paul to the Ephesian elders as he ends his ministry in Asia and prepares to go to Europe. Here he entrusts the care of the flock to those the "Holy Spirit has made overseers, to shepherd the church of God that he obtained with the blood of his own Son." Paul's summing up, his reflection on his own ministry, and his charge to those who will succeed him as leaders in the church provide important material for our continued reflection on leadership in the church. It may well be that there is no more urgent challenge facing the church today than identifying, preparing, calling, authorizing, supporting, and encouraging faithful and capable leaders. Moreover, our larger culture and society seem beset by a sense of a "crisis of leadership": the cry for "leadership" goes up frequently, though there is clearly no consensus about what the term means.

While a congregation's leaders, both ordained and lay, are only one part of the whole, they are a crucial part — a very crucial part indeed. They are the shepherds of the flock, the teachers of the faith, and the watchmen atop the city towers. This last image is prominent in Ezekiel (see Ezek. 33:6) and may be one Paul has in mind when he says, "I am not responsible for the blood of any one of you!" In other words, "I did my work, stood my post faithfully, and now the response is up to you." Note that all these metaphors for the leader are relational ones: the shepherd and the flock, the teacher and students, and the watchman and the citizens of the city. That is, leaders are community people: they guide, mobilize, direct, and support communities, whether these are groups, congregations, or institutions.

They embody community identity, they interpret community norms and sources, they symbolize a group's values and its work, and in a very real sense they "hold" a community's people. No wonder leadership is tough! It is exceedingly multifaceted in its variety of tasks, and it is always relational — engaged with people in all sorts of ways and configurations.

In this sense we can contrast leadership to a different social role, one that fares better in a technical society — the expert. Many are the experts among us; we seldom hear about a "crisis of expertise." But there is a crucial difference between the expert and the leader. The expert is, in a certain sense, someone you go to. You make an appointment, have a consultation, get an estimate, obtain a service, and that's that. By contrast, a leader is part of a community and belongs to that community. You go to see an expert, but a leader belongs to a community. The perceived "crisis of leadership" may have its roots elsewhere, in the incoherence of our varied "communities" and social groupings, an incoherence brought on by rapid social change, diminished authority, heightened personal choice and expectations, and a valuing of personal fulfillment over duty and obligation. John Gardner, founder of Common Cause and one-time Secretary of the Department of Health, Education, and Welfare, has put it this way: "If leaders cannot find in their constituency any basis of shared values, principled leadership becomes nearly impossible." Expressing that another way, the "leadership crisis" may be, in reality, a social crisis, a crisis of our communities, congregations, and institutions where shared values and agreed-on norms have been, if not lost, then certainly diminished.

Against the backdrop of the "crisis of leadership" in our society and in the church, what do Paul's parting words to those who will succeed him as leaders of the Ephesian church have to say to us? One way to frame Paul's remarks here is through the lens of the great biblical theme of "covenant." A covenantal understanding of leadership can be read between the lines of Paul's words in Acts 20. Covenants, as theological ethicist William F. May has suggested, are typically made up of four elements: (1) a primal gift, a costly sacrifice, that both marks and changes life; (2) in response to the primal gift, promises are made and obligations accepted; (3) there is life lived within the structure of gift and promise, a life that has "fidelity" as its prime descriptive quality; (4) there are occasions and events for the renewal of covenant. In Paul's parting words to leaders of the church, we can discern at least some elements of a covenant of leadership, the recovery of which may be a healthy and overdue response to the "crisis of leadership" particularly in the church.

Primal Gift

In verse 28, Paul says to the elders who have gathered with him that they are to shepherd the church that God "obtained with the blood of his own Son." As our exposition of this passage has noted, this verse is somewhat problematic in construction, and its precise meaning is unclear. Nonetheless, this much is clear: the church has its origins in a primal and costly gift, a sacrifice, a blood mark. There are some, of course, who will recoil from such seemingly primitive language and would dispose of the entire idea of sacrifice. But for Paul, this is not an option. The church begins in a primal gift, a gift of grace that has claimed believers and even rescued them from perdition.

The point may be less about blood or sacrifice, ultimately, than about the core theological conviction of the Christian faith, which is that the initiative is God's. God has made the first move. God sought us, "died for us," while we were yet sinners. God reached out to us in Jesus Christ. Thus the first word is never about us, about what we must do; it is about God and what God has done. It is about a primal gift: "We love because God first loved us." And such love is costly. Such a sentiment and understanding is not limited to God's love for humanity and the world. It is also evident in lesser dramas: the costly love of parents for their children, the teachers who have sacrificed themselves that we might learn, the historic political leaders who, at great risk and sometimes loss of life, have given themselves to a dangerous but noble cause.

It was the crucified and risen Christ that encountered Paul on the Damascus Road; that is, it was the Christ who had suffered and died. Such a primal gift and sacrifice marked Paul's life, and his leadership was "by way of response." That is, it didn't originate with his own idea, nor in his desire for prominence or a particular status. It originated in this costly, primal gift. Leadership for the church today, and in all times, can only be adequately founded in such an understanding and experience, from a source and story that is larger than our own, from a vision so grand that it has changed the world — not by force of arms but by the force of love and the gift of grace. When you get right down to it, leadership can be — in fact, often is — thankless. It is thus better for us to understand leadership not as a way we will gain thanks or recognition or praise (some days we will, but often we won't) but as a way of giving thanks and as an expression of gratitude.

Promises Made

Paul said to the elders of the church: "I do not count my life of any value to myself, if only I may finish my course and the ministry that I received from the Lord Jesus, to testify to the good news of God's grace." What shapes and defines ministry and leadership for Paul, beyond the primal gift, are the promises he has made. His life was given shape by Christ's call and charge. That is, he was placed under a divine charge: he had "promises to keep."

Perhaps in a time when leadership seems to have so much more to do with managing resources — not to mention managing perceptions — this language of gift and promise will seem hopelessly idealistic or romantic. And yet, in order to endure and to do so with integrity, leaders do require some ground that doesn't shift, some foundation amid the shifting sands of success and failure, of perception and reality, whether or not people are happy and satisfied. Sometimes leaders, by definition, will have to challenge their followers, their communities, and their constituencies. They will have to proclaim to those who elected them or who work for them or who listen to them preach, not what they want to hear, but what they need to hear. Sometimes leaders will have to challenge the very people they have come to love, the very values and ways that they, too, have come to value. Ron Heifetz has said: "You appear dangerous to people when you question their values, beliefs, or habits of a lifetime. You place yourself on the line when you tell people what they need to hear rather than what they want to hear. Although you may see with clarity and passion a promising future of progress and gain, people will see with equal passion the losses you are asking them to sustain."[1]

In order to take these kinds of risks, that is, in order to lead — which is not the same thing as "occupying a leadership position" — one has to be grounded in something other and deeper than the latest popularity poll. In a world as cynical as our own, Paul's words here, "but I do not count my life of any value to myself, if only I may finish my course and the ministry that I received . . . ," may sound hopelessly idealistic. But perhaps the problem is not in the words of Paul. Perhaps the problem is in us — in our cynicism and manipulations. Leaders are those who are grounded in some-

---

1. Ronald H. Heifetz, *Leadership on the Line* (Cambridge, MA: Harvard Business School Press, 2002), p. 12.

thing deep: in a primal gift, in a promise made, in a source of meaning and authority that are not, in the end, completely of this world or of the present age.

Fidelity

The third element of a covenantal understanding of leadership is of subsequent life and practice shaped in accord with the primal gift and the promise made. There seems to be no better word to characterize Paul's varied remarks about ministry and leadership in Acts 20 than *fidelity*. He was faithful to his calling and charge; he was faithful in teaching "repentance toward God and faith toward our Lord Jesus" (v. 21) and "the whole purpose of God" (v. 27); he was faithful in his way of life, which was devoid of coveting the silver and gold of others (v. 33). In other words, he exemplified willing work and service and care for the weak in the community of shared goods.

To tease apart the various strands of this exemplary life of the leader, we may begin with a phrase Paul uses twice in his parting words. In verses 20-21, Paul says, "I did not shrink from doing anything helpful, proclaiming the message to you and teaching you publicly and from house to house, as I testified to both Jews and Greeks about repentance toward God and faith toward our Lord Jesus." Later, in verse 27, he uses the same phrase: "I did not shrink from declaring to you the whole purpose of God." In our own time, when it appears that many leaders have shrunken — become small, timid, and cautious lest they offend anyone — Paul's "I did not shrink" is a provocative picture of leadership for the church.

Paul avoided shrinkage, and indeed practiced something we might think of as "fullness," in two senses. In the first sense, he did his work and did not shrink from the tasks to which he had been called, whether "doing anything helpful" or performing his ministry of teaching from house to house. An old pastor once said to me that many pastors seem to forget one simple thing: "You just have to do your work." He meant that there is, in the end, no substitute for simply doing the work that belongs to each of us. That work is seldom glamorous, even if "your work" is the work of pastoral leadership. There are visits to be made, reports and sermons to be written, classes to be prepared, meetings to be organized, and sometimes boilers to be fixed. Being a leader does not mean — as some seem to understand but others do not — being exempted from the work, from getting one's hands dirty, from having to show up and follow through. Leadership, at least Christian leadership, is not about being privileged to have someone else do all the nitty-gritty work while you take your place at the head table.

But in the second sense, Paul, as a leader, not only did not shrink from the work; he also did not shrink in the face of opposition. He "endured trials" and "did not shrink . . . from testifying." As the previous chapter and the story of the mission in Ephesus makes clear, the gospel definitely does create controversy. While leaders in the church must be careful not to seek some kind of masochistic self-justification in controversy and opposition, neither should they shrink from it. Keeping people happy is not generally the same thing as leadership. Leadership requires courage.

In this connection, Paul warns that, following the departure of a strong and effective leader, there will be challenges: "I know that after I have gone, savage wolves will come in among you, not sparing the flock. Some even from your own group will come distorting the truth in order to entice the disciples to follow them" (vv. 29-30). The familiar, almost stereotypical nature of this biblical metaphor — flock and wolves — should not obscure Paul's realism about the challenges that follow the departure of a strong leader. A vacuum is often created, and as it is true that nature abhors a vacuum, so it is in congregations. In the absence of clear, effective, and faithful leadership — or simply in times of leadership transition — some will try to take advantage of that vacuum or transition to further their own ends. Paul does not hesitate to call them "savage wolves." Furthermore, he is careful to note that the wolves do not always come from outside the congregation; sometimes they have been waiting and biding their time within it. And what is the mark of such false shepherds, of the wolves? They will "distort the truth" in order to "entice disciples to follow them." That is, they will not be faithful to the essentials of the faith, and their teaching will not be "sound" (see 2 Tim. 1:10). Moreover, they will be more interested in creating a personal following than in building up the body of Christ.

Paul's language may sound antiquated or even somehow romantic, but congregations should take seriously his warnings regarding leadership and the dangers in times of leadership transition. Congregations are particularly vulnerable to "savage wolves" — who may nonetheless appear attractive and alluring. There are many out there who do prey on the vulnerable, who want and need disciples for themselves, who will take advantage of others, and who find in congregations an attractive opportunity.

Not only did Paul not shrink from doing his work or from boldly proclaiming the gospel, he was clear on matters of money and possessions and how leaders relate and don't relate to them. That narrator Luke, who is consistently aware of the danger of possessions and wealth, should see this theme worked into Paul's parting exhortation is no surprise. But this is a matter that needs some honest attention in our era of "celebrity CEOs" who make millions annually and in our culture, where "our salary is our report card." It's true that "making millions" is not a problem many church leaders have to worry about. But leaders in the church, in living a life of fidelity, do have to come to grips with money in both its negative and positive potential. In verse 33, Paul notes that he did not covet the gold or silver or possessions of any in the church. He wasn't in it for the money. This is not to say that clergy should not be paid fairly or adequately; they should. But not only was Paul not looking to feather his own nest at the expense of the congregation; he was mindful of the positive potential of financial resources in the community of shared goods. He gives as an example the support of the needy and the weak in the community (v. 35).

In many congregations today, people appreciate it if their leaders don't say much, if anything, about money or personal stewardship. Note that this was not Paul's style, nor should it be that of leaders in the church today. Sometimes the polite silence that accompanies the subjects of money and possessions are simply a way of protecting the haves, of permitting "a strong habit of weak giving" to go unnoticed and unchallenged. Paul provided leadership, in part, by speaking directly of the role of money in his life and of his stewardship. Leaders who shrink from such subjects are unlikely to be very effective leaders — not just in the financial area, but in every area. To put it more positively, a clear and consistent witness regarding the faithful use of money and possessions demonstrates and strengthens all of a person's leadership in the church. This certainly does not mean that a church leader should talk about money all the time, nor that she should boast of her own stewardship. But it does mean that such a leader knows that money — how we understand and use it — is an unavoidable part of an authentic life of faith.

Under this third aspect of leadership within the framework of covenant and a life of fidelity, we should make the final point that character counts. Often today, when they seek leadership, congregations inquire about particular skill sets, areas of expertise, and bodies of experience. This is understandable, and it's probably a good idea. But skills, expertise, and experience will not overcome flawed character, untrustworthy behavior, or a lack of basic integrity. In fact, skills, experience, and expertise can be gained if basic character and integrity are firmly in place. While it is not always easy to assess character and trustworthiness, congregations should perhaps keep these qualities at the top of their list when seeking leadership. After all, trust is the currency of leadership: without trust born of being trustworthy, not much will be accomplished.

Paul spends a fair amount of time in these parting words speaking about matters of character. Some contemporary readers may be put off by his remarks, perceiving Paul as boastful. Many leaders certainly are capable of blowing their own horns. But another way to look at this is that Paul is pointing out how important character is to leadership, that leadership, while it is not less than skills or certain kinds of expertise and experience, is always much more. Rabbi Edwin Friedman, in his several works, encourages leaders to practice "self-differentiation," which boils down to knowing who you are and being able to communicate who you are and what you care about to others. Leadership, claims Friedman, is not in the end about expertise, partly because none of us in leadership positions can ever really know enough. We cannot master or become experts in all the materials and techniques. We simply can't know it all. But we can know who we are, and we can communicate that with authenticity to others. That, says Friedman, is what leaders do. They know who they are, what they are about, and they are able to convey that to others with an appropriate blend of modesty and conviction. It remains true that character counts, and that the lives of leaders are characterized by fidelity: fidelity to the gifts and promises that have authorized them as leaders and fidelity to the work and tasks that comprise their particular calling.

Covenant Renewal

We have noted before how often a change or decision in Acts is followed by some public ritual, whether it be the apostles laying hands on the new elders in Acts 6, the baptism of the Ethiopian eunuch in Acts 8, or the celebration of worship in the homes of Cornelius and the Philippian jailer. Thus it should come as no surprise that this powerful moment of transition and succession in Miletus should end with all of them on their knees in prayer and embrace. True, this is not the formal covenant renewal that a wedding anniversary or renewal of vows service may be for many couples. Still, there is a way, given Paul's recitation and exhortation, that the covenant is reaffirmed and renewed. Paul has reminded those who will follow him in leadership as shepherds of this flock of their calling, their tasks, and the need for good character; and he has pointed out some of the dangers, both internal and external, that will come. This whole passage, Paul's parting speech and succession narrative, is in a sense a covenant renewal.

"Leadership is not necessary," someone has said, "if you aren't trying to do anything." If, on the other hand, you are trying to accomplish something, then leadership is important and necessary. Leadership is not dominating others or disempowering them. On the contrary, good leaders empower their followers and the communities and organizations they lead. But leadership can be very challenging for just that reason. True leaders point the way to the future and mobilize people to take on their toughest problems and challenges. Sometimes, it seems, we prefer "leaders" who tell us that we're great, that everything is just fine, that there's no need to take any risks. But that is not leadership. Leadership, especially in the church, will be deepened when we become aware of its covenantal nature: leaders are in covenant with the communities they serve. And in the church, leaders are in covenant with God. These covenantal understandings of leadership remind us that it is not about us — not about the leaders. We have all received a great primal gift: it's about God and what God has done and is doing. Like all Christians, leaders have also made promises. "I have decided to follow Jesus," we sing, "no turning back." "I would be true, for there are those who trust me." We are people under promise, and we have promises to keep. As leaders, then, in response to the gift and under the promise, we are to live lives characterized by fidelity. Periodically, we remember and renew these promises — at ordinations, installations of officers and pastors, and anniversary celebrations.

We have not emphasized techniques or strategies of leadership in this chapter, partly because we have discussed those things elsewhere in this book, especially in the chapters on "Conflict Resolution and Decision Making" and "The Challenge of Change in the Church." In keeping with Paul's own themes in Acts 20, however, we emphasize here the covenantal quality of leadership and the character of leaders. Now more than ever, we need leaders who are faithful to the vows and covenants in their lives. We need leaders whose character and integrity we can trust. But as congregations and communities, we also need to keep our covenants: we need to be, in the phrase of ethicist Stanley Hauerwas, "communities of character."

STUDY QUESTIONS

1. Wall and Robinson argue that the book of Acts introduces and orients the reader to the letters of Paul that follow Acts in the New Testament. According to Acts 20 Paul indicates that the primary marks of Christian leadership correspond to the primary problems facing a congregation: purity, possessions, power. Read 1 Timothy. What are the threats to purity, possessions, and power enumerated in this letter, and how does remembering the Paul of Acts contribute to an effective leader's response to these problems?

2. In your view, how important is leadership to a congregation? What are the qualities or characteristics of good leadership?

3. Good leaders, according to Robinson and Wall, do not always tell people what they want to hear, but what they need to hear. Think of an example of this in your experience. How did you respond to this at the time?

4. Of the four elements of covenant (primal gift, promises made, fidelity, and covenant renewal) and their application to leadership, which one intrigues you most? Why? Which one intrigues you the least? Why?

14

The Uneasy Relationship
of Church and State

PART I: INTERPRETING ACTS 25:1-12 AS SCRIPTURE

The church's relationship to political authority is an important theme in Acts. Peter's retort to political pressure, "We must obey God rather than any human authority" (5:29), is arguably Scripture's most-used warrant in support of a believer's civil disobedience. However, the interpreter must take care to use this text in full awareness of both its nearer compositional context and its wider canonical contexts. Within Acts, the apostles are responding to a particular kind of political pressure, which is carefully drawn by the narrator. The apostles have characterized Jerusalem's priestly authority as hostile to God's purposes, unrepentant and tyrannical, and therefore clearly unfit to lead the household of Israel into the new era of God's salvation that has dawned after the empty tomb.

In today's world, political authority is rarely as sharply drawn as it is in Acts, and Peter's response to Israel's high priest can rarely be glibly made. For this reason, Peter's defiance of political authority is an exemplar for today's Christian only with several qualifications. We must note first of all that, according to Acts, his comment introduces the proclamation of God's gospel. Civil disobedience serves redemptive and not political ends. The apostles are not leaders of a protest movement against the Roman occupation or against the leadership of official Judaism. Peter and John lead a movement of God. And so it is with every leader of the earliest church, whose Spirit-enabled tasks were missional rather than political, even if they sometimes did have unintended political repercussions.

In a wider canonical context, the interpreter will note the variety of ways in which Scripture defines the relationship between church and state. In the famous passage in his letter to the Romans (13:1-7), for example, citizen Paul writes with some irony that Roman authority is divinely sanctioned to serve the good purposes of God in the world; in an ideal world the church should obey and gladly support civil authority because the state maintains God's shalom in advance of Christ's return (cf. Rom. 13:11-14) by locking up troublemakers and rewarding loving neighbors (cf. Rom. 13:3-10). Yet Revelation 13 drafts a more realistic picture: using dark and evil images, the prophet draws a portrait of a political "Babylon" (i.e., Rome) ruled by an unholy trinity, where the people of the Lamb are persecuted and even martyred because of their courageous opposition to civil rule. Martyrdom is the evidence of faithfulness in those places that oppose God's redemptive purposes for the world.

Within Scripture, Acts mediates between these two extremes and helps to maintain their self-correcting interplay within the church. Following the exhortation of either Romans or Revelation — to the exclusion of the other — leads, and has led, the church in dangerous directions, whether to easy acquiescence to fascist regimes or to violent revolution. Acts reminds its readers of the church's uneasy relationship with civil authority, but a relationship that, if properly maintained, can serve the church's missionary interests.

No portion of Acts is better suited to an exploration of this idea than the story line of Paul's legal problems — his arrest, imprisonment, and various trials — that is plotted across the final quarter of the narrative (21:27–28:31). And no episode of Acts' story of prisoner Paul is more perceptive of the church's politics than this passage in Acts 25. Nero's appointment of Porcius Festus around 60 C.E. as procurator of Judea signals an important shift in the politics of Roman Palestine. Festus is a cunning man, full of energy, whose administration is characterized by his fairness toward the Jews, especially when compared to his greedy predecessor, Felix. Unfortunately, there is not a corresponding change for the good among Jerusalem's priestly elite. Two years after Paul's arrest, Israel's elites continue to plot an assassination attempt against Paul, this time with Festus playing their dupe (vv. 1-5; see 23:12-22). The persistence of unrepentant Israel to subvert the influence of Paul's message in the Holy City and beyond implies his continuing importance in Jewish politics. Much as it is in contemporary America, the mingling of religious conviction and national destiny by Israel's ruling elites makes Paul's interpretation of God's redemptive plan — which diminishes Israel's national prerogatives — controversial and makes him a marked man.

As a citizen of Rome, Paul is granted freedom to receive visitors while under house arrest in Roman Caesarea (see 24:23). There is an indication in his letters that, even from prison, he routinely delegated the daily business of his mission to trusted associates (see Philemon): his delegates would mediate his spiritual authority beyond the prison walls. Moreover, rumors in Jerusalem of his mission beyond Palestine (see 21:21-24) imply his importance, even if embattled, within the Jerusalem church. Some think that the narrative's silence about what role the Jewish church played during Paul's imprisonment reflects their lack of support of Paul — even perhaps their effort to silence him. This is plausible. But the keen attention paid Paul by the religious establishment of Jerusalem, according to Acts, even provoking pious men to use subterfuge to assassinate him (see 23:12-15), can only be explained if he has remained an important player in Jerusalem politics.

No doubt Festus has heard from Felix of this earlier failed conspiracy against Paul; and Festus knows something of the Jewish case against him as well (see 24:5-6). He is thus duly cautious in his responses and actions in dealing with the Jewish leadership team in Jerusalem. After all, his prisoner is a Roman citizen in good standing, which he has also no doubt learned from Felix (v. 12), and the legal case against him failed to convince his predecessor of Paul's guilt. Even so, Festus listens to the ad hoc case against Paul and to his rebuttal (vv. 6-8) before tendering Paul the choice: "Do you wish to go to Jerusalem and be tried there before me on these charges?"

As we have noted, biblical narratives provide very little information about the inner motivations of their characters; the reader simply does not know what "favor" *(charis)* Festus thought he was granting "the Jews" by asking his prisoner such a question. He is a clever politician, and he makes a strategic decision as the new ruler of an intractable region. Perhaps he presumes that Paul will not leave Jerusalem alive. The reader is left to speculate — but not for long.

Nor does the reader know why Paul chooses this particular moment to make his appeal to the Caesar in Rome. Is he afraid for his personal safety in Palestine, making this appeal his ticket to the safety of Rome? That is doubtful. Is he prompted by judicial propriety since sedition is the only relevant charge leveled against him, and such an allegation against a citizen should be properly heard by the emperor? That is plausible. Or is Paul motivated by his heavenly call to "bear witness in Rome" (23:11) as an act of obedience to God? That is the most probable. Luke does not tell his readers the reason for Paul's appeal; he is concerned only to narrate the appeal — "I appeal to Caesar" — and its immediate result: "To Caesar you shall go!" Readers are simply mistaken if they conclude that this legal maneuver backfires in light of Agrippa's concluding verdict (26:32). In this particular narrative world, Paul's decision to appeal to Rome triggers a series of events that will result in a Roman mission, which accords with God's plan, and a mission that realizes Jesus' prediction that the gospel of his resurrection will be proclaimed to the "end of the earth" (i.e., Rome: 1:8).

In any case, Festus hits the ground running. Three days after arriving in the provincial capital, he departs on an official visit to Jerusalem, his region's other principal city, where he meets with "the high priests and the leaders of the Jews" (v. 2). The haste of his visit may well indicate the political urgency of Paul's case. Felix has left Palestine an unstable province and a breeding ground for terrorist activity, especially among pro-Israeli groups. No doubt Paul's "the Way" is painted by his Jewish opponents with inflammatory brush strokes, since they think his mission to the nations threatens to have corrosive effects on Israel's theological beliefs and social practices.

The change of designation from religious "elders" (see 24:1) to political "leaders" *(prōtoi)* connotes a wider spectrum of leadership, which may indicate a broader, better-organized attack against Paul. Festus meets with Jerusalem's chamber of commerce to strategize with them over the "Paul problem." The positive implication is that his message is pervasive and touches every institution of Jewish life. The plural "high priests" here is unusual, but it probably reflects the continuing role that retired high priests play in the city's religious and political culture.

Acts states the business of their private meeting sharply: they "gave Festus a report against [*emphanizō kata*] Paul" (v. 2). The repetition of *emphanizō kata* (from 24:1) indicates the resumption of the Jewish case against Paul. We get the impression that the change of procurators in Caesarea prompts a renewed effort to destroy Paul and the influence of his message about the risen Jesus. With this motive in mind, they "appealed to him and requested a favor": transfer Paul to Jerusalem for a new trial (v. 3).

This is the second of three times (in the space of just ten verses) that Paul's Jewish opponents "request a favor" of a Roman ruler (see v. 9; cf. 24:27). Such triads in Acts underline important elements of the story line. Since the reader knows that granting this "favor" would again place Paul in harm's way, the repetition of this theme casts his Jewish opposition in a bad light. Likewise, the similar responses of the Roman procurators to Jerusalem's request for favored treatment depict Rome in a good light, however softly it shines. Finally, the prophet must lean on God for support.

Initially, Festus insists on his prerogatives as Roman procurator: the provincial seat of his administrative and judicial power is Caesarea, not Jerusalem; therefore, "come with me and press charges against the man in Caesarea" (vv. 4-5). If Festus has an inkling of the murderous motive of the Jewish leaders, he has no intention of being their dupe. In clever compromise, however, he does tacitly agree to reopen Paul's case on the condition that "there is anything wrong [*atopos*, literally "out of place") with him."

And so it is in Caesarea, seated on his *bēma* (seat)[1] with the leaders of the anti-Paul movement surrounding him, that Festus orders Paul to be brought to him for interrogation. The narrator leaves the details of this legal hearing to the careful readers of Acts, who already know well the "many serious charges" the Jews have against Paul (v. 7; cf. 21:21, 28; 24:5-6) and the details of Paul's apologia (v. 8; cf. 23:6; 24:10-21). The final element of this fresh summary of Paul's defense is new and interesting: "I have done nothing . . . against Caesar." The effect of Paul's response is twofold: most obviously, it prepares readers for the climax of the story, namely, Paul's appeal to Caesar, thereby wiping his case off Festus's docket and rendering this venue irrelevant; yet it also seems true (from the previous trial before Felix, as well as Paul's various court hearings during his mission in the Diaspora [16:21; 17:7]) that Paul is well aware from personal experience that the most serious charge against him is that of sedition. A close look, then, reveals that Paul has succeeded in clarifying the prosecution's case against him!

Festus now proposes a further, deeper compromise. In the immediate context, the requested favor of a change of venue is no mere legal maneuver. While it is certainly true that a Jerusalem trial, preferably conducted by

---

1. The *bēma* is variously translated and understood by commentators. It refers to a portable rostrum or raised platform placed wherever the judge can sit above the crowd to render a verdict in dramatic fashion. Josephus, *Jewish War* 2:172; see Acts 18:12.

the Sanhedrin, would be the most favorable legal option for Paul's opponents, their implied motive is Paul's assassination and not a change of court venue or trial judge. The Jews would be more than happy to accept Festus as judge, which he evidently requires (". . . be tried before me"), as long as Paul's case is transferred to Jerusalem (v. 3).

It seems obvious to most interpreters that Festus is disingenuous when he asks Paul to decide between Jerusalem and Caesarea: he surely understands well the implications for himself and for Paul, but he chooses to ignore them for reasons of political expedience. This is Festus's choice to make — and one he is inclined to make in any case — based on his initial response to the request (v. 5). His duplicity is characteristic of his role in Acts, and as a representative of Rome he contributes to the overall negative portrayal of Rome's relationship to Paul and his mission. While Roman law safeguards Paul's appeal to Rome (while he is under the constant threat of unrepentant Jews) and is thus an unwitting collaborator with God in achieving God's purpose for Paul, Rome's pagan leaders are presented as untrustworthy and self-interested.

For this reason, Paul's response to Festus's question must be considered a sharp rebuke of the latter's political self-interest: "This is where I should be tried . . . as you very well know" (v. 10). Paul makes his implied charge of Festus, rooted in moral ground, more convincing when he expresses his willingness to pay the death penalty if his crimes justify it under Roman law. His sense of Roman justice commands this same treatment from this Roman leader. Most interpretations of Paul's statement in verse 11 ("no one can turn me over to them") miss the important wordplay between the earlier request for Festus to grant Israel a "favor" *(charis)* and Paul's challenging retort that it is illegal for him to "turn over" *(charizomai)* an innocent man in protective custody to his known enemies. The narrator shapes Paul's retort to recall a triad of requested "favors" (24:7; 25:3, 9) to condemn Festus's political expedience. God's prophet does not tolerate Rome's self-interest.

The most crucial right of Paul's Roman citizenship, however, is that which allows him to demand a fair trial before Caesar. More critically than his judicious exercise of a legal right, Paul recognizes that he must respond to allegations of seditious activities against the empire; and the emperor is the final judge in this matter. After he has spent two years in prison, the idea of "protective custody" must have been wearing thin; without the Caesar's involvement, Paul would continue as the prime player in this game of political football between the Judean Roman procurator and the leaders of his Jewish opposition. His sharp retort to Festus's lame question would seem to indicate that he does not trust Festus to call an end to this legal game. It is perhaps as a frustrated citizen, then, that he concludes contrary to the procurator's suggestion to change the trial site: "I appeal to the emperor" (v. 11). By Roman law, all legal wrangling stops when a citizen appeals to the emperor, who alone has authority to render a final verdict. With characteristic irony, the narrator uses the political idiom to score a theological point: the appeal process constituted in Roman law is the means by which Paul arrives in Rome, the city of his destiny and the place where he will realize God's prophesied plan (see 23:11).

The unnamed Caesar to whom Paul appeals is Nero (54-68 C.E.). Festus would have known informally from Felix that Paul is a solid citizen, and also by now officially from the court records of previous interrogations and notes made of his various defense speeches, which are summarized in Acts. Though the narrative mentions no sigh of relief, Festus must have felt the burden of a "no-win" situation lifted from his administrative shoulders. His subsequent conference with his legal advisors must have been relatively brief and perhaps only over the precise wording of his response: "You have appealed to the emperor; to the emperor you will go."

PART II: ENGAGING ACTS 25 FOR TODAY'S CHURCH

What kind of relationship should the church and believers have toward governing authorities? How are believers to handle themselves in the world of power politics? What do Christians believe about the proper role and function of governments and political leaders? Should Christians and the church seek political power or avoid it? When should Christians support governments, and when should they resist them? As is true for many of the questions that arise in the course of the Acts narrative, the questions above are also quite contemporary issues for believers and for the church today.

As we have noted above in the exposition section of this chapter, Acts might be thought of as "referee" between "the 13s," that is, Romans 13, with its apparent counsel of deference and obedience to civil authority, and Revelation 13, with its apparent incitement to resistance and martyrdom.

These two extremes no doubt have their place and time; but Acts clearly locates the church somewhere in between. In Acts the state and civil authorities (or nation) are not seen as self-evident instruments of God's will; nor are they seen as the inevitable antagonist of God's purposes. In this sense of occupying a middle ground, Acts addresses the ambiguities that most often characterize the realistic relationship of believers to governing authorities. One might sum up the view of Acts as follows: governing authorities have a legitimate, important, and divinely mandated authority and responsibility; but they are not God, nor are they to be conflated with or confused with God.

This broad theme and wise counsel play out in three sub-themes that are discernible in this book, particularly in Acts 25 and its story of Paul in the dock before the Roman procurator, Festus. The three themes that are able to guide and instruct believers today include: (1) prophetic calls "to account" directed at governing authorities; (2) freedom in relationship to those same authorities; and (3) the abiding conviction that God can use the powers of this world, whether they know it or not, to accomplish God's purposes. Let's look at these three themes of the relationship of Christians and the church to civil authorities in greater detail.

Calling Civil Authorities to Accountability

As we have noted throughout this study, the apostles who follow Jesus from the very first chapter of Acts are characterized as "prophets like Jesus." In the Gospels we find both Jesus' prophetic forerunner, John the Baptist, and Jesus himself confronting governing authorities and calling them to account for their actions. In Acts this pattern continues and is even amplified. When Paul and Silas visit Philippi (Acts 16), all manner of things happen to them: they are falsely accused, beaten, imprisoned, miraculously freed, and then quietly, almost casually told that they are free to go on their way. But we find that Paul is not willing simply to accept his freedom and let bygones be bygones. When the newly converted jailer reports that the magistrates have decided to let Paul and Silas go, Paul is quick to say, in effect, "No way!" "They have beaten us in public," he says, "unconemned men who are Roman citizens, and have thrown us into prison; and now they are going to discharge us in secret? Certainly not!" (16:37). Paul understands his rights as a Roman citizen, and he knows that these rights have been trampled. That is, he knows that the magistrates have not been faithful to their own calling and responsibilities; they have not stuck by their own laws. Will Paul simply act as though nothing has happened, thankful just to escape jail and further trouble? Hardly. The apostle announces his citizenship and demands an apology from the magistrates. This "prophet like Jesus" calls the civil authorities to account for their actions.

The same element is operative in his encounter with Festus, if not quite as emphatically. When Festus, not only fully aware of the priestly interest group from Jerusalem but also of that lobby's political power, poses his question to Paul — whether he wishes to be tried in Jerusalem or in Caesarea — Paul is not meek and mild in response; he is assertive: "This is where I should be tried . . . as you well know" (v. 10). Paul sees through the political machinations and calls on Festus to do his job and do it properly. He is neither deferential nor defiant. Instead, understanding that the civil authorities do have a legitimate role and responsibility, he calls on them to do their jobs as they are supposed to be done.

Here, then, is a clear and appropriate — if risky — role for Christians in relationship to civil authorities. The authorities do have a legitimate role and important functions in society; but they often forget their proper tasks, cut corners, and are subject to the manipulations of powerful interest groups. Prophets-like-Jesus, and thus members of the community of faith, need to remind them of their legitimate responsibilities and call them to exercise those responsibilities faithfully for the common good. A twentieth-century example of such prophetic "calling to account" was the work of Martin Luther King, Jr., who called both civil authorities and an entire nation to make good on the promises and mandates of its founding documents and their assertions that "all men are created equal and endowed by their Creator with certain inalienable rights, including the rights to life, liberty and the pursuit of happiness." Like Paul before him, King was not content merely to be released from jail. He continued to call civil authorities and a nation to account before the standards of its own laws and professed ideals. Another modern prophet who called civil authorities to account was Karol Wojtyla, later Pope John Paul II, who stood up in the face of corrupt Communist party officials in his native Poland. And there are many contemporary stories of African Christians, Latin American liberation theologians, and Asian believers who have called their countries' political leaders to account.

This theme of Acts suggests that Christians do properly find themselves in the chambers of the city council, the meetings of the school board, and the halls of justice. There we are to recognize the legitimate roles and authority of such entities and offices. And yet we are to recognize and respect that authority to such an extent, if you will, that we will hold it to its own highest standards. We will insist that the law be applied even-handedly, and we will insist that each person gets his or her due. Christians should not use such settings simply to further their own perceived self-interests, becoming another special interest group or lobby (as the Jerusalem faction is presented here). Rather, as a prophetic conscience, we are called to an impartial role.

In this we can see a continuity with what may be the best-known biblical account of the relationship of king and prophet, that of King David and Nathan. In the wake of David's having his way with Bathsheba and then shamefully arranging for the death of Bathsheba's husband, Uriah, Nathan confronts David. The prophet does not protect the king from his own actions and their consequences; nor is he part of the cover-up, as many religious leaders have been in relation to political leaders and powers in American and world history. He does not serve as part of the apparatus of legitimacy for the erring king. Rather, Nathan names David's failure, announces the judgment of God, and calls on David to repent (2 Sam. 1:11-12). In much the same way, though less dramatically than did Nathan, Paul fulfills a prophet's function in Acts. He calls on the civil authorities to do their job faithfully.

Reaching further back in Scripture to the stories of Abraham, we are reminded that, at least sometimes, the call to accountability and ethical behavior can move in the other direction. After Abraham, afraid for his own life, had lied and told Pharaoh that Sarah was his sister (Abraham had thought he would be killed and Sarah taken for Pharaoh's harem), it is Pharaoh who admonishes and corrects God's chosen patriarch, Abraham (Gen. 12:18-20). Lest Christians become arrogant or self-righteous, it is important to remember that, at least sometimes, those in positions of power understand very well their responsibilities and the requirement of ethical behavior, and at least sometimes they will call the church and Christians to account.

Here in Acts we find useful guidance for the church and Christians in today's world. Are we to be indifferent to the civil sphere, or are we to try to take it over and use its power to our ends and perceived interests? If Acts is to be believed, neither is the case. Rather, we are called to function as prophets, speaking truth to power, reminding the powers that be of their own standards and laws, and thus reminding those same powers that there is a higher power to which all earthly power is accountable.

The Inner Freedom of the Christian

A second theme emerges from the behavior of the apostles in relation to civil authorities in Acts. These are people who understand that, even though they may be subject to the civil authorities, these same authorities are not the final or the ultimate authority. The result of this conviction is an inner freedom they have even during outward imprisonment. In Acts 25 we can hardly miss the way Paul, though in chains, seems to be the most free person of those present. The priestly group from Jerusalem is captive to its perceived self-interests, to its shaky grip on power, and to its own fears. Likewise, the Roman official, Festus, though he has the power of an occupying force over these Jews, seems hardly free or powerful. He is very much aware of the pressures of the Jerusalem lobby and of his own precarious position as a new official, and thus he is trying to get this thorny and potentially disruptive matter out of the way quickly.

As in the Gospel accounts of the trial of Jesus, there is a deep irony here in Caesarea: the one in chains is the only one who is truly free. How can this be? Because that one, whether Jesus or Paul, knows that the power of the civil authorities is not ultimate. Thus in the Gospel of John we find the following exchange between Pilate and Jesus: "Pilate therefore said to him, 'Do you refuse to speak to me? Do you not know that I have the power to crucify you?' Jesus answered him, 'You would have no power over me unless it had been given you from above'" (John 19:10-11). Amid the swirl of pressures and power, of fury and fears that is Jesus' final week, only one man is free — the one in chains. In somewhat the same way, Paul seems the most free of those present in the courtroom in Caesarea.

It is, one might say, a question of true and false fear. Scripture makes a distinction between them: "Do not fear those who kill the body but cannot kill the soul; rather, fear him who is able to destroy both soul and body . . ." (Matt. 10:28). True fear is the fear of the Lord; false fear is deference or submission to lesser powers. This is captured in a contemporary benediction,

"May you love God so much that you love nothing else too much;
May you fear God enough that you need fear nothing else at all."

We hear a similar conviction in Luther's most famous hymn, "A Mighty Fortress is Our God": "Let goods and kindred go, this mortal life also; the body they may kill, God's truth abideth still, God's kingdom is forever."

Those who trust in God have an inner freedom that no civil authority can take away. Such has been the source of power for the witness of Christians in the face of threats and intimidation throughout the ages and across the globe. It is a high standard and aspiration, but it is one that derives logically from our faith that God alone is God and that God alone has the power to give life and to take it away.

God's Hidden Purposes Accomplished
through the Powers of This World

A third theme that emerges from Acts — and Acts 25 in particular — is the conviction of Scripture and of Christians that God is able to use the powers of this world, sometimes in spite of themselves, to accomplish God's purposes and to bring about the fulfillment of God's plan. Luke asserts this, albeit quietly, in the nativity story early in his Gospel. Luke 2 begins in the following way: "In those days a decree went out from Emperor Augustus [Caesar] that all the world should be enrolled. This was the first registration and was taken when Quirinius was governor of Syria. All went to their own towns to be registered. Joseph also went from the town of Nazareth in Galilee to Judea, to the city of David called Bethlehem, because he was descended from the house and family of David." Without any explicit word of commentary, Luke makes his point powerfully but implicitly: the great Caesar, called "Lord" by his subjects, does the bidding of the one true God without even knowing it. Thanks to the emperor's census, the Messiah will be born in Bethlehem, prophecy will be fulfilled, and Jesus of Nazareth shall also be Jesus of Bethlehem. Thus does Luke disclose the proper order of things and put worldly powers in their proper place. They are not ultimate: they serve, even unwittingly, the plan and purpose of almighty God.

In the exposition of this passage we have made a similar point: "With characteristic irony, the narrator [of Acts] uses political idiom to score a theological point: the appeal process constituted by Roman law is the means by which Paul arrives in Rome, the city of his destiny and the place where he will realize God's prophesied plan." It will be courtesy of Festus ("You have appealed to Caesar, to Caesar you will go") that Paul gets to Rome and fulfills the words of Jesus at the beginning of Acts: "And you will be my witnesses in Jerusalem, in all Judea and Samaria, and to the end of the earth" (Acts 1:8). Paul will now go to what was, for that time, the end of the earth — distant Rome. God's will shall be done, God's purposes fulfilled, declares the book of Acts, even through the deeds and devices of unrighteous men. Thus the story concludes by pointing to, as do all biblical stories in the end, the sometimes visible, sometimes hidden God.

In his stimulating book *The Art of Biblical Narrative*, the scholar Robert Alter argues that the genius of the Bible is to hold in unresolved tension two truths: freedom and design — or to put it another way, human choice and divine purpose.[2] By this Alter means that both qualities are evident and honored in Scripture. Human beings are both free and responsible; we do make choices, and our choices do matter. And yet it is also true that a plan and purpose of God, however dimly it is perceived at times, is unfolding within history. It is the gift and genius of the biblical story, Alter maintains, that it never fully resolves this tension in favor of one or the other affirmation. Both are simultaneously true, and both are expressed in Scripture. Festus acts freely; Paul exercises his right as a Roman citizen to appeal to Caesar. And yet another plan is being brought to fulfillment, a larger purpose served. In the realm of civil and governing authorities, Christians hold to, sometimes cling to, this confession: God is able to use even sinful people and sinful powers to fulfill God's purposes.

What is the proper and faithful posture of Christians and the church relative to governing authorities and civil powers? Is it to isolate ourselves, to exist in a world apart? Not according to Acts. Christians participate in the civil arena, and God has constituted legitimate governing powers. Is it, then, to try to take over such powers and use them for God's purposes, at least as we understand them? Acts gives no basis or reason for entering the political realm as yet another party, player, or faction. Acts gives no reason for seeking a new Christendom or advancing Christian dominion. Rather, Acts suggests that we are to be like Peter and Paul, prophets-like-Jesus who call the governing authorities to a responsible use of their powers. In this

2. Alter, *The Art of Biblical Narrative* (San Francisco: Harper, 1981).

the church is to be, as Jesus tells his disciples in the Sermon on the Mount, "light to the world and salt to the earth" (Matt. 5:13-14). Acts envisions neither a sectarian isolation nor a Christian nation.

We are to be bold witnesses in the face of civil powers and authorities, for we know that their power over us is not ultimate or final. And we are called to point, through our stories and our lives, to the one whose power is ultimate and whose purpose will be accomplished.

STUDY QUESTIONS

1. What do the images of the imprisoned Paul of Acts contribute to the reader's understanding of Christian discipleship?

2. Characterize Paul's uneasy relationship with Rome and Rome's uneasy relationship with Paul in Acts. How does this characterization square with the church's relationship with the state that Paul defines in Romans 13? How does the relationship between an unholy state and the church envisioned by Revelation 13 correct and balance Paul's teaching?

3. Can you think of a contemporary example of the church, or church leaders, calling civil authorities to be accountable and to do their job? Is this an appropriate role for the church and its leaders? Why or why not?

4. What implications do you see in the way Luke and Acts portray God as using the powers that be to accomplish God's hidden purposes?

15 *Concluding Reflections*

PART I: TEACHING ACTS AS SCRIPTURE

Throughout this book we have referred to the importance of teaching Acts as Scripture. While careful and informed historical and literary investigations of biblical texts often illuminate their "original" meaning, the primary role these texts perform within the church is ultimately a contemporary and sacred one: to "teach, reprove, correct, and train" current readers to understand God's way of ordering reality. Any biblical text, when studied as Scripture, will pursue its spiritual meaning: the interpreter becomes a partner with God's Spirit to hear the voice of the living God, which is instructive of an "obedience of faith."

The modern period of biblical studies has rightly been concerned to limit the possible uses of these sacred texts for fear that their inherent multifaceted meanings will allow interpretations that are not only misguided but self-serving. For this reason, modern biblical criticism has sought to limit the "official" meaning of a biblical text to the one intended by its author for his first recipients. But in fact, during the long history of the interpretation of the Acts of the Apostles, commentators have sometimes rendered its plot line in ways that are contrary to the gospel and subversive to Christian unity. Acts criticism, especially during the twentieth century, diligently attempted to reconstruct the narrative's "original meaning" in order to understand what the anonymous narrator had in mind when telling his story to its first reader, Theophilus.

This "critical" approach to Acts seems mistaken to me, not because it is unprofitable or impractical but because it misplaces Scripture's timeless referent — that is, God — for the particular historic moment of a text's composition. On the other hand, Scripture's faithful readers discern the theological meaning of a biblical text when rendered as sacred Scripture, not by the rules of critical methods, but rather by the church's Rule of Faith — its grammar of theological agreements.[1] Thus the normative meaning of a biblical text is not delimited first of all by an author's intentions, stated or implied, but by the church's reasons for including and placing a book within the final form of its biblical canon.

Within its canonical bounds, then, we no longer read Acts as Luke's story for Theophilus but as the authorized medium of God's living word for God's people. For this reason, we must use Acts carefully today within congregations of believers to facilitate their theological and moral education. Sometimes a biblically shaped rendering of the real world, conveyed with the Spirit's aid and a gifted teacher's concern, will comfort those who are afflicted; at other times it will afflict those who are comfortable. Whether for priestly or prophetic results, then, a faithful interpretation of Acts — if it truly is a word on target — will always aim its readers, no matter where they are spiritually and socially, toward obedience to God.

Israel's Scripture as a Narrative Theme of Acts

The indispensability of Israel's Scripture for defining and defending the faith of God's people is an important theme of Acts. Whether quoted directly or alluded to, the entirety of Scripture discloses God's Word to those who hear it proclaimed and publicly interpreted. For this reason, the personal credo of the exemplary Paul of Acts is that he worships Israel's God and believes "everything laid down by the law or written in the prophets" (24:14). Reading and heeding Scripture is an act of worship precisely because the very identity of the God who is worshiped is disclosed in it.

The Scripture referred to in Acts is Israel's Scripture, the church's Old Testament. While believers routinely confess their confidence in the spiri-

---

1. See R. W. Wall, "Reading the Bible from within Our Traditions: The Rule of Faith in Theological Hermeneutics," in *Between Two Horizons*, ed J. B. Green and M. Turner (Grand Rapids: Eerdmans, 2000), pp. 88-107.

tual authority of the Old Testament, the actual practices of most congregations belie their confession: they consider the Old Testament infrequently, and they marginalize its teaching about God under the uncritical presumption that the New Testament portrays a God whose responses to humanity, especially toward sinners, are more gracious and generous because of Christ Jesus. Given this seemingly irrepressible supersessionism within the church, we should read Acts today as a biblical corrective to current practice. And more than simply supplying readers with an apologia for the continuing importance of the Old Testament, Acts clarifies an interpretive strategy for using Israel's Scripture in the church's preaching of the gospel.

Perhaps more important for our present purpose, however, is the way Scripture is used in Acts, which constructs a biblical typology of scriptural authority.[2] Therefore, before defining the strategic role of Acts within Scripture, we need to understand the role of Acts as Scripture. The following catalog of observations intends to draft a working typology of Scripture's authority in forming a congregation's faith and witness: how Acts depicts Scripture is roughly analogous to the pattern by which Scripture may be used to disclose the ways of God to the people of God.

1. Against the view of modern criticism that biblical authority is predicated on historical veracity or literary artistry, Acts links Scripture's ongoing authority to its sacred roles in maintaining a community's covenant with God. Although "narrative theology" has only recently become fashionable, Acts quotes or summarizes Scripture to legitimate the church's most important events; and the most important speeches of Acts speak of God as the central character of Israel's biblical story (7:2-53; 13:17-41).

Moreover, Peter's Pentecost commentary on Joel's prophecy has consistently provided the modern church with a useful template of the core convictions of the Christian gospel. This interpretive practice merely follows the advice of the Paul of Acts, who insists that what he proclaims is precisely what Jesus had proclaimed before him, which in turn is "nothing but what the prophets and Moses said would come to pass: that the Christ must suffer, and that, by being the first to rise from the dead, he would proclaim light to both the people and to the gentiles" (26:22-23; cf. 17:3).

2. Against the modern notion that Jesus is best understood within a

---

2. See also J. Jervell, *The Theology of the Acts of the Apostles* (Cambridge: Cambridge University Press, 1996), pp. 61-75; L. Alexander, "'This Is That': The Authority of Scripture in the Acts of the Apostles," *Princeton Seminary Bulletin* 25, 2 (2004): 189-204.

critically constructed social world of first-century Palestine, Acts pairs Scripture with the church's kerygma — its proclamation of the gospel — to interpret the importance of the history of Jesus (2:22-36; 3:17-26; 10:34-43). Whether to "prove" the church's claims about Jesus or to retrieve the typical patterns of God's activities in the world, Acts uses Scripture to locate Jesus in the history of salvation. The context for providing the gospel of Jesus' life is not his first-century world but Israel's Scriptures.

We do not view Scripture's role apologetically, that is, saying that insofar as Scripture predicts events that are then fulfilled by the events mapped out in Acts, it proves the Christian gospel to be true. While there may be an element of this perspective at work, Acts uses Scripture principally as a witness to a faithful God who brings to realization promises that God made to Israel according to Scripture. The pattern of Acts' use of Scripture, then, is analogous to following the Lectionary, according to which Old Testament and Gospel lessons are read together to remind God's people with clarity that God's promises to Israel have been faithfully fulfilled because of Jesus. In other words, Acts recalls the biblical account of God's way of saving Israel as continuous with God's messianic way of saving the world (3:20-21; 17:31). This realization inspires worship and obedience.

The deep logic of God's way of salvation as disclosed in Israel's Scripture is, therefore, consistent with and interpretive of kerygmatic claims made about the Messiah's career. Thus, when Paul asks Agrippa, a secular Jew, his stunning question ("Why is it thought incredible by any of you that God raises the dead?" [26:8]), the God he has in mind, of course, is the biblical God (see 26:2-3, 27).

3. Against the modern ideal of the interpreter standing over the biblical text, ever suspicious of its continuing authority and relevance, the characters in Acts are prophets-like-Jesus who stand before Israel's Scripture trusting that its prophetic oracles will reveal God. Understood typologically of Scripture's performance (rather than literally of its production), this prophetic depiction includes three important elements for a contemporary consideration of biblical authority. First is the inextricable relationship between Israel's Scripture and God's Spirit. It is the interpreters' being filled by the Spirit that enables them to interpret Scripture after the mind of God (2:4, 14-36). This is logical because it is the Spirit who speaks in Scripture (1:16; 4:25; 7:51-53; 28:25) or through the prophetic "authors" of Scripture, such as David (2:25-32; 13:22-37) and Moses (7:42, 52), Israel's prophets par excellence. Second, the theological subject matter of

Scripture coheres to the principal interests of Israel's prophets in God's way of saving all the families of earth (3:17-25), even to the end of the earth (1:8; 13:47). Finally, the prophetic word is edgy, exposing people's spiritual ignorance while calling them to repentance.

4. Against the Protestant preoccupation with *sola Scriptura*, whether in devotion or suspicion, the members of the church in Acts learn God by their real experiences of divine activity, which Scripture then confirms. There is never an instance in Acts when biblical teaching leads the church toward theological reform; rather, it is the light of what God has done that exegetes the meaning of Scripture. The early prophets-like-Jesus use Scripture to supply the working grammar of their missionary speeches, whose end is conversion; to supply the language of prayers, whose end is the outpouring of God's Spirit; and to supply the background for the community's resurrection practices, whose end is witness. New meanings of Israel's Scripture are always revealed to the community's teachers after the fact — in the light of those "things that have happened among us" (Luke 1:1). For example, Pentecost's experience of the Spirit's "signs and wonders," while illuminated by Joel's prophecy, is the necessary prompt by which Peter recalls and rereads the prophecy as relevant for the "last days" of Israel's history. Again, the meaning James retrieves from Amos's prophecy of Israel's restoration, while confirming the status of repentant pagans within God's Israel, is itself prompted by the conversion experiences of Paul's mission to the nations. The past of God narrated in Scripture confirms the present of God experienced in the church's mission in the world. While these new actions lead Spirit-filled interpreters to discover new meanings in Scripture that were heretofore hidden from view, the patterns of God's activities are ever constant. Scripture does not dictate what course of action to take; God does. Scripture's role is to confirm that the road taken has been approved by divine plan as scripted by Scripture. Experience clarifies what is a "divine necessity."

5. Against the modern liberal notion that every individual has the authority and ability to render Scripture's meaning for himself or herself, Acts envisions something more like a dialogue between the human and divine dimensions of biblical interpretation. If Scripture is not self-interpreting, neither is it interpreted by the "critical" autonomous self, but only as the individual interpreter is guided by the Spirit in order to guide still others (8:26-40). Although traditional readings of Scripture are considered (8:34), the radical nature of the Jesus event, which both illumines

and is illumined by Israel's Scripture, requires that explosive new meanings of that Scripture be made.

Moreover, Scripture is typically read publicly and within communities (17:1-4, 10-12), even though often in ways that divide their membership (28:23-24). Within Bible-believing (Jewish) communities where the authority of Scripture is not contested, the Christological interpretations of Scripture are controversial and divisive. The typological point is this: the so-called battle for the Bible is a misnomer if we suppose that ecclesiastical conflicts over beliefs and practices will be settled by agreeing on a particular account of biblical authority (a false claim often made by religious conservatives). While the source of disagreements between believers remains extraordinarily complex, they usually reflect the different political and social ideals and "rules of faith" extant within the church catholic. Hope for Christian unity is rooted in the church's catholicity, not its uniformity.

6. Finally, against the modern tendency to seek meanings at the point of a text's origin and freeze them there, Acts reads Scripture as the current word of the living God. Peter says that "God spoke from the mouth of all the prophets from eternity" to "you who are the children of the prophets about the covenant that God gave to your ancestors" (3:21-25). Scripture not only mediates a dialectic between human and divine but between time and eternity. While the Bible comes to us encased in its own social world, which we should seek to understand and then to relativize, as sacred text it encases heaven's eternal truth, which continues to inform how we should respond as God's people to our own social worlds. The faithful readers of Scripture are these same "children of the prophets" through whom the living God continues to speak "from eternity."

In this regard, James A. Sanders describes Luke's interpretive strategy as "comparative midrash." By this he means that Israel's prophets are called on by the characters in Acts to help their ever-changing audiences — at ever-changing social locations — to interpret what it means to be a people belonging to Israel's God, the only God.[3] According to Sanders, the community's belief in Scripture's continuing authority and the continuing relevance of its teaching about God are mutually inclusive claims. The role of the faithful interpreter is to make this connection always clear and cogent for the present congregation.

---

3. C. A. Evans and J. A. Sanders, *Luke and Scripture* (Minneapolis: Fortress Press, 1993), pp. 4-13.

For this reason, Scripture is not often quoted verbatim in Acts, but it is interpreted and even rewritten to make clear the importance of a particular event or experience as that reveals God's Word. The authority of Scripture as the medium of God's Word depends on its capacity — and that of its Spirit-filled interpreter — to clarify the theological meaning of "those things that have happened among us." While negotiating this dynamic interplay between biblical text and social context, the interpreter must not lose sight of the revelatory nature of this sacred text, whose principal role is to bear witness to Israel's God, who is the same yesterday, today, and forever.

St. Irenaeus and Reading Acts as Christian Scripture

In Chapter 2 of this book, we brought up St. Irenaeus as the first to recognize the enduring importance of Acts; he remains the central character in the narrative of the church's recognition of Acts as Scripture. In *Against Heresies,* his seminal book, Irenaeus used Acts to formulate a normative account of Christian origins (or "apostolic succession") to legitimate his definition of the church's Rule of Faith, a grammar of theological agreements to which every Christian teaching and teacher must cohere.

Since the source of this Rule of Faith is Jesus, who revealed God fully as witnessed by his apostles, Irenaeus was mostly interested in defending the theological unity of the different "Gospels of the apostles" as supplying the church's authorized biography of the life of Jesus. While three of these apostolic Gospels — Matthew, Mark, and John — were already in wide circulation by the middle of the second century, Luke's Gospel was not, quite possibly because it had been only recently composed and was still in a state of literary flux. Furthermore, Luke's Gospel was linked by tradition to Paul, who was himself a controversial figure within the early church, not only because his teachings were used to defend heresy but because he had not known Jesus personally and thus lacked this crucial apostolic credential (see Acts 1:21-22).

Nonetheless, Irenaeus pressed for the unity of a "fourfold Gospel," which included Luke, not only against those who used a different version of Luke for heretical ends (e.g., Marcion), but against any other Christian teacher who would give any one Gospel priority over this full fourfold portrait of Jesus' life. In Irenaeus's mind, this kind of myopia would surely lead the church in "heretical" directions, and he used Acts as a corrective to plot a narrative of apostolic succession from a common Christological spring to defend the theological unity of all four apostolic traditions that lie behind the "Gospels of the apostles."

The design of Irenaeus's commentary on Acts in Book Three of *Against Heresies,* which is almost certainly the first commentary on Acts ever written, envisions two relevant properties. First, his interpretation of Acts is polemical against the perceived "heresies" of particular teachers or groups — for example, Marcion, Valentinus, the Ebionites, and other second-century Gnostic movements within the church. While his reading of Acts provides an excellent example of patristic exegesis, his commentary per se hardly has normative value for today's church. In fact, we will likely find his reading of Acts deficient because it is so thoroughly shaped in response to his own social and intellectual world.

Second, however, and more important, Irenaeus's commentary remains useful because it supplies a typology for relating the church's different apostolic traditions (especially the Pauline and Petrine traditions) together in a manner that unifies them by common succession from the same Christological spring and in service of the same missionary vocation. This typological appropriation of Acts had continuing significance during the entire canonical process and has come to us, centuries later, as an important means of clarifying the theological motive of the historic process that ultimately produced the Christian Bible in its present form.

The consensus of contemporary criticism is that Luke and Acts should be read together as a continuous Lucan narrative, packaged within the narrator's own particular social world and unified by his theological beliefs. There is no evidence, however, that such a Luke-Acts combination was ever intended by the church. While Irenaeus certainly believed that Luke and Acts were written by St. Luke, his interest was clearly not to prove the unity of Luke-Acts; rather, his primary interest was to demonstrate the unity of the four "Gospels of the apostles," which included Luke's Gospel, with a distinctive role to perform as a collection within the church's Scripture different from that of Acts.

Independent of any theory of a unified Luke-Acts, then, the ancient church's reception of Acts as divinely inspired Scripture followed an independent path into the New Testament canon for different reasons and with a different role to perform from that of Luke's Gospel or that of the fourfold Gospel within which it circulated and was canonized. Those few canon lists, mostly in the East, that begin the fourfold Gospel with John's

Gospel and conclude it with Luke's Gospel, and then place Acts adjacent to Luke's Gospel, perceive a "canon logic" that is incidental to a critically constructed Luke-Acts. The apparent theological motive of these lists was to grant priority to John's Gospel for identifying Jesus as the incarnate Logos. To make the case for an intentional Luke-Acts and to review the reception of Acts on this basis as a phenomenon of the canonical process is an anachronism of contemporary biblical scholarship. From the perspective of the biblical canon, there is simply no Luke-Acts: Acts is a stand-alone book with its own role to perform in shaping Christian discipleship.

But what is that role? In order to understand why Irenaeus used Acts as Scripture, it is first necessary to understand what two characteristics he required of a biblical book. First, the book's subject matter agrees with the church's Rule of Faith; second (related logically to the first point), the book's author must be linked to one of Jesus' apostles, since the Rule of Faith originates with Jesus and passes through his apostolic successors to the church catholic.

And therein lies the great deceit (or conceit) of heresy-making: heresies come adorned with ecclesiastical respectability, if not with presumptive theological superiority, because their proponents appeal to the religious authority of a particular apostle, usually against all other apostles. By retrieving a definition of Christian unity from Acts, Irenaeus was able to point out that the content and performance of any one apostolic tradition (e.g., Pauline) agreed with all others (e.g., Petrine); therefore, to use only one apostolic Gospel or Epistle against all others would not only subvert Christian unity but also the church's profession of the Rule of Faith, which is the very hallmark of God's covenant community in the world.

The issue at stake, then, is not whether a teacher appeals to authorized apostolic teaching in support of a particular belief or practice; even the heretics did. The relevant point made by Irenaeus is that orthodoxy cannot be properly freighted and framed by a single apostolic tradition. Even though Pauline teaching is true in everything it asserts regarding God's gospel, it is true in part, not in whole, and it requires additional apostolic teaching for the full articulation of God's gospel. For example, to embrace only Paul's interpretation of the gospel as true and then to reject the teaching of the Jerusalem pillars, "James, Cephas, and John" (Gal. 2:7-9) would likely produce Marcionism.

Irenaeus's definition of multiple but unified apostolic traditions derives from Acts and generates his claim that these different apostolic traditions work together in forming a whole greater than the sum of its particular parts. While we should leave open the historical possibility that such theological myopia is not intentional (the result of the conscious editing of or excluding of traditions), the typology Irenaeus advances makes any theological warrant that appeals to a single church tradition problematical. Such authorizations only create disunity within the church catholic and foster relationships between different apostolic traditions that are adversarial rather than constructive. The root of heresy is not the attenuation of the apostolic tradition per se in a movement's teaching, worship, or spirituality; rather, it is the granting of priority to one tradition above all others. The corrective to heresy, then, is to use a pluriform collection (e.g., fourfold Gospel, multiple Epistles) in which all parts of the whole cohere to the church's Rule of Faith and are linked to apostolic traditions. This kind of reading practice will protect the church against theological myopia and thus heresy. The value of Acts is that it allowed Irenaeus to speak of the incompleteness of any single apostolic tradition that is used without benefit of all the others that draw from a common Christological source and bear witness to one Rule of Faith.

Reading Acts in the Context of the Biblical Canon

With Irenaeus's typology in hand, the student of Acts should hardly regard its strategic role within the biblical canon to be the accidental consequence of an arbitrary decision. Indeed, its placement within Scripture between the fourfold Gospel and two collections of letters helps us envision the role the church has given Acts in guiding the theological formation of Scripture's faithful readers.

Aristotle teaches us that every coherent story has a beginning, middle, and an end. The Old Testament begins Scripture's story of God's way of saving the world; the fourfold Gospel about Jesus plots its climactic middle; Acts and the New Testament letters that follow are the story's denouement, leading to Scripture's apocalyptic ending in its last book, Revelation. Our earlier observations about Israel's Scripture as a narrative theme of Acts suggest a pattern for reading the Old Testament as Christian Scripture. Let's conclude with the following brief reflections about the way Acts should influence our reading and use of two other parts of the New Testament to which its narrative is strategically related within the biblical canon

— namely, the fourfold Gospel and the two collections of New Testament letters.

The Fourfold Gospel and Acts From the opening sentence of Acts, the story's narrator presumes a prior reading of the "first book . . . about all that Jesus did and taught." (As a canonical category, this "first book" refers to the fourfold Gospel.) First of all, then, Acts is to be approached as a continuation of the Jesus story and a "commentary" on it. Not only does the story of Acts function as a substantial proof of Jesus' resurrection as "Lord and Messiah" (2:36), without which there would be no story to tell; it also issues a normative response to the theological crisis for Christian discipleship occasioned by his bodily absence (cf. John 13:31–14:31). That is, those disciples who follow after the exalted Lord are to continue in the power of the Holy Spirit to do and say what Jesus began (cf. Acts 1:1-2).

In this regard, the importance of retaining the final shape of the New Testament's fourfold Gospel rather than combining Luke and Acts as a single narrative is easily discerned by the significant roles in Acts performed by Peter and the Holy Spirit in the absence of Jesus — roles for which Luke's Gospel does not adequately prepare the reader of Acts. Peter's rehabilitation at the end of John (John 21:15-17), as well as the teaching about the Spirit's post-Easter role by John's Jesus (John 14–16), suggest the important role that John's Gospel performs in preparing the reader for the story of Acts. Moreover, what it means to be a "witness" of the risen Jesus (Acts 1:8) is now more fully understood by the reader in the context of John's Gospel (John 15:26-27; cf. Luke 24:48).

Most importantly, the fourfold Gospel story of Jesus supplies the cotext with which the church's proclamation about the history of Jesus recorded in Acts is more fully understood. This is true in a couple ways. First, there is a direct correspondence between what is said about the history of Jesus in the speeches of Acts and those events narrated in the fourfold Gospel. The effect of reading Acts and Gospel together is that the gaps of the church's kerygmatic claims about Jesus' life are filled in by the Gospel's narrative, and the deep logic of the missionary speeches in Acts is made clearer. Second, there is indirect correspondence between what Jesus taught and did according to the fourfold Gospel and what his successors continue to teach and do according to Acts. The reader who comes to Acts having read the fourfold Gospel easily recognizes how the ministry and authority of Jesus' apostles bear a striking family resemblance to his mission, to his gospel, and to the conflict and controversy he provoked. The plot line of the fourfold Gospel continues to unfold in Acts, mindful that Jesus' mission continues in the church.

Plot lines of coherent stories can unfold casually. The Gospel story of Jesus is kept ever before the reader of Acts, not in testimony of Jesus' past but of his living present. The effect of this impression on faithful readers is to remind them that the plot line of the fourfold Gospel story, which continues to unfold in Acts, continues still to unfold in their own personal stories.

Acts and the Pauline and Catholic Letter Collections   The book of Acts is placed immediately before the two collections of New Testament letters for a very good reason: it offers biographical introductions to the authors of the letters. In canonical context, such biographies serve a theological purpose by orienting readers to the spiritual authority of the implied authors who are presented in Acts as exemplary carriers of God's Word. While some have challenged the historical accuracy of those portraits, their devotion to God and their ministries' rousing successes only confirm and commend the importance of their letters. Even the church's expansion into pagan territory, which Acts narrates with profound optimism, anticipates normative Christian practices. The meaningful issue is not whether Acts fails as a historical resource but that it succeeds as a theological resource that contributes to the church's understanding of its vocation and ongoing identity in the world.

In this regard, Acts provides an angle of vision into the Pauline letters and Catholic Epistles that follow.[4] For instance, Acts' depiction of the relationships among Peter, John, James, and Paul, and their respective missions, cues how the interpreter arranges the intracanonical dialogue between those New Testament writings attached to each leader. The similarities and dissimilarities in emphasis and theological conception that we see when we compare the Catholic and Pauline letters may actually correspond to the way Acts narrates the negotiations between the reports from different missions, and to the theological convictions and social conventions required by each (e.g., Acts 2:42-47; 9:15-16; 11:1-18; 12:17; 15:1-29;

---

4. Even though the anonymous NT Letter to the Hebrews is not an "official" member of either collection, it includes important emphases of each and forms a solid bridge between them. At the very least, Hebrews reminds us that the two letter collections are read together rather than in isolation, and as partners in a mutually enriching conversation rather than as adversaries or competing definitions of Christian faith.

21:17-26). Even though the modern discussion has emphasized how a narrator committed to the practical requirements of an "early catholic" church softens the disagreements between the leaders of earliest Christianity, what has often been overlooked is that the church collected and eventually canonized a Pauline corpus whose principal letters are often polemical and potentially divisive. The question is never raised why these Pauline letters were included in the canon of an "early catholic" church if the aim was to shape theological uniformity. Might it not be the case that the church recognized the importance of Acts in introducing the apostolic writings not so much to smooth their disagreeable edges as to interpret them?

Indeed, perhaps the canonical role Acts best performs is explaining rather than tempering the very diversity we see in the two collections of biblical letters. According to Acts, the church that claims its continuity with the first apostles tolerates a rich pluralism, just as the apostles did — not without controversy and confusion. What they achieved at the Jerusalem Council is a kind of theological understanding rather than a theological consensus. The divine revelation given to the apostles, according to Acts, forms a pluralizing monotheism that in turn informs two discrete missions and appropriate proclamations — Jewish and gentile (cf. Gal. 2:7-10).

Sharply sketched, Acts thus interprets the two collections of letters in a more sectarian fashion: the Pauline corpus reflects the gospel of a gentile mission, while the Catholic collection reflects the gospel of a Jewish mission. But such a theological diversity, rather than causing division within the church, is now perceived as normative and necessary for the work of a God who calls both Jews and gentiles to be the people of God. As a context for theological reflection, Acts forces us to interpret the letters in the light of two guiding principles: first, we should expect to find kerygmatic diversity as we move from the Pauline to the Catholic letters; and second, we should expect such a diversity to be useful in forming a single people for God. Against a critical interpretive posture that tends to select a "canon within the Canon" from among the various possibilities, the Bible's own recommendation is for an interpretive strategy characterized by a mutually illuminating and self-correcting conversation between biblical theologies.

Finally, the orienting theological commitments of Acts guide theological reflection on the Epistles. The point is not that a theology of Acts determines or even anticipates the various theologies found in the letters; rather, our point is that Acts shapes a particular perspective, a practical "worry," an abiding interest that influences the interpretation of the letters. For example, if, according to Acts, the church's vocation is to continue what Jesus began to do and to say, then a subsequent reading of the letters should bring into sharper focus the identity and praxis of a missionary people who respond to the Lord's demand to be his witnesses to the end of the earth. This same perspective holds true even of the Catholic Epistles, where believers constitute a community of "resident aliens" whose vocation is a costly faithfulness to God rather than a missionary witness to the needy world (which would be more Pauline).

How does the "catholicity" of Acts, then, deepen our understanding of God's people as a community of "resident aliens"? The canonical approach presumes that the connection is complementary rather than adversarial. In this case, the Pauline church, which may be inclined to accommodate itself to the mainstream of the world system in order to more effectively spread the gospel (see 1 Cor. 9:12b-23), is reminded by the catholic witness that it must take care not to be corrupted by the values and behaviors of the world outside of Christ (cf. James 1:27). That is, the synergism that comes by way of the orienting concern suggests that the diverse theologies that make up the whole biblical canon compose a dynamic self-correcting apparatus, which prevents the faithful reader from theological distortion.

PART II: CALLED TO BE CHURCH

We began by asking, by way of introduction, why Acts, why now? In the intervening chapters we have taken up texts, themes, events, and stories from the Acts of the Apostles, which we believe help the church in our own new and challenging time investigate afresh the nature, vocation, and adventure of our call to be the church of Jesus Christ. Now, in conclusion, we return to our initial query, but from a different vantage point — the perspective of those who have attempted to live within the world of Acts for a season. As the first part of this chapter demonstrates, we have attempted not only to understand Acts as Scripture but to view it within the canon of Scripture, deriving from the canon and order of Scripture itself clues to the meaning and significance of Acts for the church in the twenty-first century.

Thus emerges the following direct, simple, and powerful answer to our initial question of why we should study Acts, and why now: Acts positions the faithful reader and congregations of faithful readers in the unfolding story of God's redemptive work and purpose. It has not been our aim to display the narrative of Acts — and particular moments within that narrative — as something we can ponder and examine from a safe, objective, and disengaged distance; rather, our fondest hope is that we may, through these efforts, discover how this narrative examines and engages us, draws us in, and reframes our vision of the world and of the church. In other words, we hope that Acts puts us, readers and reading congregations, into God's story and helps us see more clearly that God is alive and at work in our own time. We hope that as we see the apostles carrying on, under the direction of the Spirit, what Jesus began, we will also see ourselves as another unfolding chapter in this yet-to-be-concluded story.

Biblical scholar J. Louis Martyn once likened the task of biblical study to that of the modern archaeologist. Martyn imagined a team of students and archaeologists diligently and carefully working away at some dry and dusty dig to uncover an especially well-preserved and interesting mummy. The students and scientists were excited about their find and what clues it might provide to life long ago and far away. But there was one thing they were sure of: the mummy, the subject of their work and study, was dead. Imagine their surprise, observed this devoted student of the text of the living Word, when the mummy suddenly leapt up, grabbed a spade from the nearest scientist, and hit them all over the head with it. Martyn's point is that the text, the narrative of Scripture, is a living thing. It will touch us — and sometimes it will smack us upside the head. It will change us by drawing us into its world and in the process giving us a new world, a world in which God is alive and relentlessly at the task of fulfilling God's promises and purpose. Our hope is that this book may have drawn us not simply into the biblical book of Acts but into the story of God and God's faithful people — the church, the community of faith.

It is our hope that, in a time of particular danger and opportunity to the churches, posed by the end of an era and the emergence of a new time, Acts will furnish our imagination with stories of those who engaged the challenges of their own time in response to the leading and prodding of the Spirit of God. We hope that the book of Acts, and this study, will enable readers to see our own time as another chapter in the unfolding story and to approach it not with fatigue but alertness, not with a querulous spirit but with faithful curiosity, not with terminal mourning for the passing of old forms but with confidence in God's power to usher us into a new thing in God's own time and way. Why Acts and why now? To draw us into God's continuing and emerging story of new life.

On a somewhat more mundane or practical note, some readers may be wondering, Why not more — or all — of Acts? Why have you selected these particular texts, and why have you concluded without including more from the final third of the Acts of the Apostles? First of all, we remind our readers that this book is not intended to be a commentary on the Acts of the Apostles. Many good verse-by-verse, chapter-by-chapter commentaries on Acts exist already; it has not been our goal to write another one. Beyond that, we want this investigation of Acts to be accessible because it is a manageable length, a length that will allow and encourage study in congregations, classrooms, and among readers who may not have time for a five-hundred-page reference book. More important, however, our goal has been to open the text and the world of Acts to contemporary readers and congregations in a way that is suggestive and helpful for them and their communities of faith — suggestive but not exhaustive. We have thus selected from among the speeches and narratives of Acts those we believe to be most helpful in accomplishing that goal. We certainly do not discourage — in fact we encourage — Christians to read the entire book of the Acts of the Apostles; but we did not feel it necessary for our purposes to explore every episode and speech in Acts.

With that caveat, are there concluding comments for faithful readers or implications for congregational life that can be drawn? The first half of this concluding chapter is a critique of the prevailing wisdom: the view that Acts should be seen as the second chapter of Luke. Instead, we propose positioning Acts, as the Bible itself does, in its canonical place and order. Rather than seeing Acts merely as a continuation of the third Gospel, with the Gospel of John curiously interrupting the flow, we see Acts in its place in the canon of Scripture and believe that its location and its content bear important gifts to contemporary congregations and the ecumenical church.

Janus-like, the Acts of the Apostles looks both backward toward the Old Testament and the fourfold Gospel, but also forward to the two collections of Epistles and to the continuing life of faithful readers and congregations. By taking Acts' position in Scripture and the role it performs there seriously, we discern fresh possibilities for contemporary congregations, including a new appropriation by Christians of their Jewish legacy, a fresh valuation of the whole gospel with its multiple voices, and a model for the contemporary unity of the church. In particular, then, we find that Acts, viewed in the context of Scripture, addresses the following important issues in fresh ways: being communities of public practice of faith; the nature of ecumenism for our time; and the future of the emerging church in an intensely pluralistic and multicultural world. We will consider each of these three topics in turn by way of conclusion.

The Jewish Legacy and the Public Practice of Faith

As we noted in the introduction, the book of Acts plays a role in the New Testament and occupies a place in the canon of the church's Scripture that balances certain aspects of the church's gentile mission even as it is devoted to telling that story of the gospel's power to break down cultural and racial barriers in its thrust toward "the end of the earth." Even as this prominent story of gentile mission unfolds, there is another story being told — that of the preservation and valuing of the church's Jewish legacy. If generations of teachers and preachers have, in light of the gentile mission, been aware of the threat of Judaizing — that is, nullifying the gospel of grace by requiring certain requirements to be met as preconditions to grace — Acts is aware of another threat to the church's faith and witness, the challenge of "gentilizing." If Judaizing would nullify grace by setting requirements on the free movement of God's initiative, gentilizing represents the erosion of the church's identity and public practice when nothing, or too little, is expected of those who have known and experienced God's radical grace.

In significant respects, this same concern is alive in the Gospel of Matthew, which may illuminate the concerns in Acts. In Matthew, story after story, parable after parable, show those who have received grace but who have failed to respond by being gracious. We see those who have not put on a new life in visible practices of forgiveness, bold witness, and generosity. Thus, for example, in the parable of the wedding feast (Matt. 21:1-14), the parable focuses on the guest who has come improperly attired to the feast. This is Matthew's way of describing one who has received the gracious invitation and inclusion of God, an invitation to the feast, but who has not responded to the invitation by putting on the wedding garments that are symbolic of visible, public new life in Christ. The forgiven man fails to forgive others.

Acts shares Matthew's concern that grace should not become license.

Acts also counsels that grace requires a response, and the response, while never less than a personal and individual one, is finally about the shape of the community of faith and its public life and practice. Acts portrays a community of resurrection practices. These include sharing of goods, common worship, avoiding idolatry, and bold public witness under the guidance of the Holy Spirit. Acts paraphrases the rhetorical question referred to earlier to address the church, even as it is composed of individual believers: "If being the church of Jesus Christ, the community of the new age, were against the law, would there be enough evidence to get your congregation put on the list of troublesome groups?" Or, to put it more positively, does your church not only preach grace but embody the bold, interesting, and visible way of life of a community set apart by God? Clearly, this has been and continues to be part of the self-understanding of Judaism and of Jewish congregations: they are called to be odd, to be a peculiar people in the midst of the world and for the sake of the world. Augustine spoke of Christians and the church as "resident aliens," those who lived *in* but were not wholly *of* the world and the present age. Acts urges just such a possibility and self-understanding on the contemporary church and communities of faith.

The point is certainly not exclusivity or turning inward, still less a smug sense of moral superiority or self-righteousness. The point is rather to be a community that provides for the world a visible and living alternative, a way to live differently, to live as the people of God for the sake of God's world. In this way the church always has an eschatological role and function: the church is a foretaste of the kingdom, a glimpse of God's dream for all creation. Needless to say, the church often fails to fulfill this high calling; but that does not nullify the calling. That calling persists, provoking the church and evoking the Spirit even as the faithful church provokes the present world and evokes God's new, redeemed, and healed world.

Ecumenism Reconsidered

As the preceding portion of this concluding chapter notes, Irenaeus understood Acts to rest and build, not on the Gospel of Luke alone, but on the fourfold Gospel of Matthew, Mark, Luke, and John, even as these rest and build on the Old Testament. Moreover, Irenaeus found that Acts opened a door onto the two rather different sets of letters that make up the balance of the New Testament that follows Acts. In these ways, Acts becomes a pivotal witness not only to the true gospel but to the whole gospel. What do we mean by that — by "the whole gospel"?

The gospel message may be in some sense simple, but it is not simplistic. It cannot be reduced to one theme, concept, ethic, or program. Nevertheless, North America is full of congregations and preachers who try to do just that. Some congregations, for example, seem to redo the themes of Good Friday and Christ's death on the cross perpetually and without supplement or enlargement by the accounts of Jesus as teacher, preacher, and healer. It is, as some wag has called it, "jack-in-the-box Christianity. Christ died, Christ rose. Up and down. Up and down. Did he never live? Did he never speak or act?" Other congregations emphasize Jesus as teacher and moral example but seem to care little about examining the dark depths of human sin as he encountered them on Calvary. Or one congregation emphasizes the Reformation conviction of *sola Scriptura*, while another gives primacy to tradition. Who is right? Acts might well say, "Both!" The whole gospel is a rendering of the Christian faith that includes its depth and diversity and the ways in which both Scripture and the faith hold in tension different themes, emphases, and truths.

One is reminded of the story of the man who went to spend several days on retreat at a monastery in Kentucky. At dinner he enjoyed a very dark, rich bread. "My, this is good," he said to one of his table companions, a monk who lived at the monastery. "Did we," asked the visitor, "bake it ourselves or was it given to us?" The monk looked at the man for a moment, then smiled and said simply, "Yes." Both were true: it was bread baked in the monastery's kitchen, and it was a gift. Acts claims something like that for the fourfold Gospel. When we ask, "Well, which is it, the crucified Christ of Mark or the eternal Logos of John?" Acts answers, "Yes." Yes, it is both of those and more. It is also Matthew's Jesus, the authoritative teacher, and Luke's Jesus, the savior of the entire world.

Congregations and preachers are always at risk of reductionism, of seizing on a single truth and amplifying that one truth to the point that all others are drowned out and cannot be heard. But this is precisely the nature of heresy: elevating a real but partial truth to the status of the whole and entire truth. Acts helps us receive the rich diversity of Scripture and the New Testament. And Acts opens the way to our appreciation of and engagement with both the Pauline and the Catholic Epistles of the New Testament. Just as Acts rests on the fourfold Gospel, so Acts validates and holds in relationship the varied ministries — and Epistles — of Paul, Peter, James, and John. In the first chapter of Paul's first letter to the congregation at Corinth, he asks, rhetorically: "Do I belong to Apollos? Cephas? Paul? Is Christ divided?" When it identifies with one leader or apostle or another, a congregation has done just that. Acts tells us that such exclusive selecting and valuing is not only unwise but in reality impossible. We are inheritors of the whole gospel.

This has significant implications for Christian unity and ecumenism in today's world and church. There have been two predominant postures with respect to ecumenism, or the "ecumenical movement." In its modern expression, the ecumenical movement has been concerned to bring about an organic union of the many different denominations and traditions in one church, a kind of ecclesiastical United Nations. Many have worked tirelessly to end the walls of division among denominations and traditions in pursuit of such a goal. And many others have resisted the same prospect nearly as tirelessly, seeing it as a vain attempt to gain worldly power or, worse, a kind of new Holy Roman Empire that pretends to be Christian but in reality is not.

Acts suggests an alternative understanding of Christian unity and ecumenism. Instead of either organic union on one hand, or isolation and claims to be the "one, true church" on the other, Acts can help us see that different congregations and denominations, like the four Gospels and the different apostles, bring distinct gifts to the whole church. Just as Acts does not require us to choose between Peter and Paul, so we are not required to choose between Methodism or Congregationalism, Orthodoxy or Pentecostalism. Each one has the potential to bear a significant part of the whole gospel to the whole church catholic. Unity does not mean or require uniformity. The Lutherans have an important gift and witness to the whole church, and so does the African Methodist Episcopal Church. Ecumenism inspired by Acts is less about "Which is the true church?" and more about "What truth does this particular church and tradition hold for the whole church?"

Does that mean, one might ask, that anything goes, that everyone or everything that claims to be "church" is to be taken seriously and heeded? Not at all. The fourfold Gospel, the core of Christian faith, does have the capacity to make distinctions, to rule some expressions beyond the Rule of Faith. There is in the fourfold Gospel both unity, a clearly discernible core of belief and witness, and diversity, a multiplicity of voices, emphases, and perspectives. Holding the two together — unity and diversity — is both our gift and our task as the church of Jesus Christ. Acts posits a new possibility for ecumenism and for the unity of the church: unity that has room for — in fact, requires — diversity.

Acts and the Church in the Emerging Multicultural World

As we have noted in the introduction, in our attempts to understand and respond to a world that is increasingly pluralistic culturally, the churches, congregations, and clergy have often turned to every resource but the one of our own that deals most directly with such questions — namely, the Acts of the Apostles. At the very center of Acts, the early church faces its most formative crisis as it works out what the gospel means and what it means to be church in the face of two very different and sometimes hostile cultures and worlds, the Jewish one and the Greco-Roman, or gentile, one (see Chapters 9 and 10). In this conclusion we will suggest that the Acts of the Apostles offers powerful counsel to the broader church and to denominations and particular congregations as they face similar issues of cultural differences and diversity.

The last congregation I served, a predominantly and historically Anglo congregation, started a new church five years ago. That new church is by design a "multicultural, multiracial" congregation located in the most culturally and racially diverse part of the city. As plans developed for the new church, the parent congregation was confronted with the questions that adolescents always pose, but which in this situation were heightened by the different cultural and racial make-up of the new congregation. They asked, in effect, "Do we have to do church the way you do? Do we have to be organized in the same way you are? Must we emphasize the same priorities?" The answer, of course — though it came not without struggle and even pain — was that "new occasions teach new duties." Our way of being church in one culture and tradition could not, and should not, be mimicked or imitated in a very different context and situation. The new congregation had to work out worship practices, forms of organization, and even ways of defining itself that fit a very different cultural matrix and context.

The book of Acts authorizes that kind of contextual adaptation and difference, under the guidance of the Holy Spirit. What is appropriate for the gentile mission and what is fitting for the Jewish Christian Church are not the same. The Pauline Epistles are not the same as the Catholic Epistles. And yet both are there, both are parts of the whole, and both are asked to respect one another and do those things (Acts 15) that make fellowship, community, understanding, and respect possible.

Today we are hearing new expressions, such as "cultural sensitivity" and "cultural competence." It is not a stretch, we feel, to claim that the debate, testimony, and subsequent agreement of Acts 10–15 is a demonstration of these very qualities of cultural sensitivity and competence. The elders at Jerusalem do welcome the gentiles — and thus the church at Antioch. They do not doubt or question that God is at work in this mission and that the Holy Spirit has been poured out among the gentiles. At the same time, they ask that the gentile Christians be cognizant of the Jewish experience and culture and show both understanding and respect in minimal purity practices.

It is worth repeating: what is achieved at the Jerusalem Council is a kind of theological understanding rather than a theological consensus. In other words, difference is not solved or driven out; it is acknowledged, respected, and allowed. God and God's way with us is not reduced to one cultural form or embodiment. The earthen vessels are not to be confused or conflated with the transcendent power that belongs to God alone (2 Cor. 4:7). This seems to us powerfully instructive for the emerging twenty-first-century world and church. There is continuity and there is difference; there is a rich pluralism, but not without controversy and confusion. No one said it was going to be easy. But Acts shows us that we can resist the impulse toward uniformity. It is not "my way or the highway." The narrative world of Acts is nothing if not a world filled with many roads, byways, surprising turns, and unexpected encounters. Through it all God is at work to surprise, to delight, and to save. We hope that Acts, and this study, inspire just such an experience of faith and hope for contemporary congregations and communities of faith. To God be the glory!

STUDY QUESTIONS

1. Discuss how and for what purposes the Bible is used within today's culture.

2. In what ways does the use of Israel's Scripture and the Gospel's memories of Jesus recorded in the speeches of Acts either correct or support what

you have observed about the roles Scripture plays in the worship of today's congregations or in the debates on college or seminary campuses?

3. Consider again for discussion the question raised on p. 273: How does the "catholicity" of Acts deepen your understanding of God's people as a community of "resident aliens"?

4. What do you see as the implications of Acts' emphasis on the church's "Jewish legacy" for your faith and your congregation's life?

5. This chapter claims that "Acts can help us see that different congregations and denominations, like the four Gospels and the different apostles, bring distinct gifts to the whole church." If this claim is true — and it should be tested and debated — how might it establish a pattern to guide a congregation's or religion department's participation in ecumenical or interfaith dialogue?

A Few Recommended Commentaries on Acts

Dunn, J. D. G. *The Acts of the Apostles*. Narrative Commentaries. Valley Forge, PA: Trinity Press, 1996.

Gaventa, B. R. *Acts*. Abingdon New Testament Commentaries. Nashville: Abingdon Press, 2003.

Johnson, L. T. *The Acts of the Apostles*. Sacra Pagina. Collegeville, MN: Liturgical Press, 1992.

Spencer, F. S. *Journeying through Acts*. Peabody, MA: Hendrickson, 2004.

Tannehill, R. C. *The Narrative Unity of Luke-Acts, Volume 2: Acts*. Minneapolis: Fortress Press, 1990.

Wall, R. W. "The Acts of the Apostles," in *The New Interpreter's Bible*, 10:1-368. Nashville: Abingdon Press, 2002.

Willimon, W. H. *Acts*. Interpretation. Atlanta: John Knox Press, 1988.

Witherington, B. *The Acts of the Apostles: A Socio-Rhetorical Commentary*. Grand Rapids: Eerdmans, 1998.

Index